PENGUIN BOOKS

PANICOLOGY

Panicology

SIMON BRISCOE *and*
HUGH ALDERSEY-WILLIAMS

PENGUIN BOOKS

PENGUIN BOOKS

Published by the Penguin Group

Penguin Books Ltd, 80 Strand, London WC2R ORL, England

Penguin Group (USA) Inc., 375 Hudson Street, New York, New York 10014, USA

Penguin Group (Canada), 90 Eglinton Avenue East, Suite 700, Toronto, Ontario, Canada M4P 2Y3
(a division of Pearson Penguin Canada Inc.)

Penguin Ireland, 25 St Stephen's Green, Dublin 2, Ireland
(a division of Penguin Books Ltd)

Penguin Group (Australia), 250 Camberwell Road, Camberwell, Victoria 3124, Australia
(a division of Pearson Australia Group Pty Ltd)

Penguin Books India Pvt Ltd, 11 Community Centre, Panchsheel Park, New Delhi – 110 017, India

Penguin Group (NZ), 67 Apollo Drive, Rosedale, North Shore 0632, New Zealand
(a division of Pearson New Zealand Ltd)

Penguin Books (South Africa) (Pty) Ltd, 24 Sturdee Avenue, Rosebank, Johannesburg 2196, South Africa

Penguin Books Ltd, Registered Offices: 80 Strand, London WC2R ORL, England

www.penguin.com

First published by Viking 2008
Published with revisions in Penguin Books 2009

2

Copyright © Simon Briscoe and Hugh Aldersey-Williams, 2008
All rights reserved

The moral right of the authors has been asserted

Typeset by Rowland Phototypesetting Ltd, Bury St Edmunds, Suffolk
Printed in England by Clays Ltd, St Ives plc

ISBN: 978-0-141-02986-3

www.greenpenguin.co.uk

Penguin Books is committed to a sustainable future
for our business, our readers and our planet.
The book in your hands is made from paper
certified by the Forest Stewardship Council.

To the next generation –
Marjolaine, Sam and Roch –
who will live with the consequences of our actions.

Contents

Acknowledgements

Many people confided their favourite scare stories to us as we set about work on this book, and we are grateful to them for their efforts in persuading us to share their fears. Family members dutifully scanned the newspapers for appropriate alarums, gave helpful pointers or at least allowed us space to write. Our erstwhile chemistry teacher Mike Morelle surprised us with a fat file of cuttings that he had apparently been keeping on the off-chance that two of his ex-pupils might write this book. Thank you all, and particularly to our wives – Moira and Laure – for their support. A number of libraries and media databases greatly facilitated our searches. We would like to thank especially the librarians of the Royal Society of Arts, the University of East Anglia and Cambridge University. Huge thanks to staff at the *Financial Times* for supplying inspiration – and allowing Simon time off to work on the book.

We sought out experts who might inform our potential fears. The following were exceptionally generous with their time, expertise and contacts: John Adams, Tony Allan, David Berube, Petra Boynton, Tracey Brown, Derek Burke, Ian Burnett, Clark Chapman, Mike Clark, Piers Corbyn, Julian Dowdeswell, Greg Durocher, Marie Edmonds, Kerry Emanuel, Andrew Evans, Pamela Ewan, Brian T. Foley, Kenneth R. Foster, Fiona Fox, Elspeth Garman, David Gee, Mike Hulme, Peter Lachmann, Chris Landsea, John Lawton, Stephen Leatherman, Georgina Mace, Jonathan Matthews, Bill McGuire, Jeffrey McNeely, Clare Mills, Julia Moore, Lynne Moxon, Kenneth L. Mossman, Brigitte Nerlich, Lembit Opik, Julian Orford, Stephen Pacala, Hugh Pennington, Raj Persaud, Roger Pielke, Richard Robertson, Jonathan Shanklin, Tom Stewart, Karen Talbot, Chris Tyler, Craig Wallace, Brian Wynne. We are grateful to all of them. Tony Lacey at Penguin deserves special thanks for his guidance.

Hugh Aldersey-Williams and Simon Briscoe
October 2008

Introduction

'This book made me feel sick. It also, equally effectively, made me feel ashamed, despondent and anxious, increasingly disenchanted with our politicians and, above all, guilty . . . this invaluable book.'

This review appeared in a serious broadsheet newspaper. The book happens to be about over-fishing, but it could just as well be about global warming, family breakdown or hospital superbugs. Observe not merely the dire mental turmoil that the book induces, but the reviewer's pathetic gratitude at being brought into this state. As a personal response, it is a touch overwrought, but it is typical of the way increasingly we are all invited to feel about the endless catalogue of disasters that are supposed to await us.

Our book won't make you feel these things. With luck, it may even make you feel a little happier about the condition of the world.

Consider bird flu. Throughout the winter of 2005–6, this was billed as an impending human pandemic that would wipe out a large proportion of the Earth's population. Yet the H5N1 type of the flu virus has led to the deaths of fewer than 300 people world-wide, mostly in Asia where victims had come in direct contact with infected birds.

Still the media is intent on sustaining scare stories like this everywhere it can – and we lap them up.

Some days, of course, not much happens, and even the media is stumped for a scare story. Actually, not much happened throughout the whole of 2006, the year we began work on this book, in 2007 and into 2008. No suicidal zealots flew passenger jets into high-rise buildings. No hurricane destroyed a major city. No killer wave arose casually to sweep away a couple of hundred thousand shore-dwelling souls. No new plague struck. We live in a complex world and we don't want to die. And in general we are winning the battle – we are living longer and more healthily than ever.

Every year, death comes a year closer for all of us, meanwhile life gets a little better for many people. So why are we happy to panic about the silliest things?

This tendency is certainly not new. Charles Mackay's *Extraordinary Popular Delusions and the Madness of Crowds*, first published in 1841, catalogued public obsessions with witchcraft, mesmerism and tulips, as well as fears of annihilation by everything from flooding to chemical poisons. Today, read paedophiles, radiation and blueberries . . . and flooding and chemical poisons. These topics are not 'hard' news or exactly fact, even if they do have a basis in fact. They live as stories because we all love to gossip, hear a tale, embellish it and retell it. Journalism is industrialized gossip, as Andrew Marr puts it.[1] Once one newspaper's story about something extraordinary, say a killer-bee, has gone down well, others follow, rooting out killer-bee-related items that would otherwise have gone unreported, or building up killer-bee near-misses into full-blown dramas in their own right. The fact is that we love to be scared – which is why many of the topics we examine (and the bees) have their own disaster movies.

These news stories frequently give the impression that life as we know it is about to end. The nature of the threat may change – a wave of immigration, AIDS, rising sea levels or an asteroid – but the threat is always there. Life is getting harder in the media as costs are cut. Journalists sometimes over-egg their stories to get them on the front page. And sometimes they are just overstretched by the demands of 24-hour rolling news from around the world and being expected to comment in real time on topics they know little about. Mackay notes how an 'epidemic terror of the end of the world has several times spread over the nations'.[2] It has happened at regular intervals since before the rise of modern science and has continued following the Industrial Revolution. And it seems it is happening still – in some cases changing our behaviour and leading to emotional and financial costs.

What's new, then, is not the public's appetite for a good panic story, or the media's willingness to serve one up. It's the role of other agencies. A generation ago, there were concerns in the world and these were reflected in the media, but the tone was different. Individual accounts of gruesome events may have been both more factual and more bloodthirsty than would be allowed today, but the tone would have been sober, and behind it all would have been the reassuring presence of a paternalistic government.

Today, that comfort blanket has been whipped away. Now politicians and government officials seem more likely to add to our sense of panic about a given issue. And even if our public servants don't, then there are plenty of other highly vocal interest groups – scientists, health and safety nuts, corporations and their advertising agencies, non-governmental organizations and lobby groups – who will. Professor Stephen Hawking said in 2007 that 'life on Earth is at ever-increasing risk of being wiped out by a disaster such as sudden global warming, nuclear war, a genetically engineered virus or other dangers.' Did he believe this or was he just promoting his zero-gravity flight to increase interest in space travel?

Governments have a duty to warn us of dangers that they perceive, but the way they do it today often only seems to add to the alarm. They are keener than ever to regulate for a safer and fairer world wherever there might be the slightest risk to health. An initial, well-intentioned impact assessment can rapidly snowball into a firmly held policy view supported by the full weight of government. Modern-day communications in our globalized world bring us stories more rapidly than ever before. Recent years have seen government campaigns in many countries about terrorism and bird flu which have raised our fears. But we never really learn the genuine extent of the risks; nor are we told what we as individuals can do to reduce them – we are merely told to be alert – that is to say, on the edge of panic.

The courts have also helped to alter our perception of what is a reasonable risk, sometimes in laughable ways. In the more litigious parts of the world such as the United States, the old rule of 'buyer beware' has been sidelined – now the seller gets sued. Following a lawsuit, McDonald's has had to print a warning on its coffee cups pointing out that the contents may be 'extremely hot'. As we witness the death of common sense, children's playgrounds lose their more exhilarating rides and doctors cover their professional reputations by putting patients through unnecessary tests. The end result is a distortion in our fears that overlooks evidence in favour of sensation: we now fear fires more than drowning even though more people die from drowning simply because fires make better television.

The classic social scientist's equation has it that the risk of an event is the likelihood of its happening multiplied by the impact if it does. So the risk of being killed by a volcanic eruption or a terrorist attack depends on the odds of the event, the event's magnitude, your proximity to it, your protection against it, and so on. But a more recent formula begins to take account of the way the media and other agencies are raising the stakes, suggesting that risk = hazard × outrage.[3] This is simplistic, but it clearly admits an important new factor. Governments advise against visits to places they judge to be at risk from terrorist attack but are less concerned about volcanic hotspots because only deaths from the former provokes outrage.

The topics we have chosen show how this wide societal network now manipulates our perception of risks. We have selected some global and some local concerns, some that are easy to understand and others for which the state of knowledge is low. All of them have been prominent stories in the media. We have scored each topic using a points system to show how vividly each threat is portrayed in the media, how real we feel the threat is and how much we as individuals can do about it. Some of these subjects you may be worried about already. To others you may never have given a thought. Our personal and unscientific assessments might prompt you to reassess your own fears. However, by parading so many popular fears between these covers, we hope at least to show that you cannot worry about everything, and also that it is foolish to worry excessively about any one issue.

We have neglected many risks – including mad cows, child abduction and the Y2K computer scare. We have also left out the things that are likely to get you, such as cancer, heart disease, dementia or simply falling. We might have discussed the nuclear threat – it has not gone away. We might have dealt with environmental pollution, still a major concern though no longer the public mania that it was a generation ago. Rightly or wrongly, these risks do not give rise to much panic these days, and so we have put them aside.

Examining panics en masse, we begin to pick out common threads not seen when they are considered, as they generally are, in isolation. There is a general difficulty in accepting that natural events still have the power occasionally to overwhelm us. At the same time, there is an almost biblical inclination to blame ourselves for things that may not be our fault, such as new viruses or freak weather events. There is a fear of forces that (we believe) we ourselves have unleashed through our arrogant scientific optimism. There is disbelief at the limitations of medical science, expressed in outrage at the deaths of infants or the presence of bacteria in hospitals. There is a growing distrust of the government hand.

Above all, there is a paradox. Modern life has greatly reduced many of the risks that humankind has to face, and yet it is modern life that seems to spawn most of our fears – fears of chemical, biological and nuclear war, pollution, terrorism, climate change and, less directly, fears associated with immigration, ageing, loss of cultural diversity and much else besides.

As we said, the last couple of years were quiet. There were merely the millions of expected deaths from malaria, HIV, poor water quality, war and car accidents. Searching the internet, it is almost impossible to discover how many die during a year from flu – the sort disingenuously dubbed 'seasonal', as if there was not a damned thing anybody can do about it – because the figure (as many as 500,000 people) is all but lost amid completely hypothetical death tolls for the bird flu pandemic that did not happen.

We notice spectacular or novel disasters, but neglect familiar killers. This is human nature. But another reason for this is the genuine gap in our knowledge of risks. The media, just like the public, attempts to navigate the daily news flow relating to global warming or the state of immigration, but, again like the public, has no means of knowing what is right or wrong. The length of the queues forming outside branches of the Northern Rock bank in Britain in the late summer of 2007 reeked of poorly informed panic about money, and it is a wonder that the economy took so long to slow down given the doom-laden credit crunch coverage in the following year. And the problem gets worse as time moves on. New and increasingly complex technologies beyond the comprehension of most bring new risks as business may be threatened by internet-based markets or our health jeopardized by nanoparticles. Breast cancer is bad, but there are serious risks associated with just screening for the disease. In cases like these, what we would like is a quantitative statement of Robert K. Merton's famous law of unanticipated consequences: how great are these consequences compared to the negative impact of the original problem and the positive impact of its technological solution? But of course this figure is seldom calculable. Sometimes, side-effects are negligible; other times, they seem greater than the original problem.

Still, we can take heart from what we do know. Not many of the dangers we confront are absolute – very few are likely to kill many people. Most are relative risks – things like eating too much salt that might knock a few years off your life or a flood that might result in the loss of treasured possessions and a tedious insurance claim. And the value of investments can fall or rise. Yet academic studies of happiness suggest that it is the relative risks that matter to us. As the world becomes more complex and we grow better informed about events, we worry more about these relative risks. But how relative are they?

Numbers are the 'fact' generator in today's society and the currency in any debate about risk. But they are not all of equal quality – some are manipulated by governments while others are produced by people with a vested interest. Often, proper figures don't exist – they are opinion surveys or come from administrative systems that do not give us data on the definition we want, leading to poor policy and weaker assessment. Yet those who wish to make a point on television or in the newspapers do it using numbers.

Sound-bite statistics, sometimes invented and often inaccurate, seize the imagination even if they crumble under close inspection. What does a one-in-a-thousand chance of catching SARS actually mean? Where in the world are you? What precautions are you taking? Are you of a vulnerable age?

Figures are one of the main ways to spread fear. We might like to think that the figures are the hard facts, the irrefutable hard-cooked foundation for the argument, but sadly they are often not. They can be misleading or deliberately distorting. As John Allen Paulos puts it in his 1988 book *Innumeracy*, 'Mathematics is the quintessential way to make impressive-sounding claims which are devoid of factual content.'[4]

The favourite quotation of the British media is the remark attributed (probably erroneously) to Benjamin Disraeli, the British prime minister: 'There are lies, damned lies – and statistics.'[5] Yet statistical data are better than nothing – they are evidence of something, the starting point for a discussion, a way of understanding society. The numbers are not everything but they can inform analysis and provide the creative impetus needed to solve problems. The only alternative is to retreat into anecdote and hopelessly selective assumptions.

However, the cult of innumeracy remains strong among the public – and the media. One leading newspaper recently announced that there was 'about' a 50 per cent chance that Europe would have above-average temperatures in some coming period.[6] Indeed. In one of his acts, George Carlin, the American stand-up comedian, invited his audience to consider how stupid the average American is. Then he paused before observing that half of them are even more stupid than that![7]

Although statistics about the past can be dangerous, forecasts about the future are even more dodgy. Questionable data are put in a black box computer model, cranked and spewed out often, it seems, with the sole purpose of scaring us. The 'results' have authority because it is experts and academics who do the cranking. Yet history is littered with examples where economists, scientists and other specialists have got their projections fantastically wrong.

Furthermore, the same raw data can be made to yield very different projections according to the prejudices of the person cranking the machine and small adjustments made to the model's assumptions.

The difficulty we have in dealing with the numbers that express risk may be a symptom of a wider inability to evaluate risk at a human level. In part, this reflects a deliberate avoidance of unpalatable truths – smokers still may not give up smoking even though they know it will be the principal cause of death for half of them. But mostly, it's down to ignorance. Perhaps you are sitting at home reading this. If so, you probably have no idea of the hazards that confront you right now. Are you more at risk from an airborne infection, a rat chewing through the wiring and starting a fire, or an asteroid crashing through the roof? You have no idea.

We have plenty of evolutionary equipment to help us evaluate immediate danger. Our senses tell us where to tread and what's safe to eat. But even the simple act of crossing a road is not so black and white. How can we choose between driving, flying or taking the train if we want the safest journey? What about radiation, which we willingly accept in the guise of an X-ray but fear otherwise?

Given this uncertainty, it is no surprise to find that people in different countries fear different things. The Swedes worry about dangerous chemicals, the Danes about nuclear power and the Italians about radiation from their beloved mobile phones, even though the risks from each are probably broadly equal in these countries.[8] Worries also change over time. A disturbing recent survey of Australian children found their main fears were being hit by a car, being near a bomb and being unable to breathe.[9] In the same survey twenty years ago a trip to the headmaster, catching germs and falling over came top of the list.

That's a huge shift. Of course, risks change over time. Worries about terrorism and, well, anything from the following pages have replaced the Cold War worries of our parents about nuclear annihilation and communism. But, it seems, our perceptions of risk are much more changeable.

It is almost as if we have to be afraid of something, as if we carry about in our heads a bucket of worry that we are compelled to fill with whatever's available. Clearly, different individuals have different-sized buckets. But the important questions are: is the size of *your* bucket fixed, or does it expand and contract according to external circumstances? Does it expand only when there genuinely is more to worry about, or is it swelled by the media, governments and other interests? Acting collectively or individually, can we shrink our buckets? If so, how? And should we do this?

According to the anthropologist Mary Douglas, writing with the political scientist Aaron Wildavsky in *Risk and Culture*, 'people select their awareness of certain dangers to conform with a specific way of life'.[10] A society united in fear is more cohesive. One where people fear different things is liable to fragment. Our dinner-table gossip and actions based on fears such as the rise or fall of house prices and immigration serve to strengthen or weaken the social fabric. So shrinking our bucket of worry too much may have consequences for social organization.

We live at a time of unprecedented prosperity, mobility and connectivity. Most of us live at peace in democracies. It is not merely coincidental that we are also witnessing a loss of respect for authority, a fragmentation of society and rising levels of worry about ever smaller risks. They are a logical consequence of these developments. What we are seeing is people's first uncertain response to greater technological and political freedoms. We are free to choose what we eat from a bewildering range of foods, for example. Governments, NGOs and corporations pull us this way and that – cheap, organic, low-salt, high-fibre, local or exotic and so on. But the choice is ours. Sometimes, though, we wish somebody would make it for us.

What can we do? For many panic topics, we can bend the odds in our favour by being aware of controllable threats. We can free our minds by deciding not to worry about others. We can begin to weigh risks and measures to deal with them. For example, some safety measures, such as making cigarette lighters childproof or putting reflectors on lorries, have proved very effective in terms of saving life, while others, such as restrictions on hazardous waste, have merely proved expensive.

It is quite legitimate to ask whether more overseas aid money should be put into flood defences in poor countries. If we want to cut road accidents, perhaps we should ban pedestrians from crossing the road while using their mobiles just as we ban drivers. Perhaps we should have a war on obesity rather than a war on terror. If we as voters were a bit wiser, and were not so easily freaked by dreadful or unexpected deaths by means such as hijacking or BSE, we might get better government.

'Men,' wrote Charles Mackay, 'go mad in herds, while they only recover their senses slowly, and one by one.'[11] After reading *Panicology*, you will, we hope, worry less about many of our subjects; in one or two cases, you might be prompted to worry a little more. But you will have begun at least to prioritize your worries. You are on the road to recovery.

Key to scores (from 1 to 5).

Panic

Risk

Personal empowerment

www.panicology.com

1. Sex, Marriage and Children

Worrying about whether there are too many people on our planet or too few, and how we should relate to them, is at the heart of many panic stories. Mrs Thatcher told us two decades ago that there is no such thing as society, but the families we make – and break – and the increasingly diverse relationships we form, and see others form, cause plenty of concern. And don't forget how we all got here – sex – is it a problem or a pleasure?

The Birth Dearth

'A second baby? Russia's mothers aren't persuaded'
New York Times

Italian men not helping much around the house is apparently one of the principal reasons why Italian women are producing so few babies.[1] Other reasons for the birth rate of Italian women falling to be among the lowest in the world include the lack of flexible work, a shortage of nurseries and the poor provision of children's services, in a country where couples have traditionally relied on families for support. A low birth rate might seem an unlikely problem for a predominantly Catholic child-loving country, but a serious shortage of babies and the prospect of a shrinking population is affecting many developed countries, to such an extent that it could soon threaten their livelihood and viability. Mass immigration, not always seen as desirable in the West, might become a necessity.

The prospect of too few people being a problem is a far cry from the impending 'population crisis' that most of today's adults were brought up with. 'Too many people in the world?' was the provocative question on the cover of one American magazine in 1963 and typical of the genre. Declining death rates, in other words increasing life expectancy, around the world contributed to the more than doubling of the world's population since 1950 to its current 6½ billion. It is now increasing by a little over 6 million a month, roughly 200,000 every day. The consequences of this growth are enormous shortages of water and fuel, the depletion of natural resources, high unemployment rates, pressure on public services including education and healthcare, increased ill-health, damage to ecosystems and pollution.

It seems, then, that there are too few people in some areas and too many in others.

Population fluctuations and associated scare stories are nothing new. The highly influential *Essay on the Principle of Population*, written by Englishman Thomas Robert Malthus in 1798, predicted that population would outrun food supply before the end of the nineteenth century. His basic view was that population, if unchecked, increases exponentially, at a geometric rate, whereas the food supply grows in a linear fashion, at an arithmetic rate. Malthus saw the solution to rapid population growth as being 'moral restraint' – including late marriage, which paradoxically is one of the key features of the problem now facing many Western countries with low birth rates and declining population. If we failed to embrace such restraint, excessive population growth would be checked, he told us, by accidents, war, pestilence, famine, infanticide, murder and homosexuality. Well, it hasn't turned out quite that bad – yet at least. Economic progress, notably developments in food production, has kept most people nourished even if the more intensive use of the world's resources has given rise to scares discussed elsewhere in this book.

Sensible debate around the topic of population growth has been hampered by several factors. One is the population projections, which have a reputation of being fantastically unreliable – they are heavily influenced by the prejudices of those conducting the forecast, and very small differences in assumptions can make large differences to the results, due to the power of compound growth rates. Another problem has been the inability to define overpopulation. Conceptually it can be thought to arise when there is a shortage of resources leading to an impaired quality of life, serious environmental degradation or long-term shortages of essential goods and services. But how serious is serious and how long-term is long-term? As there is never a eureka moment when we can suddenly say that there is overpopulation, the whole debate is conducted in shades of grey. Population generally changes only slowly and unevenly, and the concerns or pressure points vary according to the society's location and its wealth.

Nevertheless, there have been other recent well-known works along similar lines to Malthus. These include *The Limits to Growth*,[2] the world's best-selling environmental book, published in 1972, which modelled the consequences of rapidly growing world population given finite resource supplies, and *The Population Bomb*,[3] which predicted that hundreds of millions of people would starve to death in the 1970s and 1980s. At the time there was no shortage of criticism of the books, and both appeared on lists of the century's worst books made at the turn of the millennium.

Whatever the predictions, it is not difficult to argue that, with around 1 billion people already malnourished and without access to safe drinking water and healthcare, the earth is supporting 6½ billion people only because many live in misery. Others, more optimistically, have suggested that the world has a 'carrying capacity' of nearer 10 billion, and that the falling rate of population growth in various parts of the world, coupled with progress in science and technology, means there will be no problem with overpopulation.

Rapidly growing populations leading to overpopulation might appear to be a global issue, but it is limited to a minority of geographies. Indeed, the United Nations forecasts that nine countries will account for half of the world's projected population increase in the period up to 2050. These are India, Pakistan, Nigeria, Democratic Republic of Congo, Bangladesh, Uganda, the US, Ethiopia and China, listed in order of their contribution to the growth. The growth is associated with increased urbanization, bringing a range of problems, with cities growing particularly fast in China and India – India already has more than thirty cities with populations over 1 million. These changes will cause a shift in where the world's power – in terms of population – is concentrated. All of the growth forecast for the next four decades – adding 2.6 billion to the world's population – is expected to take place in less-developed regions, with the population of the developed world remaining unchanged at around 1.2 billion.

Demographers normally measure either the crude birth rate – the number of children born per thousand of population each year – or the total fertility rate – the average number of children born to each woman over the course of her life. On either measure a number of developed countries stand out as having a problem with declining population levels. Fertility in several dozen developed countries has reached levels unprecedented in recorded history – below 1.3 children per woman in several southern and eastern European countries. By contrast, fertility at the world level stands at 2.65 children per woman, a figure that rises to 5 children per woman in the least developed countries. The world average crude birth rate is around 20 children per thousand of population each year, yet a number of developed countries, including Germany, Japan and Italy, have rates of below 10.

Countries have always feared a declining population. In the past, a large and growing population was required to develop land and generate wealth. Population increase was encouraged, often by means of conquest and enslavement. Larger armies, and increased security, required a healthy supply of youths. The pressures are different these days, but a declining population, often associated with an ageing population, is widely expected to damage economic growth and wealth generation, in turn increasing the difficulty of caring for the elderly.

The reasons for the drop in fertility are not entirely clear. The theory of 'demographic transition' suggests that, as the standard of living and life expectancy increase, family sizes start to drop. At one level, factors such as the increased access to contraception give adults more choice over when and if to have children. The tendency to get married at later ages, reflecting in part the desire of many women to have careers, also reduces the scope to have

Crude birth rate of selected countries

Rank by state*	Country	Births/000 population (crude birth rate)	Total fertility rate
1	Niger	50.7	7.5
20	Nigeria	40.4	5.5
55	Pakistan	29.7	4.0
89	India	22.0	2.7
–	**World average**	**20.1**	**2.6**
112	Israel	18.0	2.4
122	Brazil	16.6	1.9
136	Ireland	14.4	1.9
137	US	14.1	2.1
142	China	13.3	1.7
148	Australia	12.1	1.8
151	France	12.0	1.8
160	UK	10.8	1.7
169	Spain	10.1	1.3
173	Russia	10.0	1.3
–	**European Union**	**10.0**	**1.5**
174	Poland	9.9	1.2
178	Italy	9.6	1.3
180	Japan	9.4	1.4
181	Singapore	9.3	1.1
184	Czech Republic	9.0	1.2
189	Austria	8.7	1.4
192	Germany	8.2	1.4

Source: The World Factbook, www.cia.gov. The total fertility rate is the expected number of children born per woman based on 2006 age-specific fertility rate date. *According to crude birth rate.

children. And the sharp fall in infant death rates has reduced one pressure to have multiple births. The financial equation of having children has also altered: in rural areas in less-developed countries, children contribute to the economic well-being often from an early age, but in developed, urban settings bringing up children is increasingly expensive.

The low fertility trends in some countries are such that demographers are now warning of 'negative momentum', occurring when a shrinking population goes into an ever-steeper spiral of decline – fewer babies now means fewer mothers in the future. When fertility rates fall below 2.1 (each woman needs to give birth on average to 2.1 babies to maintain a developed nation's population size) and death rates are broadly stable, a country's population will decline unless it is offset by a favourable combination of immigration and emigration.

This is a situation which is now facing much of Europe. The population of many of the former Soviet republics is falling due to emigration (notably since the fall of the Berlin Wall in the early 1990s), ill-health of those who remain and relative poverty. The population in the Czech Republic, Hungary, Poland and the Slovak Republic was lower in 2005 than in 2000. The population of Germany declined in 2005 and 2006, a situation that would be reflected in several other western European countries were it not for net immigration. The future looks no more promising for most developed countries. Europe's population was estimated at 731 million in 2005 – the base from which the United Nations conducts its projections. On the 'low' scenario, Europe's population is expected to fall by over 20 per cent to 566 million, by 2050. The 'high' scenario sees a rise of 6 per cent, while the 'medium' scenario sees a fall of 10 per cent.[4] All other continents, in contrast, see a significant increase in population in even the low scenario.

A declining population will usually be accompanied by population ageing, one of the factors explaining the economic malaise of Japan and Germany in the last decade – and it's going to get worse before it gets better. The median age of the world's population is currently around 28 years, but that ranges from around 16 to 18 in many of the less-developed African countries to over 40 in a good number of European countries. Looking ahead, the problems could be severe for Europe's pensioners. Currently there are around 35 pensioners for every hundred people of working age, but by 2050 there could be twice as many pensioners, around 75, for every hundred workers. Italy and Spain could see their ratios approach one for one. In most European countries, pensions are paid out of current tax revenues, which means that taxes will have to rise sharply, with the burden falling on an already proportionately shrinking number of workers, or pensions will have to fall.

There is little doubt that countries take a decline in the popu-

Population projections, UN's 'medium' variant, selected countries

Millions	2005	2015	Percentage change
World	6465.7	7219.4	+12
The growing countries			
Brazil	186.4	209.4	+12
China	1315.8	1393.0	+6
India	1103.4	1260.4	+14
Nigeria	131.5	160.9	+22
Pakistan	157.9	193.4	+22
Turkey	73.2	82.6	+13
US	298.2	325.7	+9
Stable and shrinking countries			
Bulgaria	7.7	7.2	−7
France	60.5	62.3	+3
Germany	82.7	82.5	n/c
Italy	58.1	57.8	−1
Japan	128.1	128.0	n/c
Poland	38.5	38.1	−1
Russia	143.2	136.7	−5
UK	59.7	61.4	+3

Source: World Population Prospects, United Nations, www.un.org/esa, 2005 version.

lation seriously and try to reverse it. Russia's President Putin has described the baby shortage as the country's most acute problem and ordered parliament to give large financial incentives to women who have a second baby. Australia's 'one for mum, one for dad and one for the country' campaign and the associated baby bonus cash payment, introduced in 2004, has tentatively been declared a success with the latest figures showing a small rise in the birth rate. And many European countries, including France, Italy and Poland, also offer financial incentives to mothers or families with children. But, if the incentives in the form of cash and savings offered in Singapore and Japan over a rather longer period are anything to go by, they are unlikely to have any lasting success. With surveys suggesting that it can cost several hundred thousand euros to bring up a child, it will be surprising if cash sums of €1,000 or €2,000 have any impact on the underlying trends.

One possible solution is to encourage immigration, but that is another story with another set of issues. The poor and relatively youthful countries of North Africa and Asia that are closest to

Europe offer a large supply of potential immigrants, but will the ageing residents of Europe want them? It seems certain that continued modest migration will play a part in Europe's policy, but the numbers involved are such that immigration cannot feasibly plug the gap left by the birth dearth. Spain would need 170,000 immigrants a year over the next fifty years to maintain a constant population size. Spain's position is extreme, as it currently has few retired people but is forecast to have a large increase. To maintain a constant working age population, it would need an average 260,000 immigrants a year. But to maintain the current potential support ratio (the number of people of working age per older person), Spain would have to accept an annual average of 1.6 million immigrants every year. This is clearly impossible. Europe's predicament might not end in tears, but serious adjustment in policy and expectations is required.

Overpopulation has been a popular theme in fiction, especially in the 1950s and 1960s. Books and films have proposed that the problem can be easily resolved by embracing measures such as raising infants as food or by promoting euthanasia of everyone who reaches a certain age. So it seems paradoxical that the big issue likely to face most readers of this book is the impact of a shrinking population on their wealth and health in their old age.

Family Breakdown
'A nation of unhappy families' *The Times*

The downside of the increasing flexibility that makes later marriage more appealing is that 'normal family life' might feel like a thing of the past for most children. The media plays its part, sometimes giving the impression that society is crumbling in the face of delinquent youths, teenage pregnancies, single-parent families and a high divorce rate. But this panic-inducing story resulting from the rapid change in our society has, in contrast to many others that we live with, a distinctly political flavour.

David Cameron, the Conservative leader, has pinpointed absent fathers and family breakdown as two of the root causes of anti-social behaviour, and polls show that a majority of the public agrees with him. He has said that he does not criticize all the single mothers who work hard to give their children a good start in life, but he has pledged to change the tax and benefits system to ensure that there are real incentives for parents to get and stay married.

The Labour government has taken a different view during the past decade. It says that marriage is 'a good thing' but plans no action to support it, saying that policy must be 'bias free' when it comes to marriage, adding that love and compassion are what create strong families. While love and compassion are important, it has become increasingly hard, say the government's critics, for families to survive and flourish without the protection of the law and a supportive financial regime. Indeed, traditional families have been hard hit by Labour's tax reforms, including the removal of a tax allowance for married couples and the introduction of welfare credits that reward lone parents at the expense of low-income couples. The structure means that poorer couples, for whom income top-ups from the state are important, are much better off if they keep their relationships unofficial and, so far as the government is concerned, live separately. Getting married means that benefits are cut. One report, 'Parents live apart to cash in on benefits system',[1] suggested that as many as one million couples in a committed sexual relationship live most of their time at separate addresses, and that such untraditional family structures primarily reflect financial considerations. An unemployed mother who leaves the unemployed father of her children could experience a rise in her standard of living of between 20 and 35 per cent.

It is, of course, impossible to be 100 per cent sure of any cause and effect when it comes to behaviours in society, but a number of important trends seem to be heading in the wrong direction, damaging the fabric of society, in Britain and a number of other countries. One shocking survey suggested that working parents spend only nineteen minutes a day with their children, just enough time for a quick breakfast or reading a bedtime story.[2] Indeed, leaving children to their own devices, letting them learn about life from other teenagers and not providing good adult role models are frequently seen as being at the heart of the problem. Whatever the truth, the trends seem to be leaving a large number of unhappy and helpless families in their wake. One survey of Scotland's mothers and fathers revealed that their principal concerns are balancing jobs and home life without the benefit of an extended family near by, having nowhere to turn for advice when the going gets tough, and worrying about how best to discipline unruly offspring. Three-quarters of those questioned said that they would consider counselling if it was available.[3]

A comprehensive assessment of the well-being of children and young people by UNICEF presented a report described as a 'damning' assessment of the 'crisis of childhood that is blighting Britain'.[4] The report measured well-being across more than twenty developed countries under a variety of headings such as education, relationships, behaviours and health. The top half of the well-being table was dominated by small north European countries including the Netherlands, Sweden, Denmark and Finland. Relative child poverty was highest in three southern European countries (Portugal, Spain and Italy) and in three Anglophone countries (the US, the UK and Ireland). Roughly four out of five children in the countries under review lived with both parents, but the rates fell to below 70 per cent in the UK and the US. The percentage of children who said that their peers are 'kind and helpful' varied from above 80 per cent in some countries to less than 50 per cent in the Czech Republic and the UK. Fewer than 15 per cent of young people report being drunk on two or more occasions, but the figure rose to over one-quarter in the Netherlands and almost one-third in the UK. Over one-third of 11–15-year-olds in the UK, Switzerland and Canada had used cannabis.

Newspaper reports of the study – 'Threadbare family lives' and 'Unhappy families' were typical – focused not on Britain's top-of-the-table performance on teenage pregnancies, bullying and poor family relationships, but on the depressing conclusion that British children perceive themselves to be unhappier than their peers in other countries. Overall the UK was the country where the welfare of children suffered most, and America was the nearest rival. While politicians, think tanks and the press could build little consensus about what to do to improve the situation, it is clear that Britain has suffered from adverse trends. The country finds itself in a worse position on a number of counts than many others and is at a loss to know what to do about its delinquent children.

Among the key drivers is the fact that marriage has become seriously unpopular. Marriage rates in England and Wales are at their lowest since records began over 150 years ago. Just 23 men per thousand unmarried men got married in 2006, a drop from a rate of 28 in 2004 and 49 per thousand twenty years before. The sharp drop in recent years was explained by new legislation aimed at reducing the number of 'sham marriages'[5] and the increasing popularity of getting married overseas, but there is no mistaking the underlying trend. The male marriage rates dropped below 50 only in a few exceptional years between the 1860s, when records began, and 1984, and the rate peaked at 78 in the early 1970s. Among the marriages that are occurring, an increasing proportion have an added complexity that might serve to weaken the traditional links within society, as they bring together two different nationalities, ethnic groups or religions. The increasing occurrence of second and third marriages gives rise to ever more extended and less tightly bound families.

The pattern of motherhood has also changed dramatically in recent decades even if the number of children born each year in England and Wales has been relatively stable – within 50,000 of the 650,000 of the recent years' average. But over that time the average age of the mother has been increasing: in the 1960s British women were most fertile in their early twenties; that shifted to the late twenties and has now shifted to the early thirties. The mean age of mothers is now over twenty-nine, having increased by over three years in the last three decades, and the number of first-time mothers over thirty-five has trebled in fifteen years.

Mothers with old faces and young children are an increasingly common sight on Europe's high streets as the average age of motherhood continues to rise in every European country for which records exist. The mean age of women at the birth of the first child is now around twenty-seven to twenty-nine years in most developed countries. In Spain, 13 per cent of first-time mothers are now over forty, double the proportion in England and Wales. Later births and later marriages are a result both of some women enjoying their freedoms and careers and of some men shying away from the traditional male role of providing financially for a wife and children.

Those women who are lucky enough to fall pregnant in their late thirties or forties get no thanks. So far as many newspapers are concerned, they are simply risking their health and that of the foetus – miscarriages, ectopic pregnancies and pre-eclampsia are more common among older mothers-to-be. One doctor said that women who delay having children until they are thirty-five or over constitute a 'major public health issue', adding that they are more of a burden to society than teenage mums.

The papers now regularly report women aged over sixty giving birth. Britain's oldest mother gave birth in 2006 at the age of sixty-three but a 66-year-old has given birth in Romania and a 65-year-old in India. This is as much a freak show as anything else but does show how medical techniques are extending the age at which women can conceive, even though most clinics will not accept women for IVF treatment over the age of forty-five. Plenty of women who have their first child at an older age end up with just the one child, and the swelling ranks of children growing up without brothers and sisters are giving rise to a new group of people that is of increasing interest to psychologists.

Teenage mothers are a constant source of interest to the newspapers. One story, 'Mum believable', told of a fourteen-year-old schoolgirl who was asked to give family planning advice to her peer group after four of her classmates became pregnant in quick succession. Another told the story of a girl who had had four abortions by the age of seventeen. Yet the percentage of all births to mothers under twenty years of age has been reasonably constant in Britain at between 6 and 9 per cent for the last two decades. The UK rate is only half of that seen in a number of eastern European countries, a little below that in the US, and at least double the rate seen in a number of the main European countries including the Netherlands, Germany, France and Italy.

However, the proportion of births to teenagers that are occurring outside marriage has increased sharply – it now stands at over 90 per cent compared to under 70 per cent two decades ago and barely one-third three decades ago. The rise in the proportion of births outside marriage is even greater for the mothers aged twenty to twenty-four – nearly 70 per cent now compared to just 15 per cent twenty-five years ago. Nearly 280,000 children were born out of marriage in the latest year, double the number of two decades ago and five times the number of three decades ago.

Once married, people can divorce – and divorce rates are high in Britain, up more than fivefold from 30,000 in the last forty years. Britain is beaten to the top of the world's divorce league (when viewing divorces as a percentage of marriages) by primarily a number of eastern European countries. But the UK has a rate of over 50 per cent compared to between 40 and 50 per cent for the US, France, Germany and the Netherlands. The divorce rate in the countries of southern Europe, including Portugal, Greece, Spain and Italy, is half that of Britain. They might be seeing strong rises – Italy, for example, has seen the number of divorces rise by 70 per cent in the last decade – but they are starting from a lower point. One report suggested that Italy faced a particular problem: the normal explanations for a marriage break-up – marrying too young, squabbling over money and meeting a new partner – have been surpassed by the problems arising from the unusually close attachment of Italian men to their mothers. Modern, young Italian women are less readily able, it seems, to offer the type of unconditional love that young men become accustomed to from their mothers.[6]

One academic study did at least conclude that 'divorce works', in that a comparison of the mental states two years before marital breakdown with two years afterwards showed an improvement, albeit modest, in 'mental stress'.[7] This is not to suggest, though, that a greater number of couples should dissolve their unions as those who split were normally the less happy among the married population. It seems that an increasing number of divorces among middle-aged couples are being prompted by women in a final bid for personal freedom, escaping from unfulfilling relationships, rather than the stereotype mid-life man dumping his long-term partner for the thrill of younger flesh.

As a consequence it is no surprise that the number of children living in lone-parent households – nine out of ten of the parents are single mothers – in Britain has grown by a quarter in the last decade. Across the UK, roughly one-quarter of families with dependent children are headed by a lone parent, but the proportion is roughly double that in some deprived areas, such as inner London boroughs, and roughly half the national average in the more well-heeled commuter areas of south-east England. One study showed that a half of children of black Caribbean background are living with one parent, compared to 13 per cent of children from a white British background, and just 5 per cent of those from an Indian background.[8]

While many children are raised happily and successfully in couples that are not married, the evidence shows unambiguously that married parents are more likely to stay together and much less likely to suffer from low incomes. The children of married parents are less likely to fail at school, turn to drink, drugs or crime, have mental health problems or become teenage parents themselves.

In Britain, more than four out of ten children are now born outside marriage, a slightly higher percentage than in the United States, where the annual total of 1.5 million babies born to unmarried women was recently passed. One survey suggested that almost half of children from separated families had not seen their father at all in the last year.[9]

For all the panic about children, the majority of family units across Europe are childless. One in eight Europeans lives alone and nearly a half of European households are heterosexual and single-sex couples living without children. Some have seen their kids leave home while others will never have children, but with increasing life expectancies these couples are likely to spend the biggest chunk of their life in the company of their partner. There is some survey evidence to suggest that an increasing number of people will now only marry and start families when they are convinced that it will enhance their own lives. This is a massive change from earlier generations, who thought that only a life blessed with children was a fulfilled one.

The rapid societal changes driven by changes in family structure have made the socio-economic classifications, so loved by statisticians, almost redundant. Dividing people according to the nature of work (managerial, intermediate, semi-routine, unemployed, etc.) of the head of household now looks rather out of date. As a result, several private-sector companies have created their own so-called geodemographic systems for categorizing people and the areas in which they live. Such systems typically have as many as fifty categories.[10]

It seems that societies, individuals and policy makers are finding it hard to come to terms with the consequences of a rapidly changing definition of 'family', which is increasingly flexible with ever more diverse constituent parts. But is it any worse than before? The tip of the iceberg is delinquent children who are drug-taking criminals, forming gangs to terrorize estates, but are the apparently more widespread problems of alcohol, smoking, promiscuity, anti-social behaviour and school attendance having much effect? Solutions are not readily available, but many feel that the government's policies related to social cohesion are going in the wrong direction: people see them chipping away at society's structures when they would rather see them being reinforced and rebuilt.

The Marriage Squeeze
'A good man is harder to find' *Newsweek*

Twenty years ago, *Newsweek* magazine published a story, based on Yale and Harvard research, about the difficulties that older women have finding a husband.[1] It brought to the fore the problems of reconciling a career and children and prompted much hand-wringing, countless newspaper articles and TV debates and no doubt provoked many a tearful discussion between single women and their mothers.

It started:

The dire statistics contained in a new demographic study confirm what everybody has suspected all along: many women who seem to have it all will never have husbands. White, college-educated baby boomers in particular are victims of a marriage squeeze – a shortage of available men that adds up to a numbers game that women can't win.

It went on to say that these white, college-educated women 'born in the mid-1950s who are still single at 30 have only a 20% chance of marrying. By the age of 35 the odds drop to 5%. 40-year-olds are more likely to be killed by a terrorist: they have a minuscule 2.6% probability of tying the knot.' The catchy reference to terrorists was, it seems, journalistic licence and did not appear in the academic report.

The story sparked a crisis of confidence among America's growing ranks of single women, and the core message quickly became entrenched in pop culture, even though the study was widely criticized. The media was blamed for inventing 'a national marital crisis on the basis of a single academic experiment of dubious statistical merit'.[2] Some saw it as a backlash against feminism, with one columnist writing that the report gleefully warned women: 'Reach too high, young lady, and you'll end up in the stratosphere of slim pickings.'

The US Census Bureau responded by publishing far more promising probabilities, suggesting that thirty-year-olds had a 60 per cent likelihood of finding a husband, with the odds dropping to around 20 per cent for forty-year-olds, respectively three and eight times greater than the odds in the original article.[3] With the benefit of hindsight – two decades on we can see what actually happened to these women – and looking at the personal experiences of the two authors of this book, the notion that 'women are over the hill at thirty' looks a little bit archaic. The latest US census records show that only one in ten college-educated women now aged in their fifties has never married.

The mistake in the research was apparently a simple one – namely to assume that current and future generations would behave as past generations did. Just because, for example, most women used to be married by thirty in the past and those that did not tended to remain single, did not mean that those not married by thirty in the future would also remain single. The *Newsweek* episode offers a cautionary tale of what can happen when the media over-simplifies a complicated and less than perfect piece of academic work. Nonetheless it clearly hit a nerve as it did in part reflect the experiences of many people.

These fears and worries have been dramatized in recent years in humorous blockbusters which ensure that the marriage-prospects blues remain once the laughter has died down. *Bridget Jones's Diary* told the story of a single woman over thirty who smokes too much, drinks too much and has a tendency to say whatever comes into her mind. Her mother keeps setting her up with dorks, and she has an awkward fling with her boss, leaving us wondering if she will ever find a husband. *Sex and the City* told of the antics of four attractive female New Yorkers who gossiped about their sex lives – or lack thereof – and searched for new ways to deal with being a woman as they navigated the turn of the millennium.

So, after the magazine and big-screen-drama-induced panic, what are the facts? In most western countries, there are roughly equal numbers of men and women at the crucial ages. Although more boys than girls are born – roughly a ratio of 105 to 100 – male teenagers and men have higher death rates than their female counterparts, prompting the numbers gap between the two sexes to narrow until some point in middle age when women start to outnumber men.

In the UK, the official population estimates are very evenly balanced between the two sexes from the age of twenty up to forty-four, but the reality is probably more favourable than that for women, as it is widely believed that the population census in 2001, on which these figures are based, undercounted the number of young to middle-aged men by several hundred thousand. A slightly more favourable situation for women prevails in the US – there are 2.22 million males aged twenty-five compared to 2.10 million females, and it is only at age forty-two that females start to outnumber males.

If there are enough men, the root of the problem is changing attitudes and behaviour patterns. Marriage has been hit hard by the increasing tendency to cohabit, but unfortunately there is very little decent data telling us exactly how relationships are evolving over time. People are behaving more flexibly – moving in and out of relationships, including marriage, more frequently than in the past, making it harder to track and monitor. And the definitions are complex in any case – would people in long-term relationships but living separately, an emerging trend especially among middle-aged people with established lives, be said to be single? And what about the increasing number of people who are living an openly gay or bisexual life?

What is clear is that marriage has been pushed later with each decade for all post-war generations. While 86 per cent of men and

92 per cent of women born in the 1940s had married by the age of thirty, the early figures for those born in the 1970s suggest the rate has nearly halved, to 45 per cent and 50 per cent respectively. The striking figure is the change in the proportion of women who never married between those born in the 1960s and 1970s. For the current thirty-somethings, half are not married, compared to only a quarter of the women a decade older.

Partnership rates for thirty-year-olds by decade of birth, percentages

	Men		Women	
Decade of birth	Never married	Never partnered	Never married	Never partnered
1920s	23	22	16	15
1930s	18	17	12	12
1940s	14	12	8	6
1950s	25	15	14	8
1960s	38	15	24	7
1970s	55*	21*	50*	13*

Source: 'Roona Simpson, Living like the Bridget Joneses?', BHPS conference paper 2005.
Note:* caution to be exercised in considering these figures due to the small number of cases in the sample at this stage.

The explanations for delaying marriage and childbirth are many and varied. Increased graduation rates and changing career patterns have certainly played a part. Hard-working professional people are often expected to work hardest in their twenties and thirties, making it difficult – especially for women – to find time to marry and have children. Many people simply enjoy being single at a time when it has become acceptable, in a way that was not the case a generation ago, to set up home on your own. Indeed, one survey suggested that 97 per cent of people aged between twenty-five and thirty-four believed that it was important to live alone before settling down.[4] One rather depressing survey suggested that people do not enter relationships because they don't expect them to last.[5] And a new 'social class', dubbed the 'regretful loner', has been coined for men in their late thirties and forties who live alone and have either failed to form relationships or are the victims of failed relationships.

But for most people, being single is just a phase. If surveys are to be believed, most women say that they want to get married, but at the same time they seem to be asking themselves about the cost in terms of scaling back their careers or sacrificing their (probably) enjoyable single lives. Men, too, it seems, are also keen to marry – as indeed they ought to be as surveys suggest that married men are healthier and happier than their single counterparts. But, according to the media, 'the problem' of falling in love with someone suitable to marry is more of an issue for women. It is certainly true that nearly all newspaper articles on the issue are written by women. Whatever the truth, much of the media coverage leaves us with the impression that the men who don't marry come from the bottom of the barrel while the women who don't marry are the cream of the crop.

While the reasons for delaying cohabitation and marriage are perfectly sensible, it brings a price. Surveys have shown that single people – male or female – consume more alcohol, often work longer hours, tend to skip meals and eat less healthily and might well not have someone close to share life's problems with.[6] It is also more expensive to live on your own. Most notable, however, is the anxiety related to the biological clock and a desire that many women still cherish to have children. In essence, the more fun or the more career that a woman has, the less time she leaves to find a husband and to produce babies.

As ever, when faced with a challenge, behaviours change. Women in their thirties have set about the task of finding a mate with the same efficiency that they might bring to their professional careers. The booming singles industry, based around the internet and variants of speed dating, has emerged to cater for all needs. And artificial insemination is now widely available if the priority is to have a child.

In most western countries, the situation is not too bad: it boils down to difficult personal choices in rapidly changing social environments, and of course, a good dollop of luck. As one woman said, 'I'm not a statistic. I am one woman. I need to find one man.' Most people do, if they want to, eventually marry despite the demographic forecasts. And most manage to juggle careers and children without screwing up too badly. It is also said that hooking up with someone later in life is less of a gamble than doing so earlier on – certainly the divorce rates are lower – as both parties have matured and have a better idea what they want from life.

Whatever the problems in the West, relationship forming is likely to be much more problematic for the young in China, where a severely unbalanced sex ratio will leave millions of men unable to find brides. Sons have been traditionally preferred in China, and most couples can have only one child, so many prospective parents have, over the years, aborted pregnancies if tests showed that the foetus was female. As a result there are 119 boys born for every 100 girls in China, well above a global ratio of no more than 105. In some parts of China where the ratio has been even more distorted – as high as 134 boys to every 100 girls – programmes have been launched, largely successfully, providing benefits and cash payments, to encourage families to have girls. Meanwhile, the State Commission for Population and Family Planning estimates that there will be 25 million men who will fail to have wives by 2020. How long before a male Bridget Jones comes out of China?

Something for the Weekend?
'Sex with many partners? No thanks, we're British' *The Times*

Virtually all western homes have a toilet, a washbasin and a bath or a shower. But one item of bathroom equipment shows that hygiene habits are not universally shared. It is the bidet: 'this hygienic French invention of the 18th century has taken the world by storm,' according to the French journalist Agnès Poirier writing in the *Observer*. 'Only the USA and Britain are bidetilliterate.' Market evidence confirms the truth of this. Multinational sanitaryware manufacturers find they sell no more than two bidets for every hundred toilets in the United Kingdom, whereas in Italy they sell seventy-one.[1]

This is an astonishing disparity. But what does it mean? A dictionary definition describes the bidet as an installation for 'bathing the external genitals and the posterior parts of the body' – not, as some British holiday-makers insist, a receptacle for washing socks. So, in countries where bidets are prevalent, do people wash their genitals more often? And, more to the point, do they do it because they are getting more sex, as Anglo-Saxons suspect? Or is using a bidet just a substitute for a proper wash, something Anglo-Saxons also suspect, mindful as they are that the French buy less soap than they do and that Napoleon preferred Josephine not to wash before they made love. In which case they are probably still getting more sex, the dirty beasts.

'French are way ahead in the bedroom league' is typical of the headlines that fuel Anglo-Saxon anxiety that they are missing out compared to Latin lovers. The headline refers to a survey carried out in 2002 by the condom manufacturer Durex in which French people claimed to have sex 167 times a year, the British 149 times a year, and Americans just 138 times.

The Durex survey has grown each time it has been done. In 2005, it polled 317,000 respondents in forty-one countries. This colossal undertaking sounds authoritative, but it is not. Researchers into sexual behaviour and attitudes criticize the survey's leading questions, its biased sample of respondents limited to those with internet access who feel like filling in a questionnaire, and its apparent lack of ethical safeguards.

Its shortcomings are revealed when you try to compare the results over time – something not encouraged by Durex, which updates the results on its website and not in academic journals. Recall that in 2002 the French were claiming to have sex 167 times and the British 149 times a year. In the same survey for 1998, the figures were 141 times and 112 times respectively. But by 2005, the figures were 120 and 118.[2] What made everybody so frisky in

2002? The Chinese went from being the most faithful lovers to being the most promiscuous in the space of two years, according to the same survey. Hardly likely.

The inability to compare results from one year to the next doesn't bother the media, however. Durex's context-free findings guarantee a titillating headline. One country will always have the sexiest girls, the highest level of unprotected sex, or the most one-night stands – and if it's a different one each time then so much the better.

This kind of survey, which makes it easy to compare regions or countries (but not different time periods, age groups or social classes), encourages us to regard sex as something that it is appropriate to put in league tables, like hospital waiting lists or school exam results. This is clearly a nonsense since sex is a matter for individuals and is not administrated in this way. Whereas our grandparents supposedly grew up fearful about sex because of widespread ignorance, today we grow up fearful about sex because we are not having as much, in as many ways, with as many people, as everybody else. The recent addition to the Durex survey of a number of Asian countries, for example, reveals a greater sexual conservatism among these respondents compared to their peers in the West. Presumably the company hopes that their nations' 'low' placing in the tables may lead some young Indians and Indonesians to become more sexually active – thereby providing new market opportunities.

Many commercial interests have now seen how easy it is to gain publicity by adding the spurious authority of a 'survey' to the sure-fire ingredient 'sex'. Durex is merely the leader in an increasingly crowded field. 'Much more sex please . . . we're British' was the headline to news of a poll by a New York marketing agency.[3] This pleased the media because it confounded the usual stereotype. 'Single Britons are the most promiscuous in the world, an international survey of sexual attitudes says,' the *Guardian* reported enthusiastically. An entirely different slant could have been put on the same data. The poll showed, for example, that two-thirds of British men felt entitled to regular sex with their partners, but that less than half of women did. In the four other countries surveyed, these figures were considerably higher for both sexes. One could equally have concluded that the British are closer to giving up altogether on regular sex with their partners than the French, Germans, Americans or Chinese.

There again, perhaps the Anglo-Saxons have the last laugh. The myth of the Latin lover went limp recently when the *New York Times* headlined 'Spain says adiós siesta and hola Viagra'. The story concerned a man who held up a Madrid pharmacy, demanding the erectile dysfunction drug Viagra. The article went on to theorize that the exploding Spanish market for such drugs was due to the abandonment of the siesta and the discovery of the work ethic, leaving men too stressed to perform in bed.

Occasionally, the message of constant sex is contradicted by these polls. 'Teenagers in no rush to have sex' was the headline result from another online survey of 16–24-year-olds,[4] this one said to be supported by the Department of Health and conducted by an odd alliance of popular radio stations, MTV and the indefatigable Durex. The report noted that 69 per cent 'waited' until the age of consent at sixteen. Interestingly, Durex's separate global survey produced results not incompatible with this – giving 16.6 as the age at which most British people lost their virginity, compared to around 18 in Latin countries. But on its website Durex ignored the newspaper's take on the national result and, with an eye for the market, drew attention instead to its global result that 'the trend is for people to lose their virginity earlier'.

One newspaper at least seemed to have the measure of things. Under the headline 'Teen sex surveys ruin your love life', the *Daily Telegraph* lampooned the tendency for these heavily publicized polls to highlight promiscuity among the young: 'Many young people claim to be regularly taking part in two surveys a day, often with different research organisations.'

Newspaper readers are not all young, of course. What about something for the mature reader? 'Does great sex start at 40?' queried another headline in the *Guardian*. 'A global survey has found that sex just gets better as we get older, with those aged 40 to 80 reporting the most satisfying bedroom antics of all.' The article that followed gave the title of the survey – the portentous-sounding Global Study of Sexual Attitudes and Behaviours – and the fact that 30,000 respondents took part. It unaccountably failed to mention that it was sponsored by Pfizer, the maker of Viagra. Its target market may be older, but Pfizer's message is essentially the same as Durex's – you too should be getting more, and our products can help you get it. Both companies know that the best way to suggest this is to insinuate that your peers are already at it like rabbits.

Commercially motivated surveys may be unreliable, but, when it comes to sex, it is more frequently observed that those surveyed might be the ones being economical with the truth. This possibility affects any survey, but the suspicion tends to be raised most often with sex surveys. Men often exaggerate their experience whereas women downplay theirs. Anglo-Saxons might expect Latin lovers to brag about their conquests. There is no way of knowing unless an expert closely questions the respondents directly, but then the pollsters do not need to have the true picture in order to generate media interest.

All this represents something of a wasted opportunity. Data on sexual attitudes, properly gathered and analysed, could inform social and healthcare policies rather than merely satisfying our prurience. They might even have something useful to say about the divergence of birth rates in different countries. It is one thing to have young survey respondents boasting of their promiscuity, for example, but establishing how this behaviour – and underlying attitudes – relates to sexually transmitted infection and teenage pregnancies requires expert collection and analysis of the data. For fear that it will offend sponsors or advertisers, no popular survey is likely to have much to say about these or other important topics where little is known, such as the extent of sexual ignorance, harmful practices and violence related to sex.

Academic surveys that do tackle these trickier issues have their own troubled history. Alfred Kinsey's 1948 report 'Sexual Behavior in the Human Male' opened the floodgates for sex research. But Kinsey's follow-up study of women in 1953, and a British survey by the social anthropology project known as Mass Observation in 1949, which included both sexes, were both regarded as shocking because they reported a high proportion of women having pre-marital sex and affairs once married. The latter study did not see the light of day until fifty-six years later, when the BBC promptly dubbed it 'Britain's secret sex survey'. One in four men said they had had sex with a prostitute. One in five women admitted to having affairs outside marriage, and more than half of both men and women had had sex before marriage. Homosexual activity, then illegal, was also reported by 20 per cent of both sexes.

Trying to find out what really goes on in bedrooms remains controversial today. In 1990, a National Survey of Sexual Attitudes and Lifestyles in Britain by epidemiologists and social researchers at the University of London was reported to have been banned by Margaret Thatcher's Conservative government; it was eventually funded by the Wellcome Trust and published in the usual way. The survey was repeated in 2000 with less attendant fuss. As well as providing important information about the prevalence of HIV, AIDS and other sexually transmitted infections, the surveys showed an increase in various promiscuous behaviours over the decade. Nevertheless, by 2000 more people were using condoms, including on their first time of sexual intercourse, and the number of girls under sixteen having sex had stabilized. The 2000 report also found, in marked contrast to the Mass Observation findings, that only 2.6 per cent of respondents reported homosexual experiences while 4.3 per cent of men had paid for sex.[5]

The media gave the findings the serious consideration they give to any sex survey, combining moral indignation with facetiousness. The *Mail on Sunday* reported the finding that 'one in 20 married men had been unfaithful in the past year, while only one in 50 married women had strayed', using the figures to confirm 'the received wisdom that men commit much more adultery' – which is not quite what they say. The tone of the words 'unfaithful', 'strayed', 'commit' and 'adultery' is to be contrasted with the researchers' more neutrally phrased questions about whether married persons had taken 'new partners'.

Such national surveys can now be put together to build an international picture of sexual activity – a picture that turns out rather different from the debauch painted by Durex. In 2001, Kaye Wellings, one of the authors of the British survey, and colleagues in France, South Africa and the United States gathered survey data for fifty-nine countries.[6] Unlike Durex, they did not ask about threesomes, bondage or sex on the beach. They found, boringly, that there was no global trend towards earlier sexual intercourse and that married people have the most sex. There was a global increase in premarital sex – mainly because people are getting married later. Unlike the heavily marketed Durex survey, this global study prompted only one newspaper story, under the drearily predictable headline 'Sex with many partners? No thanks, we're British'.

Some curiosities might have aroused more media interest. Promiscuity was generally increasing in developed countries, nowhere more than among Australian women, who have caught up and are overtaking men in making full use of their single years. Everywhere, men reported more multiple partners than women, but in Brazil the disparity was so great that the researchers could only explain the result by men's over-reporting of their prowess due to the 'Latin macho culture'.

As these contrasting examples show, you learn what you want to learn from sex surveys. Academics have, in Wellings's words, 'a historically unique opportunity to describe patterns of sexual behaviour and their implications for attempts to protect sexual health at the beginning of the 21st century'. For Durex, the priority is to represent sex as a recreational activity. The beautiful twenty-somethings beaming smiles from its website and telling us about their favourite sex enhancers make that clear enough. For Pfizer and other pharmaceutical companies, sex is a huge new market opportunity. But for this market to come about we must see sex not as a mystery or as fun but as a medical problem that can be solved with the aid of drugs.

This reframing is already beginning to happen with the unthinking collusion of the media. Pfizer and Boots announced a trial scheme in three Manchester branches of the high street pharmacy whereby men might obtain Viagra over the counter without a prescription. The news made the papers in typical fashion on St Valentine's Day: 'Roses are red, tablets are blue'. The media coverage was larky and by and large approving – it did not dwell on the curious circumstance of a drug designed to treat the specific medical condition of erectile dysfunction being made available without the involvement of applicants' doctors.

The pharmaceutical industry has new plans for drugs to treat premature ejaculation, heighten the intensity of orgasms or simply make you want more sex. Though ostensibly aimed at bringing help to a minority of genuine sufferers from sexual dysfunction, these seem destined to follow the path taken by Viagra, further encouraging the public to regard sex as a problem for which drugs are the cure. If this happens, the sex surveys and the media's giggling uncritical attitude towards them will have played a large part in getting us there.

2. Health

Unless confronted by immediate danger, we generally regard our health as our prime concern. Our fear of illness is exploited by governments, who want to protect us in the most cost-effective ways, by companies who want us to pop their pills and by food manufacturers who would like us to believe that their provender is health-giving. But whether or not we worry about our health, we still die. It's worth remembering that we do so on average at a greater age than in the past, with less suffering and fewer declining years.

The Fat Thing
'The fattest children in the world' *The Times*

Obesity is a favourite panic story – the media love everything to do with the subject. Even responsible newspaper editors find stories on the subject as resistible as a child finds a chocolate bar. The story might be serious – obesity shortens life and costs national health systems substantial funds – but there is also a lighter side – stories suggesting that we will all soon be too fat to fit into airline seats and too heavy to be carried to our graves on pallbearers' shoulders.

'The fattest children in the world' was the attention-grabbing headline of an article that told us that one-third of Scottish twelve-year-olds are overweight and that one-fifth are obese. The kids are fuelled by fizzy drink and unfamiliar with fresh fruit, it seems. The Scottish rate of child obesity is above that in the US at 16 per cent, and much higher than in other European countries (for example, Ireland 9 per cent, Spain 9 per cent, France 4 per cent, Sweden 5 per cent, Denmark 2 per cent). A spokesman for the International Obesity Taskforce was quoted as saying, 'The obesity epidemic is escalating totally out of control in Scotland,' adding that this 'is more than just a warning signal, it's a red light'.

The terms overweight and obesity are generally used loosely but they do have a statistical definition, relating height to weight. A person who is 5 ft 9 inches tall (1.75 metres) would be categorized as overweight at 169 pounds (76 kilos) and obese if they weighed over 203 pounds (92 kilos). The thresholds are sometimes expressed in terms of a body mass index (BMI, or Quetelet index, after the Belgian who established the measure 170 years ago), an indirect measure of the amount of body fat. It is calculated by taking the bodyweight in kilograms and dividing it by the height in metres, squared.

Someone is overweight with a BMI of over 25 and obese with a measure of over 30.[1] At the extremes, a measure of over 40 is described as morbidly obese, while under 18.5 is thought to be underweight and might well indicate malnutrition or an eating disorder. As the measure becomes more widely used, with doctors using it for medical diagnosis, so the controversy surrounding the measure's accuracy in relation to levels of body fat has increased – it can be distorted by factors such as fitness level, muscle mass, bone structure, gender and ethnicity. Yet for all its faults, for most people it gives a broadly accurate assessment and it is often the measure used to create data.

The facts behind the bold headlines are scary. A few Arab countries and some Pacific islands have exceptionally high rates of obesity, but among developed countries it is the US that tops the table as obesity among adults has risen significantly in the US during the past twenty years. Nearly one-third of American adults – over 60 million people – are obese, and the proportion of young people that are obese has more than trebled since 1980. The US authorities want to halve the prevalence of adult obesity by 2010, but the situation continues to worsen. Louisiana, Mississippi and West Virginia might be the fattest states, but only four have an obesity prevalence rate of 20 per cent or less.

The obesity plague has not visited every developed country but it has gone global – the developing world is suffering as a result of changes in diet, physical activity, health, urbanization and nutrition, with the bitter irony that, while some developing countries continue to focus their efforts on reducing hunger, others face the problem of obesity. As poor countries become more prosperous, they acquire some of the problems along with some of the benefits of industrialized nations. A hundred years ago just 10 per cent of the world's population inhabited cities. Today, that figure is around 50 per cent. Cities offer a greater range of food choices, generally at lower prices, and urban work often demands less physical exertion than rural work. Traditional diets featuring grains and vegetables are giving way to mass-produced meals high in fat and sugar. Being overweight used to be a sign of wealth, but now it often marks poverty. The number of overweight individuals worldwide now rivals those who are underweight.

Adult overweight and obesity rates, selected countries from around the world, percentages

| | Male | | Female | |
	Overweight	Obese	Overweight	Obese
Australia	48	19	30	22
China	30	2	29	6
Czech Republic	49	25	31	26
England	44	23	35	24
Germany	53	23	36	23
India	4	1	4	1
Ireland	46	20	33	16
Italy	42	9	26	9
Japan	24	3	17	3
Russia	31	10	27	22
Saudi Arabia	42	26	32	44
Scotland	43	22	34	26
Tonga	37	47	23	70
US	40	31	29	33

Source: www.iotf.org. Age ranges covered vary between countries. Data are latest available in October 2007 and mostly relate to a year between 1999 and 2003. Some countries, such as Canada and France, are excluded as their surveys are 'self-reporting'.

The increasing rates raise concern because of their implications for health. As one newspaper put it, the weight gain 'has been so fast and so extreme that experts believe these children will suffer a lifetime of horrific and crippling health problems'. Being overweight or obese increases the risk of many diseases and health conditions, including hypertension, type 2 diabetes, coronary heart disease, stroke, gallbladder disease, osteoarthritis, sleep and respiratory problems and some cancers.[2] It can also lead to inactivity and mood disorders.[3] According to the World Health Organization, a good part of the heart, cancer and mental-disorder disease burden for the world, including that of most low-income countries, is rooted in the intake of excess sugar, fat and salt and a paucity of fruit and vegetables. Obesity is proving to be a 'remarkable amplifier' of diabetes, high blood pressure and high cholesterol levels particularly among Asian and Central American communities, it said.

Obesity is also linked to early death – although the closeness of the link is unclear. The uncertainties were highlighted in 2005, when two studies from the Centers for Disease Control and Prevention in the US produced two very different estimates for the number of deaths due to obesity – 1,000 deaths a day or only 26,000 a year. As being overweight does not kill you directly, the way a heart attack might, we will always be left with a – probably wide – range for the number of deaths caused by obesity. Even so, the message would seem to be clear. The chairman of the National Obesity Forum in the UK said that obese children are twice as likely to die by the age of fifty,[4] while a Canadian paper explained that today's children will be the first generation of kids who are not going to live as long as their parents. The World Health Organization estimates that more than one in ten deaths in developed countries is already due to overweight and obesity, suggesting a figure of about 50,000 deaths per year in England.

The 'public health time bomb' of obesity will bring a 'vast' cost to national health services around the world, in addition to the direct financial and economic consequences faced by afflicted individuals. One study suggested that the medical expenses associated with overweight and obesity amounted to over 9 per cent of the total US medical expenditures – and that was a decade ago, when the problem was less pressing. Estimates of the direct costs are only illustrative in most countries, and up-to-date figures simply do not exist. Most such analyses acknowledge that published figures are likely to be underestimates.

Measuring indirect costs is even more difficult, but they are widely thought to be several times higher. If the World Health Organization's estimate of early deaths is broadly correct, it would imply the loss of several tens of thousands of years of working life in England, and associated earnings, in addition to the cost of incapacity benefits paid to those unable to work. One official report estimated that obesity was responsible for 18 million days of sickness absence in England and that, on average, each person whose death could be attributed to obesity lost nine years of life.

Despite the very real nature of the problem, policy initiatives around the globe are modest and of limited success, reflecting in part that the explanations for the trend are complex and uncertain. Generally higher obesity levels are put down to a rising consumption of fast or unhealthy food and an increasingly sedentary lifestyle in front of television and computer screens. But there is no shortage of alternative explanations paraded in the media – obesity has been linked to a virus, meaning you can 'catch fat' from other people, too little sleep and eating just one plain biscuit a day. One American article said, 'The obesity epidemic in our country has spared no age-group, even our very youngest children,' reporting the rise in the number of children under six classified as overweight. And, of course, poor reporting can confuse. The lack of policy progress could also be due to excess political correctness and the nervousness of people across society to speak openly about weight issues with fat people. Many British doctors apparently shy away from discussing weight with children for fear of hurting their feelings.

The policies being followed include food-labelling schemes, encouraging food manufacturers to reduce the amount of salt, sugar and fat in pre-prepared meals and healthy eating advice, along with a raft of measures for schools, including improved school lunches, changes to the way children play, increased sessions of sport and the reintroduction of home economics classes, with the curriculum being used to reinforce messages about healthy eating. Television 'junk food' advertisements are being progressively banned for programmes with a significant proportion of younger viewers. The change in standards has led to some food companies introducing self-imposed guidelines on junk food marketing.

But in the face of poor progress, other more desperate measures are being dreamed up: higher taxes and insurance premiums for overweight people; a restriction on government-subsidized health care for people who refuse to lose weight; new building codes that would force people to walk further as they go about their daily lives; and the use of taxes and subsidies on bad and good foods to encourage healthy eating patterns. It has even been suggested that the advertising of weight-loss dieting fads should be banished on the grounds that they give unfounded hopes and obscure the relatively simple messages that public health professionals would like to convey.

Despite all the evidence, some people believe that the 'war on obesity' is over-hyped by government and health professionals, and is one of the clearest examples of an ever more intrusive 'nanny state'. Obesity myth articles typically set out a string of 'facts', claiming that, among other things, nobody seems to know why the rise in obesity is happening, we are eating less fat than in the past, some statistics are 'pure fantasy', and a majority of children are exceeding the recommended daily physical activity levels. They also pour scorn on the so-called 'healthy lifestyles' solution to the problem, suggesting that badgering large numbers of people to change their lifestyles is a lost cause.

The food industry itself generally recognizes that obesity is a problem, but manufacturers consider it to be their role to provide food that the public 'wants', believing that eating is an individual responsibility. As the Canadian Council of Grocery Distributors has said, no doubt speaking for many trade associations, 'supermarkets are not in the health regulation business'. Although it is fashionable to attack the retailers, many slim people probably wonder in quiet moments why it is that more fat people do not address their weight status themselves.

While some people are becoming fatter, others are eating far more healthily than at any time, benefiting from a greater selection of fresh produce in the shops than ever before and the availability of cookery books and programmes and engaging in enjoyable and structured exercise. We are witnessing the emergence of a health gap in our society to rival the existing divide caused by money.

Currying Flavour
'Cheese saltier than ocean' *Independent*

'Can flavourless food be eaten without salt?' Job complains to God in the Bible. It's a rhetorical question, but it goes to the heart of our difficulty with this essential commodity today. Sugar, fat and additives in junk food lead you to obesity, but not if the salt gets you first. For salt is now the 'hidden killer lurking in your favourite Chinese and Indian takeaway meals', according to the British tabloid *Sun* newspaper in an article headlined 'Is your curry killing you?'[1]

The headline was prompted by tests by trading standards offices. More than half of fifty Indian and Chinese meals tested contained more than the *daily* adult intake of six grams of salt recommended by the government. One dish of chicken with cashew nuts in yellow bean sauce contained 15.8 grams of salt.

Salt is a simple chemical, sodium chloride, and is the body's main source of these two elements. However, excess sodium intake has been linked to high blood pressure, a major cause of strokes and heart disease. The *Sun* is thus able to claim that 'salt-related deaths' are running at 35,000 a year in the UK, though large-scale scientific studies of diet and blood pressure find it hard to isolate salt as the decisive factor.

To clear up the confusion about salt, we need to look at why and how it finds its way into what we eat. We have used salt for millennia not only to enhance the flavour of food but also to preserve it. Chefs therefore prize salt for the same reason as the producers of junk food.

For food lovers such as Hervé This, a chemist at the National Institute of Agronomic Research in Paris and one of the founders of the culinary movement of 'molecular gastronomy', there are 'two great fears: gout and a diet without salt'.[2] Salt, he explains, 'increases the ionic strength of aqueous solutions, making it easier for odorant molecules to separate themselves from food'. In other words, it is a vehicle for bringing out other tastes. This is the case whether the other tastes are subtle and delicious, as they may be in a velouté of asparagus, or faint and banal, as in a processed cheese. It may draw out elusive and exotic natural flavours or it may simply mask skimping on costly flavoursome ingredients.

Unfortunately, the high solubility of salt in water which enables it to release food flavours is also the property that effectively disguises its presence in many foods. We enjoy snack foods because their saltiness is one flavour we seek when we choose them, but then we are surprised and maybe shocked to find that corn flakes, say, contain as much salt as potato crisps because we do not think of them as salty.

It is this disguised presence of salt in western diets that has become a major issue. Up to 80 per cent of the salt we eat is contained in processed and packaged foods such as bread and meats. 'It's actually very difficult to eat too little salt. This is because it's in so many everyday foods, such as breakfast cereals, ready meals, soups, sauces and biscuits,' according to the UK Food Standards Agency.[3] So it's not that we are choosing directly to put salt on our food. Overall UK retail sales of plain salt have actually fallen in recent years.

In some manufactured products a small amount of salt is almost essential. Bread and bakery items usually include a little salt for flavour. But there are more pernicious reasons for adding salt where it is not strictly needed. Salt enables some foods to hold more water, a phenomenon exploited by manufacturers cheaply to bulk up the weight of their product. A supermarket brand of bacon can contain sufficient salt that you would consume your entire daily allowance in no more than three rashers, whereas bacon from a 'gourmet' supplier might contain a quarter of the amount.

So how much salt do we eat? In the 1980s, before it was widely known to be associated with high blood pressure, salt consumption in the United States was between 6 and 15 grams a day, according to the American food scientist Harold McGee, 'a dosage that probably supplies 5, 10, even 25 times as much sodium as we actually need'.[4] What we need, what we want and what the food industry wants to feed us are very different things, however. The WHO target daily intake is 5 grams, but national governments are happy to sanction higher levels – 6 grams in the UK – which are reprinted on many food packets. But we still eat more salt than this. On its website the European Salt Producers' Association proudly, if perhaps a little incautiously, touts a figure of 8 grams a day per capita salt consumption. Americans still consume around 10 grams a day.

The producers are vigorous in their defence of people's right to consume as much salt as they want, in tones that at times recall the tobacco lobby. There is no need for healthy people to reduce their salt intake, they insist, while casting doubt on studies linking sodium to high blood pressure. In some cases, they point out, elderly people have died apparently because they have not been getting enough salt. Although the 6 gram daily allowance applies to adults of all ages, the elderly are more susceptible to high blood pressure and so presumably more likely to act on heightened fears by cutting out salt. Not all people should automatically reduce their salt intake, therefore.

But salt is not like smoking, because you aren't always aware of it when you indulge. The recommended daily allowance is well publicized, but this information is of little use if you cannot calculate your intake. This is almost impossible to do. Packaged foods have long been obliged to list their major ingredients, which often include salt, but they do not have to declare the relative amount of salt present. More recently, in response to concerns not only about salt, but also about fats and sugar, manufacturers have begun to include panels of 'nutrition information', and some also give overall 'guideline daily amounts' of these dietary elements. In the UK, this apparently helpful gesture has been viewed as a pre-emptive measure to head off a 'traffic lights' scheme proposed in 2005 by the Food Standards Agency to display much more readily understood red, yellow or green gradings for these substances.

But even declaring salt content is not transparently done. Some global brands such as Heinz and Kellogg's responsibly give figures for salt and for that salt in terms of its sodium content alone. Cereals are especially assiduous about displaying this information, perhaps because it is at breakfast that we are most likely to pause to consider our dietary health. But many products indicate salt *only* as sodium. In a sense, this is medically useful since sodium is the component of salt linked to high blood pressure. But it is helpful to the manufacturers too, as 5 grams of salt, for example, corresponds to just 2 grams of sodium, which makes the danger appear less to consumers not fully briefed on the chemistry. In fact, although sodium and salt can be shown interchangeably on food labels, they are not necessarily equivalent at all, as other ingredients such as baking powder also contain sodium.

Unsurprisingly, it is products high in salt that prefer to focus on sodium content. There are 7.9 grams of sodium in 100 millilitres of Blue Dragon Fish Sauce, for example. This is equivalent to 20 grams of salt, well on the way to being a saturated solution of the stuff. A single stock cube may contain more than 4 grams of salt, although the information may be given in less readily interpreted form as the amount of sodium in a (small) portion of made-up stock.

Newspapers have latched on to the problem, though their headlines can rather miss the point. 'Cheese saltier than ocean' was the

Independent's line when anti-salt campaigners looked at the label on Kraft's Dairylea Light cheese slices. The cheese does indeed contain more salt weight for weight than seawater – a level boosted by having selected for testing the 'Light' variety of the cheese, which contains proportionately more salt simply because it has proportionately less fat. Its more fattening cousin brand is a little less salty than the ocean – which of course makes for a less satisfactory headline. The reader is asked to recall how disgustingly salty a mouthful of seawater tastes and to draw the inference that the cheese tastes equally salty. However, the salt in seawater is the only thing that gives it a taste, whereas the salt in the cheese is used to bring out other flavours, and the overall taste is not overwhelmingly of salt. But, whether you realize it or not, the salt is really there – 2.8 grams of it in every 100 grams.

High levels of salt can lurk within food precisely because it mingles with other flavours. This becomes a greater problem when there is no labelling. Highly flavoured curries can hide more salt than bland food. Yet if they are bought as takeaway food they are unlabelled for salt or any of their ingredients, and, as the *Sun* patriotically put it, 'Brits don't know they are eating it in such massive doses'. In cases where the takeaway food is more standardized, this situation may be about to change. McDonald's has begun placing codes on some of its packaging that when scanned will transmit nutritional information to the consumer's mobile phone.[5]

But this elaborate routine merely makes the point of food campaigners such as Joanna Blythman, who identify an Anglo-Saxon urge to see food not as a pleasure but as 'a complex problem' for which eager manufacturers supply 'meal solutions'.[6] Continental products tend not to display panels of 'nutrition information' and so give less data about salt, but their consumers tend to be more knowledgeable about food and are more likely to cook from scratch in any case.

Blythman has an unlikely ally in the food producers, who agree that 'debate about the levels at which the UK's food regulator has set its salt reduction targets misses the point about how healthier eating habits can be achieved'.[7] They argue that it is pointless to set 'arbitrary targets, which aren't even enforceable by law' when it is consumer power, and not regulation, that is demanding lower salt levels. Manufacturers might prefer to see no targets. But it is clear from the way that salt is covered by a media keen to titillate as well as to inform a largely ignorant public that the guideline daily amounts, 'arbitrary' though they may be, serve a vital purpose when presented alongside declared or tested levels of salt in alerting consumers to potential dangers to health.

Where does this leave the health-conscious gourmet with a craving for salt? For these people there is a whole different marketing game. Most things you buy in a grocery are more or less complex mixtures of basic ingredients. But salt is one of the simplest chemicals there is. Salt is sodium chloride, and that's it. Despite this, there are successful brands that sell for four times the price of ordinary table salt based on their claim to be natural, pure and even health-giving. The pack of one French brand proclaims: 'Derived from the Mediterranean Sea, Costa Fine Sea Salt has been obtained by the simple and natural evaporation of water, aided by the warm sun and wind. It is one of the vital components of taste and contains minerals which are essential to our health.' Broste salt, another French brand extracted in the same way, miraculously contrives to contain 'a rich balance of minerals and trace elements corresponding to the composition of our own tissue salts'. Halen Môn 'is natural sea salt produced from the fresh Atlantic waters around the Isle of Anglesey'. Maldon sea salt omits to tell us that it is sourced from the muddy, shallow North Sea, emphasizing rather 'the ancient craft of panning handed down by generations of salt makers'. It is 'pure', although not so pure that it does not contain a few (unspecified) 'valuable sea water trace elements'. Even Blythman falls for the hype on this occasion. She feels that sea salt made by evaporation 'is produced in a much more natural manner' than table salt, even though the latter is frequently extracted from underground as brine and then subjected to the very same process of evaporation.[8]

Salt from other sources cannot compete with the romance of

the sea, although one brand aims to meet the challenge with the claim that its product, mined in exactly the same way as ordinary table salt, is 'millions of years old'. What benefit is implied by this claim to antiquity is unclear. Italkali's iodized Sicilian salt tries to have it both ways. 'The natural purity and richness of Sale di Sicilia with the added benefit of iodine,' it announces, a 'healthy and natural' product pure as the day it was laid down in 'sub-terranean Sicilian salt deposits'. So where does the iodine come from? Potassium iodate, a chemical related to weedkiller, is added in the factory.[9]

How is it that salt on its own can be claimed as healthy while a small percentage of it in a meal is cause for alarm? There may be traces of valuable minerals naturally present, but this does not alter the fact that it is essentially pure sodium chloride. As the Food Standards Agency warns in dispelling the myth of 'posh salt', 'It doesn't matter how expensive salt is, where it is from, or whether it comes in grains, crystals or flakes – it still contains sodium.'[10]

There are alternatives to salt that do contain less sodium. Some cite medical studies adducing their benefits on the pack. But others are committed to the familiar copywriters' nonsense. A product called Lo-Salt contains one-third of the sodium of ordinary salt because it substitutes the similar-tasting potassium chloride. Or, as the manufacturer cunningly puts it, 'natural potassium' in exchange for 'sodium salt'. The implication that one chemical element is somehow more natural than another takes this deceitfulness as far as it can go.

A Dead Duck

'Bird flu "could be in our shops"' *Daily Mail*

After a winter of increasingly hysterical press coverage of the risk of a human pandemic, Britain at last experienced the reality of bird flu when, at the end of March 2006, a single dead swan washed up on to the beach at Cellardyke on the east coast of Scotland. The bird tested positive for the type of the virus designated H5N1, present in many bird populations and which had led to dozens of human fatalities across Asia. It was with almost palpable relief that the *Daily Telegraph* was able to declare on its front page 'Britain's first bird flu zone', complete with a map showing a '1,000 square mile area at risk'. Like Chekhov's seagull or Ibsen's wild duck, the bird was surely an omen: the next autumn migration season would bring squadrons of sickly foreign birds plummeting from the skies to spread their deadly infection to anything and anyone within range. More than a year on, we are still waiting.

The story of bird flu as a real hazard to human health began in 1997 in Hong Kong, where eighteen people were infected and six died after coming into close contact with birds at the city's live markets. The outbreak took epidemiologists – the scientists who study the spread of diseases – by surprise as it had been thought that the virus could not jump from birds to humans without the help of an intermediary species such as pigs. Despite the unpreparedness, further spread of the disease and loss of life was prevented by the rapid cull of all poultry in the city. In 2003, the H5N1 virus resurfaced, now slightly altered and more dangerous, 'like the doomsday bug in Michael Crichton's old thriller, *The Andromeda Strain*', according to Mike Davis's warning book, *The Monster at Our Door*.[1] This time several members of a Chinese family died after having visited relatives who kept chickens. Similar cases began to be reported from Vietnam, Thailand and Indonesia, and the World Health Organization announced a pandemic alert.

Through the autumn and winter of 2005, human cases spread westward, recorded with mounting agitation by the European press. Russia, Kazakhstan, Kurdistan and Turkey were hit in turn, as the European Union banned the import of live birds and feathers. All the human casualties were found to have been in close proximity to birds – five Azerbaijani teenagers died after plucking a dead swan. Shortly before the Cellardyke swan made its final landfall, a German cat was found to have contracted the disease; cat-owners were told to keep their pets indoors. One British newspaper was on the point of demanding that the government distribute face masks to the population until it was pointed out that they would actually be useless against the spread of the virus.

Why such expansive coverage for a disease that had killed a little over a hundred people around the world in three years – about a quarter of the number who die annually in England from resurgent tuberculosis? The main reason may be what the media habitually refers to as the 'spectre' of the influenza pandemic that struck at the end of the First World War, perhaps infecting as many as a billion people and claiming 60 million lives. There have been human flu pandemics since – in 1933, 1950, 1957, 1968 and 1977 – but none as virulent as in 1918. Add to this the vague, residual fear that what we sloppily call 'flu' may not be simply the common cold that happens to be heavy enough to allow us to claim a few days off work but something altogether more serious.

Of course, the media thrives on the unrealized threat of mortal disease that could wipe out entire, well, readerships. Bird flu is just the latest of these – after SARS, MRSA and HIV/AIDS. But in the case of H5N1 flu, august public health officials have added fuel to the flames, pronouncing that a killer pandemic is 'inevitable'. Epidemiologists merely use the word 'inevitable' to mean that 'there were several serious flu epidemic/pandemics in the twentieth century, the virus is able to evolve into new forms against which we have no effective vaccine or natural immunity, and so there is no reason to think that the twenty-first century will be different'. Or, as the *Independent* shrieked, 'We face a century of viral pandemics'. Now it is possible – just about – to make out that the *twentieth* century was a 'century of viral pandemics', although few would define it in those terms despite the devastating advent of HIV. There is no reason to think that earlier centuries

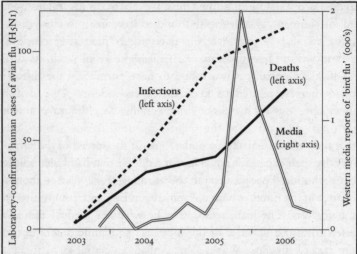

Global human infections and deaths due to H5N1 avian flu and Western media coverage of the virus. Note how media interest is higher during winter months and tails off despite increasing global mortality.
Source: WHO/Factiva database (UK, US and European news and business publications searched for 'bird flu').[2]

fared better, and so none to think that the twenty-first century should not have its share of viral outbreaks too. The question is whether outbreaks will be more frequent or more severe to earn the century this label.

This kind of language is symptomatic of an old tendency to blame ourselves for visitations of pestilence. But here it has a modern dressing of anti-capitalism. For Mike Davis, SARS and HIV were the 'deadly by-product of a largely illegal international wildlife trade, intimately connected with logging and deforestation, which mortally threatens human health as well as regional biodiversity', while avian flu has prospered 'in ecological niches recently created by global agrocapitalism'.[3] The *Independent*'s columnist Johann Hari echoes him, saying we will be 'plagued by pandemics because of the new virus-friendly ecology we have created across the world'. So it's all our own fault, then. It's our affluent lifestyles, our travelling, our migration to the cities that's doing it.

But it is clear that modern life is not mainly to blame. It is quasi-rural backyards with small flocks of chickens where people catch bird flu, not intensive poultry sheds. On the whole we enjoy better food and personal hygiene and experience less risk of picking up an infection from a non-human source than in the past. Even where the risk is still high, the solution through measures such as clean water supply is within our grasp if we are prepared to pay for it.

It is true that an outbreak today is more likely to be global. But sheer geographic spread does not mean that the virus responsible is uncontainable. The pneumonia-like Severe Acute Respiratory Syndrome (SARS) emerged in November 2002. Over eight months, it spread to twenty-six countries. In all, more than 8,000 people were infected, of whom 774 died. In the most dramatic illustration of the way disease can spread in the global village, a doctor who had attended some of the first victims in China travelled to Hong Kong for a wedding. There he passed the infection to sixteen other guests. Within a day, those people and others whom they infected in turn distributed the virus to half a dozen countries as far afield as Ireland and Canada, ultimately accounting for 355 cases.

The SARS episode now provides an exemplary case study of how a powerful virus spreads – and may be contained. For although SARS did rapidly kill three times as many people as avian flu has done, it was contained relatively efficiently by isolation and quarantine of those infected.

Preparedness in this case did not mean laying in vast stockpiles of a vaccine since SARS was a completely new virus. Nor would some of the usual government reflex gestures such as closing borders have made any difference in time. The key was openness and rapid reporting, rather than the sort of administrative denial that can give a virus time to spread unchecked. Another lesson applicable to pandemics of all kinds is the importance of accurate diagnosis and decisively taken preventive measures. In general, even very contagious diseases may be controlled by means of appropriate education as much as by high-tech medicine.

If a flu pandemic is indeed 'inevitable', it is equally inevitable that it will start in Asia. It is the high 'viral load' here that tempts epidemiologists to use the word in the first place. All of the modern global flu outbreaks began in China, where many people live crammed into unsanitary conditions, frequently cohabiting with their ducks, chickens and other livestock. The future issue for the rest of the world may be containment; the issue in rural Asia now is domestic hygiene.

Despite this reality, western governments and media continue to play to the gallery. 'If bird flu grips the nation, doctors will need guns,' screamed the *Sunday Times*. The viral load is nowhere lower than in the United States, yet this is where some of the most hysterical coverage is seen. The *New York Times* alarmed its readers with news that the vaccine being stockpiled by the US 'protects only about half the people who receive it', making it sound for a moment as if survival would be a lottery even for the inoculated. Only later in the story came the admission: 'The disease has not reached the Americas.'

In Britain, the *Sunday Herald* leaked a government study predicting the breakdown of society: 'A minimum of 25 percent of the population will become ill over each six-to eight-week period . . . Mortality is likely to be high − estimated at 1 percent of the total population.'[4] Not that there was much to be done about it. At home, nothing yet needed doing. For anywhere else, the precautions were elementary. The UK National Health Service advised people travelling to affected regions to avoid close contact with poultry and to wash their hands. Washing your hands is never a bad thing, of course, but the clueless advice hardly seems commensurate with the claimed scale of the looming disaster and media talk of stockpiling body-bags. It recalls that of the hygiene-obsessed economist Edwin Chadwick, who went to his grave restating his belief in 'soap and water as a preventative of epidemics' long after the celebrated John Snow had narrowed down the source of the 1848 London cholera outbreak to a particular street pump.[5]

So far, so terrifying. Perhaps it is more instructive to look at what you have to do to catch this disease rather than what to do to prevent it. What does it take to catch flu from a bird? Scientists discovered in 1974 that the avian flu virus thrives in the guts of wild birds, notably waterfowl. Unlike familiar forms of human-transmissible flu, which is a respiratory infection passed through the air, avian flu is passed on when healthy birds ingest water containing the excreta of infected birds. For a person to become infected, he or she must have intimate exposure to the excreta or intestines of an infected bird. Taking up voodoo and smearing yourself with the raw entrails of an infected chicken in a sacrificial ritual would thus be a good way to contract bird flu. Another successful method is to eat (carelessly prepared) raw ducks' blood sausage, which is a Vietnamese delicacy and the cause of some cases in that country. Sharing your accommodation with poultry is hazardous because the birds' excreta or remains are likely to contaminate human food. This explains the majority of human cases of bird flu – no cases have been recorded of people catching the disease from live wild birds or from cooked poultry.

In the UK, it is statistically true to say that you are more likely to die of rabies than bird flu simply because one man – a professional bat handler – died of bat rabies in 2002. This comparison may seem facetious, but both avian flu and rabies are – along with HIV, ebola and measles – zoönotic diseases, that is to say they are carried by animals but can pass to humans if the virus mutates in the right way. The comparison illustrates the fact that for both these normally animal-borne viruses a human being has to take extraordinary steps to put themselves at such a disadvantage that infection is possible.

Even then, the avian flu virus must be present in a form that is able to attack human cells. There are 144 possible combinations of the sixteen H (haemagglutinin) and nine N (neuraminidase) chemical groups that dot the surface of a flu virus. $H5N1$ is one particular combination. The previous flu epidemics of the twentieth century were $H1N1$, $H2N2$ and $H3N2$. Other combinations arise from time to time – for example, in the Netherlands in 2003 an outbreak of $H7N7$ led to a cull of eleven million chickens. One person died out of eighty-three infected by this less deadly strain. But scientists do not know what mutations are needed to produce a dangerous type of the virus. They cannot predict when mutations will appear or what they will be. This makes it impossible to prepare specific vaccines or anti-viral treatments before the new type is present in humans.

It is this mutability that makes flu dangerous. The smallpox virus, for example, has a fixed composition, which has made it relatively easy to eradicate. The H and N groups of the flu virus, on the other hand, may 'drift' into a different form if the amino acids within them are altered. Darwinian natural selection then ensures that the virus reappears each year in a slightly different version, although this change happens sufficiently slowly that the human immune system is generally able to cope with the new invader. But the virus can also 'shift' rapidly into a new type when a new H or N is introduced, for example from birds. When this happens, there is no ready immunity in the general population.

'Mutation' is also a word made for scare stories. It seems to leap straight from the pages of John Wyndham, where some malevolent biological slime manoeuvres for world domination using processes clearly outside human understanding or control. Mutation is an evolutionary process, but it is not directed. The flu virus is not out to get us, it is simply out to survive, which it already does in the bird population. A sequence of mutations is required for H5N1 to be able to thrive not in a bird's gut but in the quite different conditions of the human respiratory tract. These mutations may or may not occur. And if a human-adapted virus does result, it may or may not turn out to be highly pathogenic.

Paradoxically, a virus that is both highly infective (i.e. it spreads efficiently) and highly pathogenic (i.e. it kills a high proportion of those whom it infects) may not be very dangerous on a global level because it quickly kills too many of its host species to be able to continue spreading. The pandemic threat comes from a virus that is only moderately pathogenic but highly infective. The 1918 flu was such a virus, infecting more than half the world's population but killing only one in twenty of those it infected. The H5N1 virus circulating today is highly pathogenic (it has killed more than half the humans it has infected) but much harder to catch. If it mutates into a highly infective form, that in turn is likely to make it ultimately *less* lethal worldwide.

Recorded outbreaks have claimed single victims or small groups of people, almost all of whom can be directly linked to birds. All this means that it is extraordinarily unlikely that, for example, Princess Diana's driver was suffering from bird flu on the night of her fatal car crash, a theory reportedly entertained by the *Daily Express*. Bird flu remains essentially a disease of birds even though it may have taken the *New York Times* eight paragraphs in its story about the virus 'spreading rapidly through Asia, Europe and Africa' to remind its readers of this basic fact.

There are other reasons to worry less about bird flu. The media has repeatedly said that a pandemic is 'overdue' or even 'long overdue'. This claim is not based on any virological dictum, but simply on the historical pattern of outbreaks – one every ten to fifteen years or so from 1918 to 1977 and then a pregnant pause until now. But in fact the longer H5N1 'tries', the *less* likely it is to succeed in adapting into a human-transmissible type. Some scientists now believe H5N1 has had its chance. A virus is not like a volcano, where pressure may build up gradually, leading to an eventual eruption. And a continued non-outbreak doesn't make a future outbreak more likely or more deadly.

It seems these truths are at last being acknowledged. In February 2007, H5N1 avian flu rampaged through a Bernard Matthews turkey shed in Suffolk, requiring the swift destruction of 160,000 birds. Media talk of an inevitable human pandemic promptly vanished, replaced by a new Dunkirk spirit. When push came to shove, the outbreak was simply something that had to be – and could be – dealt with.

While bird flu has yet to claim a single human victim in Europe or the Americas, and has killed fewer than 300 people worldwide, it is perhaps worth adding that the familiar winter flu that nobody panics about claims at least 30,000 American and 12,000 British lives each year.

It's Amazing What They Can Do
'Superbug "apocalypse" warning' *Guardian*

Where would you go to catch a dangerous infection? A crowded commuter train, an aeroplane, an infants' school, a brothel? How about a hospital?

'Hospital bug that kills in 24 hours', warned the *Daily Mail* in December 2006 as an apparently new strain of the by now familiar 'superbug' MRSA claimed its latest victims, a nurse and a patient in Staffordshire. 'Hospital crisis as PVL bug kills tot', added the *Sun* five days later as a premature baby boy died in Norwich.

PVL (Panton–Valentine leukocidin) is a toxin sometimes produced in association with MRSA. It destroys the white blood cells which the body needs to fight infection and can quickly kill by causing pneumonia and other conditions.

MRSA (methicillin-resistant *Staphylococcus aureus*) was identified in the 1960s as a variant of the *Staphylococcus aureus* bacterium that had developed resistance to methicillin, an antibiotic introduced after the bacterium had already begun to show resistance to penicillin. Occasional MRSA infections were observed from this time, but newspapers began to use the word 'superbug' to describe MRSA in the 1980s, when outbreaks began to increase, especially in American and British hospitals. In 1995, in New York City alone, 7,800 people became infected with drug-resistant *Staphylococcus*; 1,400 of them died.[1] In Britain, MRSA became a major issue in the 2005 general election campaign. *Staphylococcus aureus* mainly infects open wounds, causing boils and abscesses, and is therefore especially dangerous to surgical patients. It is this that makes it a hospital disease.

So are hospitals now places to be feared rather than places of healing? The British media have widely quoted a figure of 5,000 deaths each year due to MRSA estimated by the National Audit Office. But another government organization, the Health Protection Agency (HPA), calls this figure 'incorrect', pointing out that it describes deaths from *all* hospital-acquired infections. Many people thought that MRSA was the major, if not only, such infection, hence the confusion. It is cold comfort that the death toll stands and that there are simply other infections to worry about.

Nevertheless, it was MRSA that first captured the attention of the media. The number of death certificates specifying MRSA as a contributory factor at first rose by about a hundred a year. The records start from a low base of fifty-one deaths in 1993, allowing the BBC to note 'Superbug deaths increase 15-fold' when the figure reached 800 in 2002.[2] The figure jumped from 1,100 in 2004 to around 1,600 in the last three years in England and Wales.[3]

However, deaths are not a very reliable indicator of the prevalence of MRSA. The numbers may be an underestimate if death is still ascribed to a familiar killer such as pneumonia rather than MRSA where both are present. On the other hand, better diagnosis undoubtedly accounts for some of the rise in recorded MRSA, while the fact that MRSA is much more likely to be mentioned on death certificates of people who died in hospital than on those of people who died elsewhere could arise from an excessive readiness to name MRSA because it is already associated with hospitals.

Meanwhile, the newspapers have grown shriller as nature has come up with new tricks. Unlike ordinary MRSA, which affects the most vulnerable, PVL has the impressive property that it afflicts the 'young and healthy' – among them therefore perhaps even more of their readers. 'Remember these initials,' intoned the *Independent*, putting them in letters 86 millimetres high on its front page just to make sure that we did. The first PVL fatality during this period was an eighteen-year-old who died after infection of a leg injury sustained while he was on a commando training exercise.

Microbiologists had long warned that consequences were to be expected from doctors' enthusiasm for prescribing antibiotics, as the bacteria they were designed to combat gradually developed resistance. At first, the fear was of one 'doomsday superbug', probably MRSA.[4] But more recently, it has seemed that we will come under attack by a whole range of bugs. *Enterococci*, *Clostridium difficile* and tuberculosis are among the new or resurgent bacteria that have acquired resistance to antibiotics. National statistics reported in the *Independent* under the headline 'Deaths from "dirty hospital bug" double in five years' show that *Clostridium difficile* has emulated the rise of MRSA and now overtaken it. The bacterium was linked to 8,300 deaths in 2007, double the number in 2005 – five times as many as MRSA.

In January 2007, the *Guardian* issued a 'Superbug "apocalypse"' warning'. The article that followed quoted Professor Richard James, the director of a new Centre for Healthcare Associated Infections at Nottingham University: 'We are facing a future where there will be no antibiotics and hospital will be the last place to be if you want to avoid picking up a dangerous bacterial infection – in effect, cut your finger on Monday and you'll be dead by Friday if there's nothing to prevent it.'

This pessimistic vision carries with it a sense of the medical profession's profound dismay that the antibiotic revolution trumpeted as a miracle scarcely half a century ago now seems to lie in ruins. Yet some of the reasons for this are to be found with the medics themselves. Like the rest of us, many doctors believed that antibiotics were indeed a miracle cure. The use of antibiotics in major surgery as well as in the treatment of infections of many kinds has unquestionably contributed to the public's grateful awe of doctors found in the popular expression 'It's amazing what they can do.'

Although it had been anticipated – and later was shown to be true – that bacteria would respond to hostile antibiotics by adaptation to produce more vigorous strains, it was easy to hope that antibiotics would remain good for all time like ordinary chemical medicines. Frequent indiscriminate and precautionary prescribing of antibiotics merely hastened this process of evolution. In hospitals, meanwhile, according to Laurie Garrett's book, *Betrayal of Trust*, ' "Typhoid Mary" doctors' have also been directly responsible for spreading infection from patient to patient because they are too hurried or too arrogant to wash or submit to testing.[5]

While many doctors have held unrealistic expectations of antibiotics, we have all perhaps cherished unrealistic expectations of what hospitals can do. The idea of public health was born when hospitals were 'little more than warehouses for the dying', according to Garrett.[6] During the third quarter of the twentieth century, they became rather more than that, but this period currently appears to us more like a brief interlude than the latest stage of an upward progress. In terms of infectious disease, hospitals may be reverting to type.

The reasons advanced for this reflect the range of political prejudices about how health services should be run. The transfer of power from the public health authorities to the medical profession in the United States and the reorganization of public hospitals as trusts in Britain are among the suggested factors. The introduction of privatized services, including cleaning, coincides unfortunately with the rise of resistant bacteria. Hospital mergers and centralization may also play a role, since larger hospitals tend to have disproportionate levels of MRSA, while closures facilitate the spread of superbugs as workers relocate.

A full hospital that turns beds over rapidly presumably restores more people to health than a half-empty one. But high occupancy rates are also thought to help the spread of MRSA. 'Headlines about patients dying while waiting to go to a hospital have given way to reports of patients dying simply by staying in one,' as one newspaper tartly put it. An occupancy rate of 82 per cent was cited as a maximum by the Department of Health: 'If occupancy is at 95 per cent, then no amount of handwashing will stop infections.'

MRSA levels are high in the United States and Britain, comparable with France, but twice the level in Germany or Spain.

The situation in all these countries has been compared unfavourably with that in the Netherlands and Denmark, where MRSA infection is extremely low. However, some countries have little MRSA but more of other hospital-associated infections, and it is not clear that anybody has a complete answer. Dutch hospitals operate a praised 'search and destroy' policy whereby patients are screened for MRSA on admittance and placed in isolation wards if necessary. But in Britain this has seemed to be ruled out. Avoiding any mention of isolation wards, the website of the Health Protection Agency at one time invited readers to assume that screening would simply lead to people being excluded from hospital altogether.[7] The advice has changed following a policy U-turn in 2007.

The British government's response to the MRSA crisis has instead been to promote hand-washing, reintroduce matrons to hospital wards and – inevitably – set targets. This last measure has been criticized as crude as it simply records the percentage rise or fall in MRSA. This can penalize hospitals that have cut their infection rates to low levels only to find that an 'unlucky' outbreak sends the figure soaring. In one hospital an admirably low two cases in one month was followed by a still low seven cases the next, due mainly to an influx of new patients. The 250 per cent increase meant that the hospital failed to meet its target.

It is tempting to seek parallels for the MRSA phenomenon in previous scares to do with bacteria, such as salmonella and listeria in food, as well as diseases such as BSE in beef cattle or the threat of avian flu, and a generalized fear of invisible germs. But this is to neglect the hospital connection that is so much a feature of the media coverage. Consider instead that the fear of hospital-associated infection may mask a deeper fear – that of having to go to hospital at all. The dread of surgery in particular, though seldom discussed, ranks among the highest public fears, according to Paul Slovic's *The Perception of Risk*.[8]

Another distinctive factor in the MRSA story is that at least part of the solution to the crisis is widely thought to lie with improved hospital hygiene. Unlike the transmission and treatment of infectious diseases, this is a topic on which everybody has an opinion. We see with our own eyes that many hospitals are filthy. The issue of cleanliness which emerged as MRSA infections climbed in the late 1990s gave the media and the public a campaigning focus of both practical and metaphorical value. Hospitals needed to be cleaner, but the way they were run could use a 'clean-up' as well.

The Labour government responded by rolling out a 'Clean your hands' campaign across the nation's hospitals in 2004 – with modest results. The Conservatives fought the election the following year using a number of ingenuous Joe Public remarks linked by the refrain: 'Are you thinking what we're thinking?' One of these was: 'I mean, how hard is it to keep a hospital clean?' The only mildly counter-intuitive answer is, of course, that it is pretty hard and, in terms of microbial contamination, harder than many other places.

The obsessive focus on hygiene by the media, and subsequently by politicians with an eye for cheap measures that might make a visible difference, has disguised the fact that the other part of the solution to bacterial resistance must be the creation of more effective antibiotics. For all the use of words such as 'doomsday' and 'apocalypse', there is no destined biological end point where all bacteria become resistant to all antibiotics. Instead, we need to develop new antibiotics to keep pace with the emergence of new resistant strains and at the same time remain disciplined in prescribing them only in specific circumstances so as not to spur the emergence of resistance. Sadly, this means letting go of the notion that the antibiotics of the last century are everlasting miracle cures and adjusting to the fact that bacteria adapt and change.

It's amazing what they can do. The bugs, that is.

Completing the Course
'Jab damaged our children, say 2,000' *Daily Mail*

The triple vaccine for measles, mumps and rubella (MMR) was the basis for one of the biggest recent scare stories in the United Kingdom. The story blew up not when the vaccine was introduced in 1988, but ten years later, when a doctor at the Royal Free Hospital in London published a paper that appeared to link the vaccine to autism and bowel disease.

The MMR vaccine was designed to protect against three viral diseases of which older readers may have direct memories. Measles is a highly contagious disease characterized by an itchy rash. In developed countries, the mortality rate is one in 3,000, but it can be as much as one in ten where malnutrition is rife. Measles deaths have fallen sharply this decade but, according to figures from the World Health Organization, still claimed 242,000 lives in 2006 among unvaccinated populations worldwide. Mumps produces glandular swelling and is generally less serious, but both mumps and measles can produce life-threatening complications. The principal risk from rubella is to women in early pregnancy whose babies may be born with birth defects.

These diseases have been virtually eradicated in the West since the introduction of vaccines in the 1960s and 1970s. However, a large proportion of the population must be vaccinated in order for society as a whole to be protected. For measles vaccine, the coverage required for the population as a whole to be safe from an epidemic (to reach what is called herd immunity) is 90 per cent or more because the disease is so contagious. Measles remains a major killer in developing countries simply because the vaccine doesn't reach enough people. Because it is hard to achieve the necessary coverage, and because not all vaccine doses are effective, immunization programmes frequently recommend a second dose, which greatly reduces the chances that a given person does not have at least some protection.

The measles-only vaccine introduced into the UK in 1970 reduced annual deaths from a hundred or so to an average of twenty. In 1988, just before the introduction of the MMR vaccine, there were 86,001 notified measles cases and sixteen deaths. From 1989 to 1997, MMR coverage then reached more than 90 per cent and measles deaths fell to two a year.[1]

What happened next was to derail the juggernaut of medical progress towards the eradication of measles in Britain and beyond. In February 1998, Dr Andrew Wakefield, a gastroenterologist at the Royal Free Hospital, published results of tests on twelve children with both intestinal inflammation and developmental disorders including autism. The paper mentioned work by others (and previous work by Wakefield on the measles-only vaccine) in which the viruses and/or their vaccines were 'associated' with or 'implicated as risk factors' for autism; it left similar doubt hanging in the air over the MMR vaccine. 'We did not prove an association between measles, mumps and rubella vaccine and the syndrome described,' the authors wrote in the *Lancet*.[2]

Not only did Wakefield not prove an association, he did not produce *any* evidence to support one. Wakefield simply wrote: 'Onset of behavioural symptoms was associated, *by the parents*, with measles, mumps and rubella vaccination' (italics added). That was all. There the story surely would have died a death but for the fact that at a press conference Wakefield then pursued this idea of a link and suggested that parents might wish to have their children put through three courses of separate vaccinations rather than undergo the triple vaccine.

The story hit the headlines immediately, but grew only slowly in ferocity for reasons largely unrelated to the quality of the original science. 'Measles vaccine's link with autism studied' was the anodyne way that *The Times* put it as the *Lancet* came out. Two months later new work appeared to refute Wakefield, and another paper countered: 'MMR study dismisses fears as groundless.' At this point, the *Daily Mail* got the scent of a David-and-Goliath battle between put-upon consumers and medical authority. 'Vaccine experts clash again', reported its sister paper, the *Mail on Sunday*, noting that the row 'is set to intensify'.

Through the rest of 1998, worried parents sought single

vaccinations against the three diseases, or vaccination solely against measles. Supplies of single vaccines ran out in less than a fortnight while the government insisted that people rely on the combined vaccine. The *Daily Mail* took up aggrieved parents' cause, championing their attempt to win the right to choice in court: 'Parents shun MMR jab over health fears'; 'Jab damaged our children, say 2,000'; 'Parents' fear as the single measles jab is withdrawn. Drug company denies giving in to government pressure.'

The scare was unusually effective for a number of reasons: the public trusts what doctors say, but does not like being told what to do by governments; parents seek their children's safety and well-being; people naturally fear immunization; and autism was apparently on the increase. The numbers of people identified with autism had begun to rise in the 1970s in the United States and in the 1980s in Britain, largely coincident with the respective dates of introduction of the MMR vaccine. Autism was doubling every five years, partly because of better diagnosis and more inclusive definitions of the condition, but partly, it seemed, because of unidentified, possibly environmental, factors. Identifying links with other conditions might help scientists understand the causes of autism, and it was understandable that people should light upon one potential link where it was easy to lay the blame.

The immediate consequence of the press campaign was a fall in immunization levels. Coverage fell from 91 per cent of two-year-olds in 1998 to 88 per cent the following year. It continued to decline steadily, reaching a low of 80 per cent in England and Wales by 2004, and much less in some areas. No evidence has been presented to support Wakefield's theory, while many large studies, including one in the *Lancet* as early as 1999, could find no link. These culminated in a review of thirty-one studies, each involving hundreds, and in one case half a million, subjects, by an international team for the Cochrane Library, an organization set up to evaluate medical research.[3] This received a fraction of the coverage of Wakefield's study of twelve children, although the *Sun* put it in plain English under the headline 'MMR in clear': 'The Cochrane

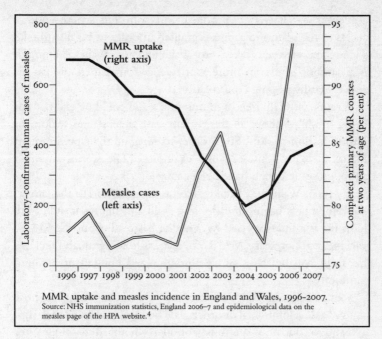

MMR uptake and measles incidence in England and Wales, 1996-2007.
Source: NHS immunization statistics, England 2006–7 and epidemiological data on the measles page of the HPA website.[4]

Review analysed 31 studies from around the world and said there was NO evidence to back up the fears.'

As evidence grew refuting Wakefield's claim, Wakefield himself was accused of having been paid £55,000 by lawyers for the families who had brought their children to him, an interest he had not declared to the *Lancet*. Most of his co-authors publicly dissociated themselves from him. But the *Daily Mail* still backed him. 'MMR safe? Baloney. This is one scandal that's getting worse,' opined Melanie Phillips in a typically strident column.

Catching Phillips out on science is like drowning rats, but somebody has to do it. So, here goes (and you can repeat this check for yourself). Phillips writes that Wakefield's discovery of autistic enterocolitis, the condition supposed to explain the link between MMR, autism and bowel disease, 'as a completely new syndrome has now been replicated in studies around the world'. Let's see. The simple expedient of a search on Google Scholar, the academic search engine, produces forty-one hits where enough access to the scientific papers is granted in order to be able to take a view. Six references take a pro-Wakefield line, Wakefield himself is an author of eleven more, but twenty-four papers dismiss his result. Hardly ringing confirmation.

Parents with children of immunizable age could be excused for being muddled about all this. In any case their stories seldom fit into neat clinical slots. So in order to imagine their predicament it may help to consider some examples. (The stories are true, although some details have been changed.)

It's 1999. William, a bookie, has his first addition to the family. He remembers having measles as a child and figures it didn't kill him. He is a little worried by what he has read about the MMR vaccine, but notes that MMR coverage is holding up and reckons his child will be safest of all unimmunized but reliant on herd immunity.

2001. Fiona, a florist, has a two-year-old son beginning to show signs of a developmental disorder. The boy had his first MMR shot a year ago, but now she must consider whether his young sister should have her first shot in a few months' time. The boy's disorder may be genetic, but there again, perhaps the MMR was respon-sible. She decides the girl should have the vaccines singly in a private clinic. As the doctor gives the jab, he vouchsafes that, by the way, his children had the combined vaccine, and he thinks it's safe.

2002. Juliet, a busy actor, has a daughter who had the MMR jab and now must decide whether to do the same with her eighteen-month-old son. She remembers reading an article a couple of years ago in *Private Eye* recounting the conviction of a parent of a child who had developed autism that it was the MMR vaccine that must have caused it. Her 'blind faith' in medicine is rocked. 'I had learned how vigilant you have to be as a parent because you are responsible for this little life.' She books her boy in to a private clinic to have the three vaccines separately: first measles, then rubella and finally mumps.

How did these children fare? Fiona's daughter is protected against measles and turns out not to develop her sibling's disorder.

William realizes that protection against contagion is actually frighteningly low where he lives – against Department of Health advice, people are holding 'measles parties' so that their unprotected children might get the disease over with. He belatedly puts his child in for the MMR jab. Fortunately, the child has not caught measles in the interim. Juliet (who is in fact the actor Juliet Stevenson) duly takes her son to a crowded, disorganized clinic for the measles and rubella shots. By the time that she is free of work commitments and can think about the final shot for mumps, she calls the clinic only to find that it has closed some months ago. The doctor who ran it has been arrested and charged with forging the results of blood tests. An independent test shows that Juliet's son actually has no protection against measles. 'Now I don't know what to do. Do I get him single measles again, or forget the whole thing?' she wonders aloud to the *Mail on Sunday* while promoting her role in a cathartic drama about the dangers of MMR.

As the example of mothers like Juliet Stevenson shows, the relative safety of a vaccine shown by statistical evidence is not always persuasive. Vaccination allows a pollutant to enter the body and so breaks a deep taboo. Vaccines do not work in all cases and produce adverse reactions in some. For these reasons people have feared vaccination since its invention – an occasion commemorated in a lurid caricature published in 1802 by James Gillray showing people receiving Edward Jenner's smallpox vaccine erupting in bovine buboes.

This timeless fear is overlaid by characteristically modern concerns that seem bound to surface afresh with each new vaccine introduction. 'Vaccines come under greatest scrutiny when they are successful,' as one doctor pointed out in the *Guardian* at the height of the single vaccine rush. When they are the only alternative to a nasty disease, they are uncritically accepted. But today we – including many of our doctors – have forgotten what it is like to suffer, or witness suffering, from many of the diseases that we now immunize against. Smallpox was the biggest killer disease in the West during the eighteenth century, tuberculosis in the nineteenth, both eradicated by vaccination.

Without unpleasant reminders of what vaccines are for, we have the luxury of speculating about side-effects and links to other disorders. Combined vaccines – which are likely to become more of a feature of immunization in the future – mean fewer jabs, but excite fears of chemical 'cocktails' and overloading of children's immune systems. As Stevenson told her interviewer, 'There are hundreds if not thousands of parents in this country who deeply believe that their children were damaged by this vaccine, yet they have still not been given credibility.' But most parents are not immunologists, and while the depth of their belief is not in question, its basis in reliable observation most definitely is.

Autism is an obvious focus for parents' fears because it is often first observed at an age shortly after children have had their first immunizations. (Before MMR there were fears that other vaccines might be linked to autism.) However, a closer look at the timing of autism diagnosis in relation to immunization reveals an interesting pattern, with parents tending to spot signs much sooner (around six weeks) than health professionals (six months or more).[5] Yet if there was a link between MMR and autism, one would expect the professionals to notice the signs as soon as the parents. Alternatively, if there is no link, one would again expect everybody to notice signs at the same time – when they appear. The fact that the experts observe the signs later could conceivably point to professional conservatism, incompetence or denial. Perhaps the parents' earlier observation can be attributed to entirely natural anxiety. Sadly, this does not mean that the autism is not real, but it does suggest that the link with the MMR vaccine is imagined.

Blaming the MMR vaccine for autism rather than one's genes, or sheer bad luck, is a complicated displacement that implicates science and technology, the medical establishment and modernity in general. But it is also a pernicious way of blaming ourselves – we as parents put the child to the needle – and it is this tendency above all that the media exploits so cynically in scare stories of many kinds.

The effect of the anti-MMR campaign was to add to the

defaulters who did not have their children immunized out of ignorance or idleness a large number of 'active resisters', who were, according to Michael Fitzpatrick, a doctor who wrote a parents' guide to MMR and autism, 'middle-class, well-educated parents who had chosen not to have their children immunized'.[6] These parents pitched themselves against a government that refused to give the option of single vaccines, as is sanctioned in some other countries. The combined effect of these two groups pushed immunization in Britain well below the safety threshold for herd immunity.

It began to seem that matters would only be resolved the hard way. Cases of measles rose sharply in 2002–3 and again in 2006, and to nearly 1,000 in 2007 – a level not seen since before introduction of the triple vaccine. In March 2006, a thirteen-year-old boy became Britain's first child measles fatality since 1992. Among the papers joining the chorus of alarm was the *Daily Mail*: 'Measles epidemic fears as cases rocket'. The story that followed neglected to mention the paper's own role in sustaining the MMR controversy that had produced this unhappy situation, and even nonchalantly dropped in a reference to Wakefield's *Lancet* paper: 'research that has been widely discredited.'

Sudden Death

'Cot death link to lone parents' *Daily Express*

Immunization is not the only worry facing parents of new-borns. Sudden infant death syndrome (SIDS) is any sudden and unexplained death of an apparently healthy infant aged over one month. The term cot death is often used in the UK and crib death in North America. The diagnosis of cot death is a so-called definition of exclusion, applying only to an infant whose death remains unexplained after the performance of post-mortem investigations, including an autopsy. Generally, the infant is found dead after having been put to sleep and exhibits no signs of having suffered. The fear of sudden infant death means that new parents regularly visit their sleeping baby to check that he or she is still breathing.

The extent of parental worry does not make much sense as SIDS is responsible for very few deaths. In the US, it accounts for roughly 50 deaths per hundred thousand births. The rate is a little higher, around 60, in Scotland, and a little lower, around 40, in England and Wales. This is far fewer deaths than caused by congenital disorders and disorders related to short gestation, though it is the leading cause of death in otherwise healthy babies aged one month to one year, albeit a category in which there are very few deaths. Moreover, the incidence of sudden infant death syndrome has fallen in all developed countries in recent years, in some cases dramatically. A fall of nearly 90 per cent in Australia over fifteen years is particularly noteworthy.

But the worry remains very real, reflecting both the horror of losing a young child and the 'incomplete' medical explanation for the event when it does occur. Very little is known for sure about the cause of SIDS, and there is no proven method for complete prevention. That said, many studies of babies around the world that have died suddenly and unexpectedly have identified a number of risk factors. Pre-natal risks include inadequate nutrition, a smoking mother, teenage pregnancy, alcohol and hard drug abuse and an interval of less than one year between subsequent births. It is striking that the rate of unexplained infant death in England and Wales is four times greater for children born to mothers aged under twenty than those born to mothers in their thirties, and six times higher for those children registered at birth only to the mother than for those children born to a married couple. Studies in the US have also shown that African American and Native American infants are two to three times more likely to die from SIDS than white infants.

Post-natal risks include low birth weight, exposure to tobacco smoke, excess clothing and overheating, excess bedding, soft sleep surface and stuffed animals and sharing the parental bed. It also seems that boys are more likely to suffer than girls – nearly two-thirds of deaths are accounted for by boys. Putting young children to nap in their own bedroom is also thought to be a risk.

Laying an infant to sleep on his or her stomach is widely thought to be one of the greatest risk factors. Accordingly, many govern-ments have introduced 'back to sleep' campaigns, encouraging parents to put their children to sleep on their backs. There are various theories supporting the risk of prone sleeping. The first is the idea that small infants with little control over their heads may, while face down, inhale their exhaled breath or smother themselves on their bedding. A second theory suggests that babies sleep more soundly placed on their stomachs and are unable to rouse them-selves when they have an incidence of sleep apnoea, breath holding, which is thought to be common in infants. It has also been sug-gested that the victims of SIDS might have abnormalities in or delayed development of the arcuate nucleus of the brainstem, contributing to their death. Whenever 'back to sleep' campaigns were introduced, in the early 1980s in the UK and the early 1990s in the US, SIDS death rates fell, often sharply.

Death might also be caused, some researchers say, by the toxic nerve gases produced through the action of fungus in mattresses on the chemical compounds frequently used to make mattresses fire retardant. A major plank in this explanation is the widely observed phenomenon that the risk of cot death rises from one sibling to the next. After one cot death in a family, the risk of recurrence for a subsequent child is up to five times the rate of the population more generally. No satisfactory biological explanation for this has ever been put forward. But the toxic gas explanation fits this neatly as parents generally buy new bedding for their first child, reusing it for later children, with a greater chance that there will be fungus which has become resident in the material, in turn leading to a higher chance of cot death. Single mothers or poorer families might borrow used or buy second-hand cots, perhaps accounting for the higher death rates among these groups.

A decade ago, the New Zealand government issued advice recommending that new parents either buy bedding free of the toxic compounds or wrap the mattresses in a barrier film to prevent the escape of gases. It is claimed by those supporting this view that no case of cot death has ever been traced back to such a manufactured or wrapped mattress. Of course, face-up sleeping could well reduce the death rate if this is the cause for SIDS, as the dense gases that cause death diffuse away towards the floor – a baby sleeping face-up is less likely to inhale them.

More recently a brain abnormality has been found in the victims of SIDS that could cause the babies to suffocate if they become smothered by bedclothes. The US researchers claimed that this was 'the strongest evidence yet of a common cause for cot death'. The debate rumbles on.

One particularly sensitive issue is the link between cot death and child abuse. All professionals involved in cot deaths accept that there are a small number where a parent or carer has done something unlawful to contribute to the death. A number of paediatricians have said that they believe that some cases diagnosed as SIDS are really deaths resulting from child abuse. Their suspicions are particularly aroused in the case of multiple cot deaths within a family. Indeed a dictum known as 'Meadow's Law', after the well-known former paediatrician, says that 'one cot death is a tragedy, two cot deaths is suspicious and, until the contrary is proved, three cot deaths is murder'.

During the 1990s and early 2000s in the UK, a number of mothers of multiple apparent SIDS victims were convicted of murder. At one of the trials, Sir Roy Meadow, speaking as an expert witness for the prosecution, made one of the most infamous statistical statements ever in a British courtroom. He claimed that the chance of two children in the same affluent and non-smoking family both dying a cot death was one in 73 million. In a complex, confusing and emotional case, the statement provided something definite to hold on to and was widely headlined in the national press. The mother, Sally Clark, who had had two children die of cot death, was convicted of murder.

Unfortunately, the figure was in all probability wrong and certainly misleading. The statistic was derived from the Confidential Enquiry for Stillbirths and Deaths in Infancy, a study of baby deaths in England in the 1990s. It estimated that the chances of a randomly chosen baby dying a cot death are one in 1,300, falling to around one in 8,500 if the child is from an affluent, non-smoking family, with the mother aged over twenty-six years. If, and it is a big if, there is no link between cot deaths of siblings, then the chances of two children from such a family both suffering a cot death is obtained by multiplying the odds, namely one in 8,500 by one in 8,500. This produces the probability of one in 73 million.

But all the evidence suggests that there are links between such deaths, which are not independent. If the odds of a second cot death in a family are around one in 100, the odds of a double cot death would fall to about one in 130,000. Since around 650,000 children are born every year in England and Wales, we might expect as many as five families on average each year to suffer a second tragic loss. This paints a far less dramatic picture than the one in 73 million figure. Interventions from a number of quarters including the Royal Statistical Society led to some high-profile acquittals at subsequent retrials. Sally Clark died of alcohol intoxication in 2007. A family statement after her death said 'she never fully recovered from the effects of this appalling miscarriage of justice.'

The ambiguity, uncertainty and complexity in defining SIDS incidents has had an impact on the statistics we use to define the issue. Statistically in Britain, sudden infant death syndrome did not 'exist' until 1971, when the Registrar General first accepted it as a cause of death. Prior to that time, we had no idea of the true incidence of such deaths, and that in turn hindered the search for an explanation of those deaths that did occur. (Many of the infant deaths prior to that time were – wrongly – attributed to respiratory disease.) Throughout the 1970s and 1980s, the annual total of the newly defined SIDS deaths was stable around 1,000, but the 'back to sleep' campaign has contributed to a reduction in the numbers so that they have recently dipped in England and Wales to below 200 a year.

But defining cause of death is sometimes an imprecise science, and fashions change over time. In the last decade, while the number of sudden infant deaths in England and Wales has halved, the number of 'unascertained deaths' has increased from barely any to over 100. The rise in this category probably reflects the suspicions that some paediatric pathologists have that parental or adult intervention may have occurred in some of the cases where an infant dies suddenly. The Office for National Statistics concluded in a 2005 study that changes in certification practices meant that it had become so difficult to distinguish between the two causes of death that both groups are now presented together in any analysis of unexplained infant deaths. This means that, taking the two definitions together, the number of deaths has fallen but less steeply, from around 400 to 300 each year since the mid-1990s.

Several British government reports in recent years, notably the 2004 Kennedy report, have suggested that the parents of babies whose deaths are labelled as 'unascertained' unfairly face stigma which could reflect nothing more than differing practices among coroners. It recommended that the term 'sudden infant death syndrome' should continue to be used where appropriate, with 'unexplained pending further investigation' or the broader category of 'sudden unexpected death in infancy' being used for all other cases. The report called for a compulsory national protocol along these lines. It is quite possible, therefore, that the number of deaths in each category will change in the years ahead even if there is no underlying change in circumstances.

Whatever the definitional issues relating to the figures and the resulting trends, the bottom line would seem to be that parents can reduce to next to nothing the chances of an infant dying unexpectedly by putting it to sleep on its back, on a properly wrapped mattress and with little else in the cot. The odds also seem to favour girls, first born to a thirty-year-old couple compared to the second or third son born to a teenage mother. Nevertheless, while uncertainty about the causes of unexpected infant death remain – and money is thrown at researchers to pursue such a wide range of avenues – the media will stir up concern, leaving parents of young children with a nagging doubt for years to come.

As the children grow up, the parents can leave behind worries of SIDS but can begin to worry about the emerging phenomenon of 'adult cot death' or sudden adult death syndrome, which seems to strike mainly those in their teens and twenties. Evidence is emerging that the number of people who collapse and die suddenly without explanation could be much greater than is recorded in the official statistics, with the cause of the tragic deaths remaining a mystery. One study suggested that no cause could be identified for around 150 of the 3,500 apparently healthy adults who die suddenly each year in England. Campaigners say that this condition needs to be given a 'name' so that the problem will be addressed more seriously, as was the case with sudden infant death from the 1970s onwards.

3. Passing the Time

Pastimes designed for relaxation can also be panic inducing. Alcohol is a well-known demon, but art can also kill. Modern technology might threaten the cinema as we know it but it has made collecting easier.

Art Is Dangerous
'Art – or accident waiting to happen?' *The Times*

Artists have always relished the idea that their work is 'dangerous'. Picasso, Duke Ellington and Anthony Burgess are among those who have made this claim in as many words. But the artist's idea of what makes a work dangerous is perhaps not quite the same as everyone else's.

When Carsten Höller became only the seventh artist to fill the vast Turbine Hall of London's Tate Modern art gallery in October 2006, his temporary installation was greeted not with the usual gasps of awe but with whoops of glee from most – and trepidation from a few. *The Times* was most concerned. Was the piece 'Art – or accident waiting to happen?' Höller's work, *Test Site*, was essentially a set of five glorified helter skelters, finely constructed in stainless steel and clear plastic. The longest of the slides was 55 metres, and it took just twelve hair-raising seconds to descend through its chutes and spirals. But were gallery visitors taking the ride possibly on 'a slippery slope to disaster'?

The story originated on press night, when sliders reportedly emerged from the tubes at high speed with 'swollen ankles, friction burns, grazed knees and bruised elbows'. Extra cushioning was hastily added. Nobody was going to worry much about a few injured journalists, but the safety of the public was naturally a concern as the slides were being assembled. Fortunately, the artist was able to offer solid reassurance: 'These are built to German safety standards which the British inspectors are very happy with because they have the reputation of being the best in the world.'

As art critics were bruising their bottoms on Höller's slides, controversy was also growing concerning Antony Gormley's *Another Place*, an array of one hundred larger-than-life cast-iron standing figures staring out to sea, dotted over several square kilometres of the beach at Crosby in Lancashire. The pieces farthest out to sea were said to pose a hazard to navigation as well as to admirers, who might become so enraptured by them as to forget the advancing tide and be swept off to Davy Jones's locker. Citing the danger to health and safety, the local council voted to have the work removed (it later won a reprieve). As this was due to take place, a woman viewing the figures did indeed become stuck in the mud, requiring the services of the Liverpool Coastguard. In reporting the story, a local newspaper exonerated the art with the headline, 'Iron men not to blame for beach hazards, say rescuers'. The article quoted a lifeboatman, who pointed out: 'Beaches are always a hazard.'

But perhaps there is good reason to be wary of art. A few months before these incidents, two women had been killed and a three-year-old girl badly injured when a giant inflatable artwork that they were exploring broke free from its tethers and flew off into the air before snagging on a nearby CCTV mast. The work, *Dreamscape* by Maurice Agis, was on display at a park in Chester-le-Street, County Durham. The PVC structure consisted of colourful chambers linked by a network of tunnels. Wearing equally colourful capes, people could wander through the maze, 'disappearing' when their location matched their costume. Since 1996, versions of the work had been exhibited in Denmark, Italy and Spain without mishap, as well as in Liverpool, where it was vandalized with knives.

But the most notorious cases of death by art were in 1991. In October of that year the artist Christo, best known for his colourful wrapping of edifices such as the Pont Neuf in Paris and the Reichstag in Berlin, unveiled a massive installation of specially

constructed metal umbrellas on either side of the Pacific Ocean –
1,760 yellow umbrellas in California, 60 miles north of Los Angeles,
and 1,340 blue ones at Ibaraki in Japan.

The installations in California had been open little more than a
week when they had to be closed to the public due to high winds,
which were beginning to damage the umbrellas. Crews struggled
in the gale with the dangerous job of cranking the giant metal
objects into a furled position. People continued to come and see
the artwork, however, and a few days later a woman was killed
when one of the 200 kilogram structures blew free of its foundations and crushed her against a boulder, forcing the complete
abandonment of the ambitious project. 'Christo umbrellas close:
crews dismantling project after woman is killed in accident,'
reported the *San Francisco Chronicle*.

Worse was to come a few days later. As the Japanese umbrellas
were being dismantled, a crane operator was electrocuted when
the boom of his crane struck a high-voltage power line. 'Japan
crane operator killed dismantling Christo umbrellas,' noted the
same paper four days later.

What is the problem with art? Does it really pose a mortal
danger? And why is the problem apparently getting worse? The
main factors are easy to identify. But the true nature of the phenomenon is obscured by the attitude of the media. Disproportionate
coverage of accidents of this type – compared to, say, accidents
suffered by members of the public on building sites or while at
leisure facilities – reflects newspapers' pretended bafflement over
'conceptual' art.

Art in galleries is the province of the critics and may safely
be ignored by the rest of the press corps. But when art escapes
these boundaries, it becomes fair game for any philistine reporter,
especially when the work has been paid for with public money.
Thus, the *Guardian* lost no time in dubbing Agis's *Dreamscape* 'the
Arts Council-funded PVC installation'. Gormley's *Another Place*,
though also partly funded by the Arts Council, avoided this tag in
the *Liverpool Daily Post*, which was campaigning to keep the work
in the area.

The first reason that art goes wrong is that, at some level, it is meant to. Art is risky. Part of its job is to revive in us a feeling of visceral sensory connection with the world, and this in principle includes its dangers. Carsten Höller produced a French sociologist who claimed that one merit of his work was its ability to induce 'a kind of voluptuous panic upon an otherwise lucid mind'.

After the double tragedy of the umbrella deaths, Christo acknowledged he was saddened by the loss of life that his work had occasioned, but then offered this brazen piece of post-rationalization: 'All my works of art are created to challenge normal views of art. [*Umbrellas*] challenged the view that art is safe. They're not make-believe. The risk is real – almost like climbing the Himalayas.'[1] It is perhaps curious then that on his personal website, in an otherwise detailed chronicle of the setting up and taking down of the umbrellas, Christo makes no mention of the deaths that he seems to believe validated his work.

Art is different in this respect from architecture. The media tends to regard the more substantial and widespread problem of architectural failures as deserving of serious treatment. With cata-strophic building collapses, the press may occasionally rejoice in the misfortune of the architect and developer, but any hazard to the public is taken seriously. This is because, unlike art, where our expectations are uncertain, we expect buildings to perform properly and are shocked if they don't. Where fatalities occur, as in the wave of collapses of sports halls and similar buildings prompted by exceptionally heavy snow in eastern Europe during the winter of 2005–6, the tone is appropriately sombre. The media's handling of building failures only resembles that of its art coverage when the architecture concerned is self-consciously avant-garde and when it is judged that lives are not seriously at risk. Thus, the wobbling of Norman Foster's Millennium Foot-bridge across the Thames between St Paul's Cathedral and Tate Modern, which came to light when the first pedestrians crossed it, was treated with broad good humour.

While it might be considered desirable that art should involve the sensation of taking a risk, then, any actual risk must of course be minimized in the same way that it is for other facilities open to the public. Ignoring Höller's sociologist, the administration at Tate Modern was therefore keen to stress not the feelings of panic that *Test Site* might have induced, but the stringency of the safety checks that the work underwent. And even the artist himself felt driven to point out of his slides: 'They are much safer than stairs; stairs are quite dangerous.'

But perhaps this is to overemphasize the need for safety. Many people seem unexpectedly prepared to make allowances for art. Even at the time of the umbrellas tragedy, Californians seemed to sympathize as much with the artwork and its creator as with the human victims. 'It was just an accident of nature. Why should it ruin everything for the rest of us?' responded one visitor to the site, a retired construction worker, when questioned by the *San Francisco Chronicle*.

Some time later, the lifestyle supplement of the *Los Angeles Daily Times* headlined: 'Umbrellas: a year later shock of deaths wearing off'. The article discussed Christo fans' plans to commemorate the short-lived art installation and took the unusual step of quoting a professor of art on the matter of risk assessment. 'People get killed in building roads and bridges and no one thinks about it. Art should be judged on the same scale,' he felt.

In fact art *is* judged on the same scale because accidents involving art are not so numerous that they warrant a category of their own. Because he was at work, the Japanese crane operator on Christo's umbrellas is regarded as just another construction industry fatality. The death in 1983 of a studio worker of the New York sculptor Beverly Pepper, who was crushed when one of the artist's iron sculptures fell on her, was likewise an industrial accident because it happened in the workplace.

When members of the public are the victims, the situation becomes less clear. In the UK, the Health and Safety Executive records the 200 or so fatalities a year at work in gory detail. But the 12,000 or so other accidental deaths each year are simply logged by where they happen, mostly 'at home' or 'elsewhere', rather than by cause. The US National Safety Council does list deaths by 117 accidental means, including 'bitten or crushed by reptiles'. Christo's Californian victim would simply have been 'struck by or striking against object'.

Two more conclusions may be drawn from these examples. The first is that art simply becomes more dangerous as its scale expands – when it becomes very large or massive, when it requires numerous crew to set it up and take it down, when it covers large areas, when those spaces are unrestricted to the public, when those spaces present wild or unfamiliar terrain, and so on. In the case of Christo's umbrellas, two unconnected deaths make the art look dangerous indeed. But, set against the scale of the work, the coincidence is less remarkable.

The final reason for the apparent growing danger posed by art is its growing popularity. If nobody visited these works, there would be fewer human injuries. Half a million people were reported to have seen Christo's umbrellas in Ibaraki. Seven thousand turned up on one day in California. Each week, 44,000 rides were taken on Höller's slides at Tate Modern. There was a surge in visitors to Gormley's seaside 'iron men' when it was announced that they were to be removed. It was one of these visitors who became stuck in the mud.

Cheers!
'Binge drinking deaths soar' *Daily Mail*

'Binge drink deaths soar' and 'Quarter of children so drunk they have passed out' are typical of the recent headlines in British newspapers. The problem – known as the 'English disease' – seems to affect adults, youths and even children. One foreign journalist describes pub closing time in an English town: 'When the pubs shut, the drinking tribes charge out like wounded bulls, piss in the alleyways, wrestle with the rubbish bags, smash bottles on the pavement, break the occasional shop window and do a lot of braying.'[1] Other countries have heavy drinkers, but the gratuitous violence and vandalism are not on the same scale.

The tendency for people to drink more on the occasions that they do drink – 'binge drinking' – is higher now in virtually every country compared to a decade ago. According to the International Center for Alcohol Policies,[2] a not-for-profit organization funded by leading alcohol producers in America, there are diverse definitions of binge drinking, more formally referred to as heavy episodic drinking. One of the increasingly common thresholds is for men drinking five or more drinks or for women four or more, on one occasion. Canada defines binge drinking as the consumption of eight drinks within the same day, while Sweden considers half a bottle of spirits or two bottles of wine on the same occasion to constitute a binge. Such serious drinking usually occurs in large groups.

There are some occasions, and some cultures, where heavy drinking is accepted: for example the rites of passage into adulthood (Japan and the Pacific Islands), certain university cultures (in the US and Canada), at sporting events and for exceptional celebrations beyond conventional behaviour, such as weddings, New Year's Eve and Mardi Gras celebrations. In Europe, binge drinking is most prevalent in northern Europe, notably Scandinavia, and least common in the southern part of the continent, in Italy, France and other Mediterranean countries.

But it is Britain and Ireland where the culture of drinking has changed most for the worst in recent years – and has a grim reputation. David Ginola, the talented French football player of the 1990s, said that he would not bring up his children in England because 'I don't want my daughter to be an Englishwoman'. He observed that across the country he saw women trying to keep up with men, drink for drink, usually concluding with unsavoury behaviour such as 'vomiting in the streets'.[3]

Survey data seem to support Ginola's view. A sample of teenagers aged between twelve and seventeen suggests that 5 per cent have been so drunk that they have had their stomachs pumped and a further 13 per cent admitted suffering from such a bad hangover that they had played truant from school.[4] The problem, according to the charity Alcohol Concern, is not that more young people are drinking alcohol than before but that those who do drink drink more. As official figures show that over nine out of ten fifteen- and sixteen-year-olds have drunk alcohol, there is little scope for the participation rates to rise.

Heavy drinking is associated with a series of negative outcomes. Some of these are medical in their nature, leading one EU-funded report to say that 'Alcohol is public health enemy number three, behind only tobacco and high blood pressure, and ahead of obesity, lack of exercise or illicit drugs.'[5] Dangers of alcohol include an increased risk of stroke and other cardiovascular problems, neurological damage and adverse effects on the health of the foetus of a pregnant woman. Drinking can, of course, also damage the liver – one British newspaper noted a 37 per cent rise in the number of drinkers dying from alcoholic liver disease in the last five years, with hospital admissions for the condition doubling in a decade to over 35,000 a year. Alcohol can also lead to poisoning. An article titled 'Hospitals swamped by young drinkers' told us that at least twenty youngsters are diagnosed every day with alcohol poisoning or behavioural disorders because of excessive drinking. The paper also told the story of a seven-year-old treated for alcohol poisoning.

However, it is the adverse social consequences that generally attract more attention in the media. An EU report estimated that the tangible social costs of alcohol in Europe were around €125 billion, equivalent to an annual cost of €650 for every household.[6] These include: unemployment, absenteeism, traffic accident damage, criminal damage, the cost of police, courts and prisons, and the medical bills. It estimated that the costs in the workplace, along with those due to crime and traffic accidents, were in total at least four times as great as the health-care costs. The addition of the more intangible costs, such as the loss of healthy life, impaired professional and academic performance, anti-social behaviour (and hooliganism at football matches) and relationship difficulties including the suffering of domestic violence victims, would add considerably to the cost.

Young people are, for a variety of reasons, at increased risk of harm due to excessive drinking. Many risks stem from young people's relative inexperience with alcohol consumption and a greater tendency towards risk-taking, but still-growing young people are also more susceptible to brain and other physiological damage. Young drinkers also have a greater chance of alcohol dependency later in life – or so we are told. The *New York Times* ran a story, 'The grim neurology of teenage drinking', which explained that children drinking heavily at age fourteen or younger have a 50 per cent chance of becoming an alcoholic – a risk roughly five times greater than for the general population.[7] The problem is that people who start drinking that early are often very different in a whole host of ways from those who don't. They are more likely to have at least one parent with alcoholism – itself presenting a 40 per cent risk of alcoholism for the child – and are more likely to come from chaotic homes and to have suffered from child abuse.

According to one American newspaper article, under-age drinkers find it easy to get hold of alcohol via the internet. One article told us that 'one in 10 teenagers have an under-aged friend who has ordered beer, wine or liquor over the internet'.[8] It also told us that more than a third thought they could easily do it and nearly a half thought they wouldn't get caught. All of this sounds pretty scary, but closer analysis suggests that the survey, which was paid for by the Wine and Spirits Wholesalers of America, a group that competes with direct sellers of alcohol, perhaps tells another message that suited the sponsors less well and would have had less media impact.[9] Despite most teenagers using the internet daily and often spending many hours online, and despite almost half believing they could buy alcohol online, only 2 per cent had ever done so. This is not a very large proportion given almost half of those surveyed were between eighteen and twenty years of age.

Heavy drinking is clearly a problem that we could live without, and the press regularly debates the available policy options. One senior British judge criticized the levels of weekend drink-related violence on the streets during his summing-up in a case arising out of a Saturday-night brawl, and suggested that pubs close at nine o'clock in the evening. Higher taxes, especially on the drinks favoured by young people, could also play a part in reducing consumption. And a Scottish community is hoping to reduce crime by encouraging local shops to ban the sale of alcohol after 7 p.m. Others advocate that premises only be granted a licence to sell alcohol if there is plenty of seating, on the grounds that bars with standing room only encourage more rapid consumption of alcohol. But pessimists argue that the problem runs deeper than drinking regulations and is rooted in a working-class tradition of loutish youths 'moving in packs' – groups that are at their most visible when travelling abroad as football hooligans.

Treating the English disease is definitely proving difficult. In 2005 a British government initiative removed the traditional eleven o'clock closing time of pubs, allowing them to apply for licences to stay open later. They argued that this was 'the European way' and that by easing pressure of last orders, bingeing would be reduced. Those against the change said that it would merely pro-long the misery and cause more damage. One year on from the change, the impact seemed not to have been significant one way or the other – although the government, which has learned to manage the news flow, did leak to the press prior to the publi-cation of the figures that the number of drunk and disorderly people decreased in the period immediately after the change in the law.[10]

The EU report advocated more extensive random breath testing of drivers, higher taxes on alcohol, shorter opening hours for the sale of alcohol and restricting the extent and content of alcohol advertising. It also wanted tougher measures aimed at young adults.

There is no doubt that one constraint on government's pursuit of such policies is the size of the developed world's drinks industry, which takes advantage of its association with prestige products and even national identity to foster close contacts with ministers. There are roughly three-quarters of a million jobs in Europe's drinks production industry, with many others indirectly linked to the business working in shops and bars, and it produces billions in tax revenues annually. France and Italy together account for over half of the world's wine exports, the UK and France account for over half of the world's spirits exports, and the Netherlands and Germany account for over one-third of the world's beer exports. Governments end up treading very carefully.

Social attitudes might change. In the nineteenth century, European elites were faced with a situation of urban squalor that included unprecedented public drunkenness. This led to the growth of temperance movements across Europe. Initially they were focused on the idea of drinking in moderation and only later moved on to the idea of prohibition. Finland, Iceland and Russia were among the countries that adopted some form of prohibition, while other countries allowed individual areas to vote on prohibition. Might we again see bans on alcohol? The City of York Council, for one, has drawn up proposals for an Alcohol Exclusion Zone in two parts of the city in response to pleas from residents who have experienced alcohol-related disorder.

While there is no doubt that consumption of large quantities of alcohol is damaging for health, there is some evidence – especially popular among wine drinkers – that modest quantities of alcohol can give beneficial effects. A study in the *Lancet* over twenty-five years ago compared the death rates of men in their fifties and sixties from heart disease in a number of countries. It found the highest death rates were in traditional beer-and spirits-drinking countries, while France had the lowest number of deaths and the highest wine consumption. A Danish study of 24,000 people also found that drinkers of wine, as opposed to other forms of alcohol, benefited from an overall reduction in deaths from all causes. But the village of Gers in south-west France seems to provide the conclus-ive evidence that wine is good for you – it has double the national average of men aged ninety or more. This is put down to the wines being very rich in procyanidin, which somehow seems to counter the otherwise negative effect on life expectancy of the French diet, which is typically high in saturated fats.

This positive view of moderate drinking is not new. The Greek physician Hippocrates was using wine as an antiseptic, diuretic and sedative 2,400 years ago. Louis Pasteur, no less, said in the mid-nineteenth century, 'Wine is the healthiest and most hygienic of drinks,' and in an era predating modern manufacturing and sterilizing processes, wine provided products with a stability and cleanliness that water could not. Even before Pasteur, a serving of wine each day on the convict trips from England to Australia contributed to a reduction in malnutrition and scurvy during tran-sit. So successful was this that some of the British doctors involved started their own vineyards in Australia.

There might be some good news on binge drinking in the UK as the latest year's official figures showed lower rates of heavy drinking.[11] The percentage of men exceeding the government's daily sensible drinking benchmarks (three to four units on at least one day in the previous week) fell from 39 per cent in 2004 to 35 per cent in 2005, having been broadly stable in the previous four years. Women are less likely than men to exceed the benchmarks – 20 per cent did so in 2005. Perhaps changes in drinking habits are finally taking place in response to the increased availability of coffee shops and other cafés for social drinking. There are also signs of consumer preferences shifting as lower-alcohol beers increase their market share at the expense of premium lagers.

Meanwhile, those of us who have long since left teenage years (and binge drinking) behind will hope that none of the measures that could be introduced to restrain the abuse of alcohol would affect the – essentially immeasurable – pleasures associated with alcohol. The trouble is that some old people cannot be trusted. 'Too old to booze' was the headline of the story saying that pensioners in East Sussex were being sent letters warning them against heavy drinking after research showed that they were particularly prone to falling over after a tipple. There seems to be no easy solution.

The Death of Cinema
'Coming soon, the end of a cinema near you?' *The Times*

The arrival of digital videos and cameras, now typically available in mobile phones, and internet hosting sites means that film-making is no longer the preserve of a few Hollywood barons. The phenomenal success of YouTube, the site launched only in 2005, where people can watch and share original videos, exemplifies the way creative possibilities have opened up for the masses. But does it mean the death of the cinema?

We will certainly never be short of recorded moving images. In 2000 alone, it is estimated that 1½ billion hours of moving images were created, roughly 200,000 hours of film every hour. That represents a doubling compared to a decade before, but nothing compared to the forecasts for the years ahead. Within twenty years we could be creating 100 billion hours of moving images every year – equivalent to over 10 million hours of film for every hour of the day.[1] Such a volume of material presents a range of difficulties, not least choosing what to watch and what to archive and save for the future.

Meanwhile, the increasing availability of DVDs, often free or at very low prices, and improvements in home entertainment are contributing to the fall in cinema attendances. This in turn is putting considerable financial pressure on the entertainment market and prompting much head-scratching about how to maintain revenue streams going forward. In the same way that digital technology has changed the production of film, for example in editing and the creation of special effects, it will surely have an impact too on distribution, projection and home delivery. This could be viewed as a positive development, not least because the lower costs allow new, independent directors to produce films. But where will we watch the new films?

The movie business has already been through – and survived – a number of transitions during its relatively short life. The early publicly shown movies – silent and black and white, probably part of travelling exhibits or acts in vaudeville programmes, often only a minute long, perhaps showing a single scene, authentic or staged, shown largely to working-class audiences – would be unrecognizable to today's cinemagoers.

The First World War wrought many changes, notably dealing a devastating blow to the European film industry and giving the Americans – with the rise of Hollywood – the chance to earn the dominance in the mainstream industry, a dominance that it still has today despite many other countries and cultures having more or less thriving genres at various times. The hundred-year history of cinema shows the coming and going of many styles, techniques and fashions, and no shortage of people who say that things just aren't what they used to be.

The economics too have changed. Cinema-going in the US reached its peak in the 1940s, when it was estimated that Americans spent nearly one-quarter of the money available for recreation on going to see films, compared to no more than one-fiftieth, 2 per cent, today. The widely accepted principal explanation for this decline was the mass arrival of televisions – between 1950 and 1955 the number of televisions in America increased eightfold to over 30 million. Although it is likely that increased urban sprawl (most cinemas were in urban areas) and anti-trust action (studios were no longer permitted to own theatre chains) also played a part.

But the long-term decline in the number of admissions stopped and rose for a couple of decades, due mainly to the arrival of the multiplex screens, which offer both more films and more viewing times for the same film. The number of screens in America increased by over 50 per cent to 37,000 during the 1990s, with a similar rise in the UK a little later, as multiplexes were rolled out. But for all the positive medium-term trends, the very recent past has seen declines in admissions again, reigniting concerns about the future. In the US, admissions peaked in 2002 at over 1.6 billion and have since declined to 1.4 billion, returning admissions to the 1997 level. The fall in Britain over that period was smaller – though 7 per cent through to 2007 – and much smaller across Europe. Such declines are noteworthy but hardly amount to a death. In any case, attendances continue to rise in the Asia–Pacific region – up by 22 per cent in the last four years. The strength in the Asian market is encouraging for the business as it comprises around 60 per cent of global admissions.

The number of films released for a week or more during 2007 – 516 in Britain – is 40 per cent up on the 2001 figure and would seem to suggest that the industry is healthy. The increase was, however, in good part being driven by foreign-language films, with Hindi topping the list, designed often for minority communities. The top twenty films drive the business as they still account for roughly half of box-office takings. Even so, it is clear that a greater variety of films is available than was the case a decade or two ago.

Paradoxically, one reason to be optimistic about cinema attendances is that people in many countries do not go to the cinema very often, leaving plenty of room for improvement. Britons are on a par with the French and Spanish, visiting the cinema no more than three times a year on average. That is roughly twice as frequent as Italians and Germans but somewhat less than the Americans, who manage to notch up five trips a year. Plenty of youngsters go to the cinema frequently, but attendance drops off as we age – a trend that the industry could try to reverse.

The battle fought by cinemas in the last two decades has been against the VCR and DVD. While it survived the VCR, the latest decline could be linked to the increase in DVD household penetration. The number of American households owning a DVD player has more than trebled from 25 million in 2001, an increase from under one-quarter of TV-owning households to over three-quarters. Over the same period, the average price of a DVD player halved, and the number of titles available trebled. Cinema admissions per head in America have fallen from a recent peak of 5.7 a year in 2002 to 4.8, with larger and better home TV screens, broadband internet options and more accessible illegal downloads and pirate DVDs putting pressure on numbers. On the other hand, research suggests that the households who own more sophisticated home entertainment technology tend to visit the movies more frequently than lower-tech households.

In the UK, the market for the rental of videos and DVDs has declined by over one-quarter from the peak in 2000, but that has been more than compensated for by an increase in the retail market. The total sales, of 229 million videos and DVDs in 2006, was more than double the sales seen in the late 1990s and reflected the falling price of DVDs as people have replaced the old-style video collections with the new media. The UK especially has also seen a dramatic rise in the occurrence of newspapers giving away discs – roughly 130 million units were given away in 2005 alone, with the number given away in the first quarter of 2006 being broadly the same number as retailers sold through traditional channels.

The next big advance for the cinema-goers will be the arrival of digital cinema, which will not only reduce costs for distributors and help to control piracy, but, it is hoped, maintain the viewers' experience gap with regard to the developing home cinema and high-definition TV market. This might well amount to the 'death of film', if not the cinema. Cinemas are now rolling out the new technology, and more than 20,000 d-cinema screens are expected worldwide by 2010. It sounds like an exciting enough prospect to keep drawing crowds, and, in any case, the cinema will still be a good place to take the children on a rainy day during the school holidays. Technically at least, such digitalization narrows the gap between television and film, opening the way for events such as concerts and sport to be shown in the cinema. As these events already draw much larger audiences than the most successful Hollywood film, the cinema, perhaps renamed and remodelled, looks likely to survive into the future.

Collectors' Agony

'This is a stick up' *Daily Mirror*

The 2006 World Cup football competition, hosted by Germany, was bad enough for England supporters of all ages, with the over-hyped national team going out on penalties in the quarter finals. But the real agony was reserved for the children – and the parents of children – who decided to collect World Cup stickers.

One such set of stickers, which was available in dozens of countries, was produced by the Italian-based Panini Group, a magazine, sticker and new media group. The World Cup stickers included seventeen players from each of the thirty-two teams plus various others such as team photographs, badges and stadium pictures. In total, there were 598 stickers to collect and these were sold in packets of five, costing 35p each in the UK and an equivalent amount in other countries.

There is nothing new about the publication and collection of such stickers, with the origins of the hobby traced back over 100 years, when cigarette companies put collectable cards in their packets to boost sales. But the scale of such collections has increased – there were twenty-two more stickers in 2006 than were produced for the similar collection in the 2002 World Cup, making it more difficult and more expensive to complete the collection. Indeed, there has been inflation in the number of stickers in each set since they were first produced for the Mexico World Cup in 1970, when there were 'just' 271 stickers.

One newspaper headline, 'The £100 World Cup penalty', gave some indication of the problem of completing a set. Collecting the first few hundred stickers is relatively easy, but the laws of probability mean that the nearer collectors get to completing the album, the more difficult it is to find the last few.

The cost of buying 598 stickers at 7p each would be just under £42. But the issue of duplicates – the cards are sold in sealed packets of five – increases the cost considerably. For once, however, the headlines were not dramatic enough.

Fortunately some Irish academics worked out the likely cost of buying the full set of stickers. Kevin Hayes and Ailish Hannigan estimated that it would be necessary, on average, to buy 4,170 cards, that is 834 packs, at a cost of nearly £292 to complete the set. Their simulations show that an unlucky quarter of collectors will face the prospect of having to purchase more than 919 packets to complete their album, at an estimated cost of £322, but the luckiest quarter of collectors will purchase fewer than 724 packets, at the cost of £253. They estimated the median at 815 packets (costing £285) – that is, half the collectors will be expected to spend less than this amount to complete their album, and half will spend more.[1]

The National Consumer Council in the UK was reported as complaining about the cost of filling such albums, saying it was 'far more than children can afford' and that it was a 'classic case of pester power' as the producers of these products knew that parents would give in to their increasingly desperate children. It is only fair to say that it is not only children that collect such stickers. There were plenty of newspaper reports from all corners of the world of adults collecting and exchanging in an attempt to complete their album.

In the past, children would have swapped cards in the school playground, reducing the need to continue buying, in order to find the last elusive cards. Modern technology has short-circuited the playground, and cards and stickers for collections like this can now be traded over the internet. For those willing and able to go online, this goes some way to reducing the cost. It should also be said that Panini offered a facility for buying missing cards. But with the numbers of cards that can be bought being rationed, and there being a processing and postal delay before they arrived, the solution is unlikely to have been greeted enthusiastically by many of the collectors.

A much smaller collection of disks covering just the England squad was made available by Texaco, the petrol company, in the UK. A disk was given with every £10 of petrol bought, begging the question as to how many times it would be necessary to drive from England to Germany before collecting the full set.

4. Social Policy

We are always worried about money – pensions, debt and housing are the big-ticket items at the top of the list. Get these wrong, and your life can be ruined. A credit crunch, house price collapse or commodity price hike could also spell trouble. Government economic and social policies, for example on immigration, can affect us too and so can being in the wrong place at the wrong time – if you happen to be involved in a traffic accident.

Golden Oldies' Time Bomb
'Should everyone be forced to save for their retirement?'
Independent

A generation ago the life pattern for most of the working masses in the developed world was simple – they worked until they were sixty-five, roughly pensionable age, and then they died. But increased life expectancy has changed all that, leaving people in the position where plenty have to plan for around two decades of life in retirement. This is a big change since the first universal pension in Britain was introduced nearly a century ago, in 1909. That applied only to anyone aged over seventy – a decade or more above life expectancy at the time – on a means-tested basis.

The phrase 'Pensions time bomb' has been coined to refer to the predicament we face. A growing proportion of elderly to care for, as explained in chapter 1, with a smaller proportion of workers paying taxes to fund that care means that government will be unable to afford generous pensions in the future. The reluctance, and in the case of the lower earners, the inability, to make private provision for pensions makes the situation worse. Company pension schemes are also under threat. The system in many countries is now complex, unwieldy and in crisis.

The institutional differences between countries coupled with decades of widely diverging savings behaviour make it very difficult to compare the state of the pensions provision in different countries. Many also suffer from a lack of decent statistics – and decent forecasts – setting out the state of play and the scale of any potential problem. Figures from state administrative systems and private savings schemes are often incomplete, pay-as-you-go systems have no statistics, and surveys are notoriously poor at collecting pension data as respondents rarely know the answers to questions.

Pension funds play a significant contribution in only a minority of developed countries. Four countries – the Netherlands, Iceland, Switzerland and the US – have pension fund assets that are greater in value than the annual output of their economies. Others, including Canada, Ireland, Australia and the UK, have assets of between one-half and one-third of national income. In terms of absolute value, American pension funds dwarf those in any other country, accounting for two-thirds of the global total. The UK's assets are the second-largest, almost equal to the combined value of the third-and fourth-placed countries, Japan and the Netherlands. The dominant position of the Anglo-Saxon countries – Canada and Australia also have large pension funds – reflects the maturity of the private occupational pension plans started decades ago.

The slump in world equity markets between 2000 and 2003 caused the value of these assets to fall, but the rally in the markets since has seen the value in nominal terms increase substantially (to $18,000 billion in 2005 from $13,000 billion in 2001). This rise in the value of assets and the more recent weakness means that across the industrialized nations as a whole the value of the funds in relation to national income is unchanged from what it was at the beginning of the decade.

Many countries, including Spain, France and Italy, have followed a different model, where public pensions play a dominant role in the old-age retirement system. In these cases, pension fund assets amount to less than 10 per cent of national income. Many countries with small or immature private pension schemes have introduced policies to enhance them in the last decade. Where this has happened, for example in the Czech Republic, Hungary and Poland, asset values have grown quickly, although they are still small.

In addition to private pension fund and life insurance assets, several countries have accumulated assets in their so-called national pension reserve funds, funds set aside by otherwise pay-as-you-go systems in preparation for the rising financial costs resulting from the predicted ageing of populations (and the decline in the proportion of the population that is working that can finance the pensions through their taxes) in the next few decades.

Countries need to address these issues because the levels of public spending on social benefits are already high in many cases. Four European countries – Sweden, Denmark, France and Germany – spend an amount equivalent to over 30 per cent of their national income on social benefits and will find the costs increasingly hard to meet as the demographics deteriorate.

The rise in national pension reserve funds is one of the responses from governments, which are becoming increasingly aware of the financial problems that many of their citizens will face in retirement as funding pensions from pay-as-you-go schemes becomes more impractical. There are various ways that governments can reform their pensions systems, including improving the regulatory environment to reassure savers that their money will be safe and creating a tax regime to incentivize saving. Governments have also introduced policies to encourage people to stay in the workforce longer, and age discrimination in employment is now outlawed across the European Union. Many of these policies are new, and it will take many years to see an impact on the official statistics. As it stands, average retirement ages in Europe range from sixty-three in Sweden to fifty-six in Slovenia. The gap between life expectancy and the average exit age from the labour force varies between twenty-one years in France and eight years in Latvia, with over half of the countries bunched between fifteen and eighteen years.

The trends strongly suggest that many – perhaps a majority of – people in developed countries are unlikely to have a financially comfortable retirement as they are either choosing not to save or are on incomes so low that saving is not a realistic option. It is no surprise that governments find it very difficult to introduce mandatory savings schemes on a scale that would be likely to have a material impact on future pensions provision. Company pension schemes, upon which many employees are depending, are also unlikely to be the solution. One Scottish newspaper article, 'Pensions crisis is much worse than firms say', quoted the president of the Faculty of Actuaries, Scotland's most senior actuary, as saying: 'We are kidding ourselves over the security of pensions.' He predicted that more pension schemes will collapse and pensions be lost, because companies rely upon 'wholly inadequate' yardsticks to measure solvency.[1]

AON Consulting, part of the insurance and risk management company, produces an annual benchmarking study of the European pensions systems, assessing which country is likely to find itself under the greatest pressure to make material changes to its pension system in the medium to long term. The study analyses each country according to its demography, adequacy of the state pension, affordability and sustainability of the state pension, and the availability of company pensions. The 2006 study put Denmark in the most favourable position and Belgium in the least favourable. The top countries, including Denmark, Estonia, Ireland, Latvia, the Netherlands and the UK, combined favourable demographics with reasonable private pensions. The state pensions might be poor but at least they are affordable. France, among the lowest-performing countries, combines a high life expectancy, one of the lowest retirement ages, decent state pensions and low private provision, similar to the situation in Belgium.[2]

The UK is one country that has at least conducted an analysis of the problem and identified the solutions, even if the appropriate policies have not yet been fully adopted. The Pensions Commission was an independent body set up following the Pensions Green Paper published in December 2002 to keep under review the regime for UK private pensions and long-term savings. It produced three reports between 2004 and 2006 and concluded that there was almost universal acceptance that the combination of the present state pension system and voluntary system of private pensions 'is not fit for purpose and will result in pension provision which is increasingly inadequate and unequal'. It concluded that the solution should entail some combination of higher private pension saving, higher average retirement ages and an increased percentage of national income spent on state pensions. The option of pensioners' incomes falling relative to average earnings was viewed as unattractive.

The contents of the Pensions Commission's reports have been widely welcomed, and leave the government facing a difficult challenge of deciding how far and how fast state pension reform can be afforded. The government introduced pensions legislation in 2007 which included measures to restore the link between earnings and state pensions (currently state pensions are uprated in line with inflation), an increase in the state pension age to sixty-eight and provision of access to workplace schemes, but these were small changes spread over many years.

The re-establishment of the link with earnings growth was popular but is not an easy option. The Pensions Commission estimated that the percentage of GDP devoted to pensions might need to rise by about 1.5 percentage points by the year 2050, from about 6¼ per cent today. Such an increase carries significant implications either for tax rates or other categories of public expenditure.

These measures are at least a step in the right direction, which is more than can be said for some of the government's other policy decisions. The then Chancellor of the Exchequer Gordon Brown was widely criticized when he removed the tax relief on the dividends earned by pension funds' equity holdings in his first budget statement in 1997. One report in the *Daily Telegraph* said that the 'raid on pensions' cost Britons £100 billion and created 'the crisis that has left huge shortfalls in pension pots and forced hundreds of firms to wind up final salary schemes'.[3] The Treasury's view was that the change removed a distortion in the tax system that encouraged companies to pay out their profits in dividends, rather than reinvest them. The government also failed to equalize public- and private-sector retirement ages at sixty-five and amend the civil servants' final salary scheme when it reviewed pension policy.

A cynic might think that there was little incentive for reform at the heart of government given the size of senior public-sector employees' pensions. Pensions are hard to understand and essentially dull, so if the senior policymakers are sitting pretty, they perhaps do not understand the predicament faced by the majority. One report by the Taxpayers' Alliance, a lobby group, discovered that nine senior civil servants had pension pots worth more than £1 million and claimed that 'the public sector elite is seemingly immune from the pensions crisis hitting ordinary workers across the country'.[4] The Cabinet Secretary had an accrued sum equivalent to a guaranteed annual index-linked income of £75,000.

Other countries have introduced a variety of initiatives that are likely to help: Turkey has raised its retirement age; Finland has changed the formula used to calculate benefits so that they are based on earnings throughout the working life rather than a specific shorter period of relatively high earnings; Mexican legislation has increased competition among pension fund managers and cut the costs of running such schemes; and Italy has legislated to boost the growth of private pensions. In all bar a few developed countries, the proportion of defined benefit plans, where the pension payable is related to income earned, is decreasing while the proportion of defined contribution plans, where the pension is related to the value of savings and investments made, is increasing. Schemes of the former type are generally more generous.

Despite several years of scare stories in the British media, the population does not seem to have changed its habits. It seems that paying off a mortgage, repaying a student loan or just spending money are far more appealing options than making a decent provision for retirement. Perhaps people have been frightened off the idea of saving by the stories of individual pension fund scandals. A report in 2006 on the City of San Diego's pension fund scandal told of 'years of reckless and wrongful mismanagement' and 'non transparency, obfuscation, and denial of fiscal reality'.[5] The report drew analogies with what happened at Enron and HealthSouth in the US. Such stories go back many years including the plundering of the Mirror Group pension fund by Robert Maxwell, which was discovered after his death in 1991. The pensions mis-selling crisis in the UK in the late 1980s is also fresh in the memory.

The gradual decline in the percentage of the British workforce that has any current pension provision above that provided by the state has continued, with the decline in participation rates among private-sector workers continuing at a significant pace – from 10½ million to 9 million in the last eight years. The percentage of employers making any pension provision for their employees declined from 52 per cent in 2003 to 44 per cent in 2005. Some people will no doubt have been hoping to be bailed out by their investment in property, but house price weakness means that only a minority will be saved, and many of those who have done well in the property market have probably also made some provision for a private pension.

The prospect of poverty in old age remains very real for many people. Most countries have to face up to significant policy changes or come to terms with the consequent growing inequalities in society.

Credit Crunch
'Britons piling up Europe's worst debts' *Metro*

During 2008, at the time of writing, the most talked about threat to the stability of our lives was economic recession. A combination of factors but mainly the credit crunch – the increased difficulty of getting credit following the demise of the sub-prime mortgage market in the US in 2007 – falling house prices and higher com- modity (mainly oil) and food prices were threatening to derail the world's economy. According to the Governor of the Bank of England, Mervyn King, the 'nice' decade, an acronym to describe the non-inflationary consistent expansion enjoyed by the economy until recently, was over.

Clearly one of the longest periods of sustained economic growth in Britain – about fifteen years – was coming to an end, but the question was how serious the slowdown would be. As recession loomed, the economic fundamentals were poor, especially in the UK where the Labour government had returned to the party's traditional form of excessive public-sector spending, meaning that government borrowing was already high and limiting the scope for actions such as tax cuts and spending increases to boost growth. People had borrowed heavily, too.

But the real problem was the *fear* of what might happen. The ex-Prime Minister John Major said in a television interview in July 2008: 'Fear is toxic and it is spreading.' He was right. Interest rates were a bit higher, the housing market was weakening and banks were reluctant to lend, but if recession was deep there was every chance that it would be noted as one that was brought upon us by fear rather than fundamentals.

At the heart of the problem was borrowing. Easy credit from banks at a time of low interest rates and prolonged growth had led to a binge on a scale never seen before. Britons were the big borrowers of Europe, and the figures were frightening. By the end of 2007, the country's adults had racked up over £1,400 billion in personal debt – that equated to nearly £30,000 for each adult. The amount of debt increased by 10 per cent during the year, growing at the equivalent of £200 per adult per month. The average amount borrowed on credit cards, finance deals and bank overdrafts stood at £4,700 per person, and the total personal debt was increasing by £1 million every five minutes. This might have dire outcomes for the feckless families involved, but, given the tighter credit regimes from banks since the end of 2007, the problem could push the economy into severe recession.

Given these sums, the headlines seen in the mid-2000s are perhaps unsurprising. 'Banks are warned to stop tempting families into debt' followed the publication of the annual report from Britain's financial regulator, the Financial Services Authority. Its 2006 Financial Risk Outlook warned of 'signs of growing distress among consumers, including more insolvencies, more late payments on credit cards and a rise in mortgage repossession orders'.[1] The FSA was particularly scathing of credit card companies encouraging customers to borrow when their debts are already out of control – it is said that lenders have sent out at least 100 million unsolicited but pre-approved credit card application forms between September and November each year to tempt us with Christmas spending – and the offering of so-called 'mega-mortgages', which allow homebuyers to borrow up to 125 per cent of the property price. The excesses became a real problem in late 2007 when the credit crunch started. Suddenly it was harder to refinance borrowing and lenders took a less lenient line with those who could no longer repay.

The young Britons, who are doing more than their fair share of the nation's borrowing, have been described as the iPod generation – insecure, pressured, over-taxed and debt-ridden.[2] Traditionally the young take out debt to buy their first property and the middle-aged repay the mortgage and save for old age. The elderly run down their savings and sell their assets. But that life cycle is being distorted by several factors that encouraged the young and middle-aged to borrow more than they have in the past. The large inflation-adjusted increases in house prices in recent years mean that proportionately more now has to be borrowed to get on the property ladder. Today's twenty-somethings in England are the first generation of graduates to start their working life in debt, owing on average £12,000 from student loans. The 'buy now, pay later' culture has taken a firm grip on consumers in many countries. And all the evidence suggests that those who want to have children are having to deal with costs increasing rapidly in real (inflation-adjusted) terms. One survey suggested that seven out of ten young people fear for their financial future.

This love of credit is not evenly spread across all countries. An Organization for Economic Co-operation and Development study of fifteen industrialized countries showed that only Britain, the Netherlands and Denmark had total household debt that was greater than national income.[3] Italy and Finland were at the other end of the scale, with debt levels less than 50 per cent of GDP. Except in Japan debt has increased, in most cases significantly, over the last decade, but Britain is the dominant borrower in western Europe.

The US, the Netherlands and the UK are three countries where over four out of ten households have mortgage debt – in Italy, Germany and Spain the proportion is below one-quarter. There were five countries in the OECD study where at least four out of ten households have debts other than their mortgage – New Zealand, the US, Canada, Sweden and the UK. Italy, Germany and Spain were again the countries where the proportion of households with debt was the lowest. (Debt can also be measured in relation to annual disposable income and net wealth. While the pecking order of countries will change under different measures, the main differences between countries tend to be maintained.)

One report claimed that overspending Britons were responsible for a third of all unsecured debt, namely that excluding mortgage debt, in western Europe. The £3,000 per person owed is roughly double the average elsewhere in Europe. Some experts suggested that Britain was approaching its debt 'saturation point' and that lenders would have to focus on other markets to seek high returns.

Although the British led the way, America's young were not far behind. A survey of students showed that, while one in eight most feared a terrorist attack, one-third most feared going deeply into debt and another third feared unemployment.[4] Nearly a half of those surveyed expected to graduate with $10,000 or more in college loans, with one in five saying they would have more than $20,000 to pay off.

There is nothing wrong with borrowing in itself. Indeed the

redistribution of capital from those who wish to save, and earn interest on, their surpluses to those who are willing to pay to use the money is a driver for economic growth. Borrowing, repaying debt and then saving is a common life-cycle activity for most people in developed countries. And the increase in borrowing should be expected following the progressive removal of credit rationing with the financial deregulation that started two decades ago in Britain and is now spreading to many other countries. Lower interest rates, both in nominal and real terms, have also boosted demand for credit. That said, the size of the total personal debt mountain looked worryingly large as the credit crunch took hold.

The high debt figures are already a matter of concern for a significant minority of the population. The figures are striking: Citizens Advice dealt with over 1.5 million debt problems in the last year (equating to over 6,000 people a day seeking advice); personal insolvencies are over 100,000 a year and rising, similar to the number of mortgage repossession actions initiated by lenders; one in six adults have unsecured debts of over £10,000; and on it goes. Mortgage delinquency, or default, rates have edged up in most countries from recent low points. The survey evidence makes grim reading too – nearly 4 million people admit that money worries have caused them to take time off work and over 10 million claim to suffer relationship problems because of money worries.[5]

And the problems started happening when there was a benign economic environment of low interest rates and high employment. Those in debt become particularly vulnerable when the economy weakens, at which point many more households could be pushed over the edge into financial crisis. The OECD believes that households in aggregate have become more vulnerable to adverse shifts in the economy.[6] The FSA has warned of various risk events that could affect financial markets and the ability of people to service their debts, namely a global pandemic, terrorism, financial system crisis and a significant fall in house prices or major corporate bankruptcy. Two other worries were ushered in by the 'credit crunch' of 2007, which led to higher interest rates for borrowers with lower credit ratings. The British government's decade-long claim to have put an end to 'boom and bust', itself the type of rhetoric that over-encourages borrowing, has proved to be wrong. At the time of writing most economies are on the brink of recession.

For all the doom and gloom, however, the situation might not be as bad as it seems. Households' net wealth has increased, mostly reflecting a sharp appreciation of property values and an increase in home ownership rates, and incomes have risen. It also seems to be the case that most indebtedness across the household sector is held by higher-income households that are generally better able to manage it. This needs to be taken with a pinch of salt, however, as it might be those on lower to middle incomes who have difficulty meeting their repayments in a crisis even though their debt levels are lower – those on lower incomes generally have less in the way of reserves to draw on in a time of crisis and, with inferior credit ratings, might well have access to less flexible borrowing schemes and be subjected to higher interest rates.

There is little sign to date that enough households are having difficulties meeting their financial obligations to lenders to harm the broader economy, but economists keep trimming their growth forecasts, lengthening the expected duration of the recession. It does seem, however, that an increasing number of families are engaging in what has been described as 'revolving arrears', that is, shifting debt to where it can be most easily and most cheaply handled, for example the utility companies. Over 8 million letters a year are sent to British household water customers warning that they could face legal action because of the non-payment of bills, and over 2 million households are struggling to pay their council tax.

But for all the atrocious statistics, the world economy was still growing a year after the start of the credit crunch. As Martin Wolf of the *Financial Times* said, 'The good news is that the world economy has held up surprisingly well. The bad news is that the risks remain squarely on the downside.' The recession might be shallow or short.

But even if a serious crisis is averted, borrowing has other consequences. Higher debt coupled with high property prices does serve to shift financial obligations between generations. More borrowing and less saving now by today's workers will leave them with lower pensions and less equity than they expect in the future, and quite probably a more financially stretching retirement. It will also mean that there is less money to pass on to the next generation – properties might have risen in value but so have the debts set against them.

The Housing Bubble
'House price explosion' *Daily Express*

Panic about the housing market in recent years has been widespread and came in two particular forms – first, there was the worry that prices were so high that people who are not already home-owners would be permanently excluded from the market; second, there was the worry of the economic consequences of a material fall in prices should the so-called 'bubble' burst. Either way the large increase in prices over the last decade or more will leave us with a nasty hangover – the only uncertainty being which problem we have to live with and the nature of the social and economic crisis coming our way.

At the time of writing, housing markets around the world have slowed and a few – the Irish, American, Spanish and British – have started to see price falls. The newspaper headlines would have us believe that markets are in freefall. But they are not – yet. There is little doubt that the hefty house price inflation of recent years, barring a major fall, will lead to greater social division as the rich get richer and it becomes harder for first-time buyers to enter the market. 'House price explosion' and 'Property ladder too high for 17 million' are typical of the large-print, panic-inducing headlines that regularly appeared over years on our front pages as markets kept rising into 2007. There are particular concerns for key workers and young people – how can teachers or nurses be expected to buy property in the highly priced urban areas in which they work? Commuting is often not an option for those on low pay or working anti-social hours. Labour mobility is also curtailed as people find it impossible to move from areas of low house prices to areas of higher house prices. Alternatively a price correction – shall we call it a crash? – could leave the economy in tatters, given the debt mountain and speculation (especially in the buy-to-let market) that has supported the rise in house prices.

House prices have been rising faster than general inflation and earnings in most countries for some years. With the exception of Germany and Japan, advanced countries have been in the grip of a housing boom since the mid-1990s. The Organization for Economic Cooperation and Development, the Paris-based think tank, has described this boom as unprecedented in its steepness, durability and geographical breadth.[1] *The Economist* magazine described the worldwide rise in house prices as 'the biggest bubble in history'.

The most notable growth was in Ireland, where house prices more than trebled after allowing for inflation since 1992. Prices doubled in the US in the last decade. It is daft money. In 2006, Donald Trump's Palm Beach mansion and Tommy Hilfiger's mountain home in Nevada were each put on the market for around $120 million, a figure surpassed only weeks later when a Saudi Arabian prince's ranch near Aspen, Colorado, was on offer for $135 million. Trailers on the Californian coast sold for more than $1 million. A villa in the south of France was sold for €500 million.

2007 saw several markets pause for thought and even show early signs of decline, but where are they heading? The positive housing market factors are common to most of those areas that have experienced above-inflation increases: growing demand for property (from families, immigrants and speculative investors), building land becoming increasingly hard to find especially in the more desirable areas, and interest rates and unemployment at historically low levels. The increase in immigration to the UK – three times higher in the late 1990s and early-to-mid-2000s than in the mid-1990s – has contributed to the price rise in the UK, especially in London. The government never adjusted the housing programme to take account of the extra 100,000 people a year the country is currently receiving, a consequence of the world's increasingly open borders.

The rise in property prices has given home-owners considerable equity with which to buy additional properties, often on a buy-to-let basis, inflating prices further. And up to 2007 at least, there has been no shortage of imaginative, alluring and generous financing deals from the mortgage lenders – zero down payments, low starter rates, loans higher than the valuation of the property, flexible payments, and even 'stated income' or 'self-certification' applications, in which the borrower is left to use his own imagination to describe his financial circumstances. In the UK, housing market turnover is less than half what it was at the peak seen in the late 1980s – people then moved at a rate of once every eight years, now it is once every eighteen years. One explanation for this is the large increase in stamp duty (payable by the seller) imposed in recent years, which has reduced the number of properties on the market and helped push up prices further.

This was fantastic news for home-owners. As they saw the value of their assets rise it made them feel more financially secure about the future. There are many people who for some years 'earned' more money from the rise in the value of their property than they did from their work. One article explained how the boom had seen the price of an average house 'shoot up' by £45 a day during 2006, a figure that rises to £80 a day for the typical London property.[2] The newspapers, and presumably most of their readers, loved stories telling us about the 'massive' increase – up by one-third in Britain in 2006 – in the number of people living in properties valued at over £1 million.

On the downside, housing unaffordability – measured in many different ways but essentially the cost of property relative to people's incomes – got to an all-time high, in Britain and many other countries, reducing the supply of buyers. Average property prices in Britain were approaching six times average earnings, much higher than the most recent peak of five times in 1988 and the long-run average of about 3½. The plight was particularly desperate for first-time buyers. The average price paid by a first-time buyer pushed through the £150,000 barrier in 2006, according to Halifax, the lender, compared to the average full-time earnings of 22–29-year-olds across the country of just under £22,000. The number of first-time buyers was at a 26-year low in 2006, 37 per cent down on the half million plus seen in 1997, and lower still in 2007. The last peak in the price earnings ratio in 1988 was followed by hefty nominal falls in prices, taking the price-to-earnings ratio back to its long-run average, landing thousands of people in negative equity (holding a mortgage debt higher than the value of the property) for years after.

There are pockets of unaffordable housing around the world. One study calculated the median house price to median household income ratio for a number of cities and regions in a handful of Anglo-Saxon countries. It described anywhere with a median multiple of over 5 as being 'severely unaffordable'; a score of 3 was described as 'affordable'. Three locations, Los Angeles, San Diego and Honolulu, had a median multiple score of over 10. Another twenty locations, about half of which were American, achieved a score of over 6. These included San Francisco, Miami, Sydney, New York and London.[3] Roughly one-quarter of the locations studied were deemed as affordable and another quarter as 'moderately unaffordable', leaving the other half to be severely or seriously unaffordable. None of the British locations qualified as affordable, but those in the US and Canada so defined included Houston, Atlanta, Dallas and Quebec City.

The study described the last decade's price escalation as 'unprecedented' and said that it was 'a matter for concern'. The locations studied in Australia, the UK, New Zealand and Ireland

(Dublin) had an average score of around 6, compared to 4½ in the US and just under 4 in Canada. The high scores were all the more surprising as most of the locations had ratios of around 3 as recently as a decade ago. The ratio for London, for example, had more than doubled to just under 7 since 1996. The report warned that less housing affordability is likely to lead to lower levels of home ownership, as is already evident in New Zealand.

Affordability is not the only problem. Interest rates and un-employment have risen from record lows with a commensurate impact on sentiment. Banks' lending criteria have tightened, especially following mid-2007 and the credit crisis – the require-ment for larger deposits has choked the first-time buyer market. In Britain, increases in utility bills and taxes along with increasing interest rates on record levels of unsecured debts are also starting to bite. There are also concerns that the equity and rental returns on second homes, often bought speculatively in novel locations such as Croatia, Bulgaria and Dubai, will disappoint, leading to a glut of properties and forced sellers. As mortgage arrears and repossessions rise, albeit from a low level, lenders further restrict the flow of cheap money. The fact that prices are now falling also serves to scare off buyers.

The boom in prices was spurred in good part by consumer borrowing, as discussed in the previous section. During 2006 borrowing by homebuyers in Britain reached a staggering £1 billion a day. As one paper pointed out, the value of loans made in the latest year to British homebuyers was broadly equivalent to the annual economic output of an economy such as India.[4] The median advance reached £120,000, having trebled in just over a decade. The income multiple was over 3 by the end of 2006 compared to 2¼ a decade before and under 2 as recently as 1985. 2006 was the tenth year in which over one million loans were made, lifting activity to the levels seen in the five years up to 1988, even though the value of loans made was roughly four times that of the mid-1980s.

There is never a shortage of debate about the prospects for the housing market. Analysts said at the time of the market peak that property was overvalued by anything from 10 to 40 per cent, and that further falls should be expected. There could be a major fall in house prices, or, less painfully, many years of no increases. Material nominal falls in house prices would be expected to bring on an economic recession as people grappled with negative equity, and the appetite for credit disappeared.

Others, notably some researchers from Oxford University, said that the higher price levels can easily be justified by taking into account housing supply, the changing age structure of the population, shifts in credit conditions and the level of nominal interest rates.[5] Based on their modelling, nominal house prices will only fall materially in the years ahead under 'quite dismal' economic scenarios. A housing crash would bring widespread economic misery, while continuing high prices will consign the significant minority of the population that does not own property to a life of relative poverty.

John Kay, the British academic and columnist, says that the level of house prices 'depends not just on levels of income but on social mores and the distribution of wealth' and believes that modelling house prices requires a range of skills that few people have. That said, he has little difficulty with the concept of property hotspots. He explains that:

A house provides space and shelter and, in the American mid-west, these are the principal attributes of a house. There is more land there than anyone could build on and usually not much to choose between the prestige or convenience of different areas of the spacious cities. House prices are low, stable and tend to move in line with incomes.

In contrast, in New York, California and London, most of the price of a property reflects the location rather than the accommodation – he points out that you cannot make more houses on East 69th Street or in Belgravia. With increased mobility, the high prices in the hotspots reflect 'the self-defeating character of the search for the symbols of status and affluence'.[6] House prices are, then, what economists call a positional good.

In the short term, policy makers have got their fingers crossed hoping for a 'soft landing', typified by modest falls in prices, allowing the price-to-income ratios to return closer to the long-run average. Longer-run solutions to reduce the inequality brought about by the house price inflation are harder to find.

One possible solution would be to introduce a land value tax, a tax on any house price gains. In essence the burden of taxation needs to be shifted off income and profits and on to the currently untaxed gains in property values. Economists argue that such a tax – say, an annual charge of 1 per cent on a property's value – would encourage far more efficient use of space. It would (probably) lower prices, discourage speculation and make second homes far less attractive than they are currently. But such innovative and sensible solutions are most unlikely to be introduced as govern-ments would be afraid of the shifts in price and the redistributive effects of changed tax bills caused by the transition to the new structure. The building of more homes would help, but land is limited in areas of high demand.

Meanwhile, expect house price crash stories to continue to appear in the papers. Prices will fall below the levels at the time of writing but when they have stopped falling we can be sure that life will still be tough for first-time buyers.

Migrant Invasion
'Immigrants to flood in' *Daily Star*

'Halt the tide of EU migrants', screamed the front page of one newspaper, demanding that Britain's borders be closed, while another warned that Britain's population would hit 70 million 'unless we get a grip on immigration'. One story quoted a 'top military expert' warning that 'migrant vandals will bring havoc to Britain', adding that mass population movements could lead Europe into a 'Rome scenario', in other words the collapse of an empire. These may be headlines from tabloids, but the story of immigration, and its impact on social structures and the economy, is a favourite for all newspapers, whatever their hue.

Some of these stories are reporting sound research that merits careful examination. For example, the warning about Britain's population reaching 70 million came from Lord Turner, who studied population growth as part of his respected Pensions Commission report. He said that he was 'amazed' by the 'piecemeal discussion' on immigration and the 'incoherence about the debate'. He warned that high levels of unskilled workers entering the country might have a short-term benefit but would ultimately damage the economy, saying that 'to deny that is nonsense – it just flies in the face of all economic theory'.

Other stories lack substance, but there is no doubting that international migration has jumped up most countries' policy agenda in the last decade in response to the rapid growth in immigration flows. Globalization, budget flights and more open borders, not least following the collapse of the Iron Curtain in eastern Europe and the broadening of the European Union, have increased travel opportunities and legitimate migration. Illegal immigration, via irregular or unconventional channels such as asylum seeking, fake documentation or overstaying legitimate trips as a student or a tourist, and humanitarian migration, in response to civil and ethnic conflict, have also increased.

The numbers are large. Around 3 million long-term immigrants are recorded as entering developed countries legally every year. This is giving rise to strains as some ethnic communities are having difficulty integrating into the host society. Fear and prejudice freely breed in the absence of accurate and reliable data – it is easy to fear the worst – and a lack of coherent policy from governments. In most countries there are serious gaps in available data with a too heavy reliance on imperfect administrative information and poor-quality surveys. This affects policy makers too. Mervyn King, the Bank of England governor, has said that the lack of accurate immigration figures makes understanding economic developments hard and is one of his biggest concerns when setting interest rates.

There are definitional differences between countries – how long does someone have to stay to be counted as an immigrant? – making the compilation of international comparisons a tricky task. Surveys are notoriously weak as people are often reluctant to respond, let alone give the true reasons for travelling. But the size of the flows in the future is potentially enormous. One study, admittedly from a lobby group advocating lower population for the UK, raised the prospect of some 60 million people moving from desertified areas in sub-Saharan Africa towards northern Africa and Europe in the next twenty years.[1]

The lack of decent data, in this area at least, goes hand-in-hand with generally unclear government policy. Balancing an openness to international migration with a firmness in managing inflows is a difficult task for governments to achieve. Most do not even try – they dodge the issue. This in part reflects the sensitivities surrounding the topic – one incautious remark can lead rapidly to accusations of racism.

The OECD has been developing harmonized figures for 'permanent-type' legal international migration that now cover nearly thirty countries and shed some light on the issue. Inflows were higher in most countries in the mid-2000s than at the start of the decade, notably due to a rise of one quarter over 2004 and 2005. The US had by far the largest long-term inflow of foreign nationals in 2005, the latest year for which figures are available, of over 1 million. The UK followed with over 360,000 new immigrants, and Canada with 260,000. Germany, France, Australia and Italy all received over 150,000 in the year. This represented an increase on the previous year for all these countries except Germany and France, which recorded small declines. When that year's inflows are presented as a proportion of the total population, it is the UK, Italy and New Zealand that come top of the pile.[2]

These figures do not include short-term migration, which is probably high in some countries such as the UK, and illegal immigration, which in common with any other covert activity is hard to measure with any degree of accuracy. Where estimates do exist, they put the illegal proportion of the population at between 1 and 4 per cent in many developed countries.[3] The measure is highest for the US and Greece, both of which are characterized by an extensive land border with a country of much lower per capita income – and nationals from the neighbouring countries account for a large majority of the unauthorized immigrants. Such percentage figures might not seem very high, but it is striking that illegals represent a large proportion of the overseas-born population in many countries.

Feelings about illegal immigration run high, with most newspapers being firmly entrenched on one side or the other. One US editorial, titled '11 million reasons', referring to the estimate of 11 million illegal immigrants in the US, said, 'The problem is not just getting worse, but way worse, and very fast.' Another article, 'False facts tar immigrants', said that some people in the immigration debate 'regurgitate factoids ad nauseam, all with the purpose of blaming Mexicans for just about everything wrong with America'.

Whatever the tone of the newspapers, the flows are large enough to merit attention. Net unauthorized immigration to the US is estimated to be around half a million persons per year, equivalent to the population of a decent-sized city and one half of the current annual levels of legal immigration, as measured by the issue of green cards. In Italy, a regularization programme – essentially an amnesty for illegal immigrants – in 2002 elicited 700,000 applications. If all of these entered in the years since the previous regularization, it would imply unauthorized entries of about 175,000 a year, higher than the recorded levels of legal long-term migration over the same period.

The situation is not easy for governments to manage as they do not have complete control over who comes into a country. This reflects both basic human rights – the right of residents to live with their families and the freedom to marry or adopt whom they wish – and a range of international agreements relating to refugees or the free movement of people. But governments do have control over the flow of some migrants, and they choose to exercise this policy in very different ways. Australia and Canada, for example, select people on the basis of various characteristics such as language proficiency, work experience, age and education. Their systems are transparent and often pointed to as models for other developed countries to follow.

Setting the quotas at the right level for the countries which pursue that route is another challenge – too many, too rapidly and there will be difficulties finding work and integrating; too few and the potential benefits will not accrue to the host country, with labour shortages persisting and the best migrants going elsewhere. Often where countries have set targets there is little rationale for the chosen figure, it being the result of 'political judgement' with the consequence that they fail to attract wide support. Temporary migration, based on a permit system, might be appealing to a sceptical public and might be acceptable for some categories of low-skilled workers, but such newcomers are likely to be less adaptable and integrate more slowly. Ongoing, regular labour needs are unlikely to be met most satisfactorily by recycling temporary workers.

A major focus of controversy in Europe since 2004 has been the impact of the accession of ten countries to the EU in May of that year, taking the number of members to twenty-five. Membership was increased again at the beginning of 2007 with the accession of Bulgaria and Romania. With membership came the free movement of people and an extensive debate up to accession surrounding the likely numbers of eastern Europeans – the population of the ten countries was about 73 million – who would choose to move west.

Initially, only Ireland, Sweden and the UK offered unrestricted access to their labour markets for the citizens of the new EU members. Perhaps because of the restrictions in other countries, the inflow of migrants to them, and the UK in particular, was much larger than expected. More than 170,000 people from eastern Europe applied to work in Britain in the first eleven months, and others came without permits, much higher than the official government estimates, made before accession, of between 5,000 and 13,000 in a year. The gap between the forecast and outturn was very damaging to the government's reputation for policy competence, and the size of the inflow led to arguments about funding for public housing and schooling. Two years after accession the government admitted that about 600,000 people from the new EU countries had come to work in Britain. Over half of those who came were from Poland. One government publication said that 2005 'saw the largest ever entry of foreign workers to the UK, totalling some 400,000'.[4] The distribution of the new workers within the country was very uneven, with nearly half coming to London. The emigration was so large that it has caused concerns in the countries of origin.

Much of the furore surrounding immigration, which can be a significant and beneficial activity, reflects the media and public attitudes to a relatively small number of system abuses by asylum seekers, people traffickers or others engaged in illegal activity – and might well have a racist undertone. In the early 1990s, the possibilities for migration to developed countries were very limited, but the successful flight of refugees quickly focused attention on asylum seeking as a means of entry for those seeking a better life.

The vast majority of asylum seekers – up to 90 per cent in many periods in many countries – fail to have their claim for asylum recognized, reducing the legitimacy of this route. The number seeking asylum in developed countries has almost halved compared to 2000, but still amounted to 300,000 in 2005, with over 25,000 asylum seekers in each of the UK, France and Germany. The very high and rising levels in the 1990s put national processing systems and public sympathy under considerable strain. Even so, refugees and other persons admitted for humanitarian reasons, and their accompanying families, currently account for no more than 10 per cent of long-term migration in developed countries.

Abuses of the system attract large headlines and strong public criticism. In 2006, a group of 150 HIV-positive women, mainly from South Africa, Eritrea, Uganda and Zimbabwe, refused to leave Canada, seeking asylum, having attended an AIDS conference in Toronto. Back in 2000, an Afghan airliner on an internal flight was hijacked and diverted to London's Stansted airport, at which point sixty of the 150 passengers claimed asylum. People who do not have the entitlement to stay in a country might opt to enter into a bogus marriage. The government has said publicly that there might be 2,000 'sham' marriages in Britain annually, but leaked memos from the Home Office said that there could have been around 15,000 each year,[5] itself probably an underestimate, prior to a clampdown in 2006.

Half the developed countries now have foreign-born populations representing at least 10 per cent of their total populations. Adding offspring can take the percentage with a recent immigrant background to 40 per cent or more in some countries. In practice, figures are likely to be larger since some legal immigrants and most illegal immigrants will not be counted in the official population figures. Illegal immigrants often cannot join their municipal population register, frequently the source of the numbers, as they do not have a valid residence permit, and often they will choose not to complete a census form, concealing their presence rather than risk being found. Foreign-born residents make up over 20 per cent of the officially counted population in Luxembourg, Switzerland and Australia, about 13 per cent in Germany and the US and a little less in the UK, France and the Netherlands.

Concern about the lingering uncertainty of the numbers is compounded in people's minds by the uncertainty over the economic contribution of immigrants. The newspapers do not help to clarify the situation. On the one hand, we are told '80 per cent of migrants are a net drain on the economy', arguing that only one in five earn over the £27,000 a year required to make a net economic input over the course of a lifetime. And on the other, 'Spanish study points to benefits of immigration', arguing that national per capita output might have fallen in the last decade instead of increasing at a healthy rate had it not been for the influx of immigrants. Whatever the truth, the rapid change in some parts of some cities due to the high levels of recent immigration has been unsettling to many long-term residents.

Losing Control of Your Vehicle
'Jets fly on despite engine failures' *Sunday Telegraph*

Illicit cargoes, human or otherwise, produce their share of scare stories, but the modes of transport they choose are not regarded by the media in quite the same way as many other hazards. Although some people are genuinely terrified of particular forms of transport, especially flying, their fears are not translated into headlines anticipating disaster as they are for diseases or violent crime. Why is this?

The obvious answer seems to be that transport disasters actually happen often enough to satisfy the media's demand for excitement – with speculative alerts before the event replaced by righteous fulmination after it. Each nation has its own roll call of disasters recalled in locations of rail crashes, names of ships that have sunk, or the flight numbers of planes lost.

A contradictory explanation for the absence of scare stories is that transport is too much an essential part of daily life for us to entertain them. The evidence of our continued survival of the daily car or train journey gives them the lie. Travel must be safe.

Both of these perceptions are false. Moving around is intrinsically dangerous. Transport accidents are the leading cause of accidental deaths after falls. In England and Wales, around 3,000 people typically die in transport accidents each year, three-quarters of them men.[1] Yet when measured by the distances covered and other gains to the traveller, travel is considered pretty safe, and it's getting safer all the time. Its high benefit-to-cost ratio makes us prepared to accept the real dangers of travel. This pill is sweetened by the fact that transport often lacks the essential 'dread' factor that arises in the case of risks that are 'globally catastrophic' or where 'little preventive control' is possible.[2] A transport disaster, by contrast, mainly affects those taking the transport and does have the possibility of preventive control exercised by a human driver.

Nevertheless, there are reasons why we might be alarmed. We travel ever greater distances, whether commuting to work, taking cheap flights on holiday, or making longer round trips to grander but more remote supermarkets and other facilities. It is natural to ask how safe we are. They may not inspire dread, but transport accidents do have some unpleasant characteristics that mark them out from other risks. They occur across the board to all age groups and social classes. It is therefore not easy for one community to reassure itself of its own safety because the risk is greater for another, as may be the case with illness or violence. Transport accidents are also responsible for more years of lost life than many other accidents – people tend to fall off ladders in their dotage but off bikes in their prime.

The Department for Transport collates deaths and injuries in Britain per billion kilometres travelled for many modes of transport. In the last decade, there were no fatalities attributed to crashes of UK-registered airlines. Buses and coaches were responsible for 0.3 deaths per billion kilometres travelled. The equivalent figures for other forms of transport were: by water 0.3, by rail 0.4, vans 0.9, cars 2.8, cycling 38, walking 49.[3]

Except perhaps to a statistician, these figures at first seem impossibly low. A billion kilometres is an awfully long way. With 2.8 deaths per billion kilometres for car travel, it seems you can expect to drive nearly 400 million kilometres before, on average, you meet your maker. Is car travel really this safe? How come there is carnage on the roads? The answer is simply that the roads are so busy. It is all car users taken together who rack up this number of kilometres between fatalities. There are about 30 million cars in the UK, which travel an average of 15,000 kilometres each. Based on these figures, we can calculate the average total annual death toll suffered by car occupants as 2.8 per billion × 30 million × 15,000. This comes to 1,260. The usually quoted official figure of around 3,500 deaths annually covers all *road* accidents in Britain including those involving other forms of transport as well as pedestrians.

Different forms of transport are often in competition. We face a choice of flying or taking the train on holiday. We drive, cycle or walk to the shops. This competition extends to the way that respective transport industries choose to present these already opaque statistics. Where journeys are long, it is advantageous to quote the accident rate per distance travelled, as above. Airlines come out safest by this measure. Where journeys are short, it is better to quote the accident rate per journey. By this measure, air is more dangerous than going by foot, and the bus comes out safest. By both of these measures, however, motorcycles come out as the most dangerous means of transport of those included in the survey, with 113 fatalities per billion kilometres, or 1,640 per billion journeys – forty times more dangerous than cars. The only regular form of transport popularly believed to be more dangerous than the motorcycle is perhaps the helicopter. The Department for Transport does not include helicopter travel in its survey. However, figures for US civil helicopter travel confirm this suspicion, giving a fatality rate of 6,200 per billion journeys.[4]

These data may not be strictly intercomparable since the statistics tend to be recorded in slightly different ways for each form of transport. However, they do permit some broad conclusions to be drawn. As the result for motorcycles highlights, we face the greatest risks when we ourselves are at the controls. Per kilometre travelled, motorcycle, foot, pedal cycle and car are the most dangerous forms of transport, with rail, bus and air the safest. According to the risk psychologist Paul Slovic: 'the public seems willing to accept voluntary risks roughly 1000 times greater than involuntary risks at a given level of benefit.'[5] If this is anything like true, then car travel, which is only nine times as dangerous as going by bus or train, is a freedom that we are unlikely to relinquish. This may help to explain why, despite a high level of preventable fatalities, initiatives to improve car and road safety progress only slowly.

The situation is very different in UK rail travel where a rapid sequence of tragic accidents – Clapham, Southall, Ladbroke Grove, Hatfield, Potters Bar – has focused a harsh media spotlight on 'failings' in the industry. These events attained a visibility arguably greater than that warranted by the loss of life incurred, partly because they provided a focus for broader public concerns about the effects of the recent privatization of the railways. Even including these disasters, the record of the railways before and after privatization is one of continuing safety improvement. Up until 2006, the Health and Safety Executive monitored the number of 'significant incidents' on the railways, including collisions and derailments affecting passenger services, but excluding accidents involving level crossings. These have fallen from around one significant incident per million journey miles in 1975 to 0.2 per million miles today.[6]

The statistics reflect the unequal pressures on private and public transport. All the accident rates surveyed by the Department of Transport have improved compared to those for the previous decade, except for motorcycling which has become marginally more dangerous.[7]

The improvement for other individual forms of transport – cars, pedal cycles and pedestrians – is around 10 per cent. Cycling fatalities have fallen from 44.6 to 38.0 per billion kilometres, for example – but there is still a long way to go before we reach the 12 fatalities per billion kilometres seen in the Netherlands.[8] Car travel, too, has become consistently safer in developed nations. A rare opportunity to make a long-term comparison came when the German Federal Statistics Office decided to mark its centenary of keeping track of road accidents. In 1907, there were 4,864 recorded traffic accidents in Germany, in which 145 people were killed and 2,419 injured, out of a car population of just 27,026. In 2005, 5,362 people were killed on German roads, but there were 56.3 million cars. The comparison led the Reuters news agency to draw the conclusion: 'German drivers 56 times safer now'. In Europe, deaths per kilometre driven have been declining steadily by about 4 per cent a year as the combined consequence of increasing car safety, safer roads and tougher driving tests.

Turning to public transport, rail passenger fatalities have declined by 33 per cent, to 0.4 per billion kilometres in 1995–2004 from 0.6 in the previous decade. Buses have come down by 25 per cent to 0.3 from 0.4. Water transport appears to have improved most dramatically of all, reaching 0.3 deaths per billion kilometres travelled from 2.6, although this is explained by the high figure for the decade from 1985 to 1994 due to the capsize of the cross-Channel ferry *Herald of Free Enterprise* in 1987 with the loss of 193 lives. All of these improvements are significantly greater than for individual transport.

The perception of who is in control is important in determining how we respond to transport dangers. A lone car driver takes an entirely voluntary risk when he or she gets behind the wheel. That person's passengers take an involuntary risk if they share the journey. However, this involuntariness is mitigated by the fact that they can see the driver and can take a view as to how reliable he or she is. Passengers in a train or a plane face an additional involuntary degree of separation because they must put their trust in an unseen driver. In reality, this driver may have little operational control and may only be there at all as a figurehead to reassure the public, so that passengers are in practice putting their trust in a *system*.

In September 2006, a German magnetic levitation train crashed while on a high-speed test run near the Dutch border. Most of the twenty-nine passengers on the experimental journey were killed, along with two employees of the company developing the train who were on the ground. 'At least 21 die as driverless train crashes into maintenance truck', reported the *Guardian*. The key word for the media here is 'driverless' – it was repeated in the first sentence of the story and in a text highlight. (The journalists who went to work that day on certain stretches of the London Underground were presumably unaware that they too were riding in driverless trains.)

The implication is that a driver would have seen the truck and stopped the train – which is almost certainly not the case at high speeds. Such perceptions will need to change if we are to gain an accurate impression of travel hazards in the future. Developments in transport technology already make travel generally safer. Would-be disaster headlines now betray small miracles. 'Passengers escape after 100 mph express derails', reported *The Times* in 2006 after a train (with a driver) hit a car that had been driven on to the tracks. 'Jets fly on despite engine failures' was the *Sunday Telegraph* headline accompanying 'news' that more than twenty British passenger planes had not crashed on long-haul flights over the previous five years when they had suffered problems forcing pilots to shut down an engine.

Airlines are now keen to make flying cheaper by using planes without pilots. Flight control technology makes this feasible, but it is judged that the public is not yet ready for this innovation. On the roads, the decline in car fatalities could become much sharper as cars too are equipped with computer devices to monitor and control driving. Jeremy Clarkson will undoubtedly complain that such measures cramp his style, and there will equally undoubtedly be aggrieved tales of unfortunate people who suffer accidents nevertheless and who now hold the new technology to blame for them. But overall, accidents and lives will be saved if we can bear to let go of the controls.

Death by Phone

'Mobile phone blamed for fatal road accident' *Guardian*

Death on the road, perhaps in dramatic circumstances and often involving children or young people, with a phone as a contributory factor gets expansive coverage in the media. 'Was death crash girl texting at the time?' is an example of the sort of tragic story that makes heart-wrenching reading. In one case, a lorry driver drove into the back of a stationary car while punching the keypad of his new phone, killing a young woman. He admitted dangerous driving. In another, it was the person suspected of using the phone who was killed, leaving the relatives fighting for the person's reputation. The common theme in the stories is that people's lives are ended as a result of a moment of stupidity or carelessness.

What are the facts behind the emotion? Mobile, or cell, phones have been around for a long time, but it is only during the last decade that their use has become widespread among the population. Comprehensive network coverage means that they are increasingly used by drivers of vehicles. In an increasing number of countries, including Britain, it is now illegal to drive while using a mobile phone.

But just how dangerous is it to drive while using a mobile phone? While it must be more dangerous to drive using a mobile phone than to drive not using a mobile phone, how does this particular in-car diversion compare with others? Once again we are faced with imperfect data. Information has not as a rule been collected at accident sites to assess whether mobile phone usage might have been a contributory factor – robust data would in any case be hard to collect. Breathalyser tests are now conducted as a matter of course in many countries when an accident has occurred, improving our knowledge enormously about the role that alcohol plays in such events. But as yet, information on other stimulants, such as drugs, or diversions, such as mobile phone usage, is not in general collected at the accident scene. The number of accidents where mobile phones are known and declared to have been a contributory factor are very small but in all probability are just the tip of the iceberg.[1]

Accordingly, we are left relying on specially conducted research. One early and much-quoted example in the *New England Journal of Medicine* in 1997 looked at the mobile phone call records of nearly 700 drivers who had been involved in vehicle collisions resulting in substantial property damage.[2] It concluded that the risk of collision when using a mobile phone was at least 3 to 6½ times higher than when one was not being used. It concluded that the relative risk was similar for drivers who differed in personal characteristics such as age and driving experience, and was the same during the day as the night, in winter and in summer.

'Mobiles worse than drink driving' was how one piece of research conducted by the Transport Research Laboratory was reported, which suggested 'talking on a mobile phone while driving is more dangerous than being over the legal alcohol limit'.[3] This research involved a panel of twenty volunteers using a driving simulator to measure reaction times and stopping times while using a mobile phone and under the influence of alcohol. The research said reaction times when talking on a mobile were, on average, 30 per cent slower than when just over the legal alcohol limit, and nearly 50 per cent slower than when driving sober. Drivers on the phone were also less able to maintain a constant speed and found it more difficult to keep a safe distance from the car in front. There is no reason not to believe the results of this test, although without more details and bearing in mind the small number of subjects – and the knowledge that the study was sponsored by an insurance company – the detail of the results should perhaps be taken with a pinch of salt.

Some of the other research might be a bit less robust and therefore more open to misinterpretation. One poll of over 1,000 motorists by consumer magazine *What Car?* was reported under the headline '10 million ignore the law on phone calls at the wheel'.[4] Only 58 per cent of those polled said that they fully observed the law and did not use their phone when driving – grossing up the remaining 42 per cent leads to the figure of

10 million. The article went on to say that the figures 'suggest that driving while using a handheld phone is 20 times more prolific than recent Department of Transport research claimed'. This phrase alerts the reader to a yawning gap in the message coming from two different data sources, adding to scepticism and concern, but unfortunately in this case probably erroneously. The official figures come from a survey, conducted in April 2003, suggesting that 2.4 per cent of drivers, roughly one in forty, are using a mobile phone *at any moment in time*.[5] The two figures are very different, but both are plausible as they are measuring different things.

One of the more interesting conclusions from both the *New England Journal of Medicine* and the Transport Research Laboratory studies is that hands-free kits were almost as 'dangerous' as handheld phones. The former study concluded that hands-free units 'offered no safety advantage over handheld units'. The latter study said that under normal circumstances the braking distance for a car travelling at 70 mph, the speed limit on Britain's motorways, is 31 metres. This increased to 35 metres with alcohol, 39 metres with a hands-free phone and 45 metres with a handheld mobile. It is interesting to note that, despite this evidence, legislation and public opinion in virtually all countries ignore the risk from hands-free phones while punishing those found to be driving using a handheld phone or over the limit for alcohol.

So if it is conclusive that the use of mobile phones while driving is more dangerous than not using mobile phones, why do governments – and pressure groups for that matter – shy away from the prospect of a proper risk assessment of other in-car activities? Perhaps it is because any such assessment could well conclude that there are many more practices and conditions – and perhaps even people – that should be banned. Almost any form of in-car diversion, physical or mental, such as talking, controlling children, map reading, loud music, smoking or eating, ought to be studied and, if appropriate, be banned.

There are also other less obvious risks while driving. One such example, resulting from research conducted in the Czech capital, Prague, suggested that the significant minority of the population with latent toxoplasmosis – cysts in neural and muscular tissues – had an odds ratio of between two and three times higher risk of an accident. And often accidents are not the fault of the vehicle driver. Many of the road accident deaths are of pedestrians, some of whom may have been talking on a mobile phone while crossing the road. Would it be sensible to introduce laws to dissuade people from speaking on the phone while crossing the road?

The research on driving while using mobile phones is more advanced in America than elsewhere. One piece of research estimated that each day mobile phones in the US accounted for nearly 1,000 reported collisions, 1,700 total collisions, 317 persons with injuries, two deaths, and 99 lost years of life expectancy.[6] The research concluded that regulations controlling the activity 'may be justifiable because the benefits and harms do not always involve the individual who has a cellular telephone', but also noted that other regulations, such as limiting the access of teenage males to cars, could be more cost-saving to society.

The risk of being killed as the result of a road accident caused by the driver using a mobile phone is not large. Regulations making illegal the use of a handheld phone while driving came into force in the UK in December 2003 and have also been brought in in many other countries. But even if the number of these types of accidents stabilizes or declines, it seems likely that the keen human interest element in such stories means that they will still feature strongly in the media.

There are two other factors that are likely to see such stories prosper. The first is the refusal of a minority of the population to accept the new laws. A *National Post* story headlined 'Selfish cellphone users have Toronto police fuming' quoted a number of senior members of the community explaining in forthright manner why they would not support a ban. One even suggested that he would set up a business selling tinted windows so that those using their phones while on the move could not be spotted by the police.

The second is the advent of new technology and the application of existing technology for use in the car, which could lead to a whole new round of scare stories. A report in a Seattle-based newspaper suggested that a significant minority of local residents already had internet access in their cars and used it for e-mail and web surfing, sometimes while driving. The rising use of DVD players and gaming machines in cars is also causing concern as some drivers are apparently dismantling the systems that prevent them from playing while the car is moving and installing them in a place, such as the dashboard, where the driver can see the screen. The article reported the case of a man in New York who was stopped for watching pornography on a screen in his passenger-side sun visor. It wasn't the simultaneous driving and viewing that the state objected to, but the public display of sexual material!

5. The Workplace

Money makes the world go around, and when we perceive a threat to our livelihoods we tend to panic. Globalization is a relatively new cloud on the horizon, but discrimination of one sort or another – we discuss that between men and women here – has been around for much longer. Too much work can lead to stress – and of course work itself can be dangerous.

No Work or Low Pay
'Profits of doom' *Financial Times*

'Black Thursday, as 1,500 jobs go', was the headline on the day after three leading British firms announced their plans to shift production abroad. The spokesman of one of the companies said that there was 'no commercially viable alternative' to the move of production to China. The trade union representative said, 'British workers are once again paying the price of globalisation without any perceived benefit.' One American worker faced with down-sizing at a Detroit engine plant said, 'It's a helpless kind of feeling.' His union leader said, 'The Chinese are coming.'

One of the unwritten rules of capitalism is that the workers in companies with rising profits are rewarded with higher pay. But this tacit arrangement has taken a new twist as multinationals across the industrialized world enjoy very high profit growth while the wages of many workers in their home markets in the West, and especially those on low earnings, are failing to keep up with inflation. The hit has been felt in the last couple of years, when taxes, interest rates and energy prices have been rising, straining household budgets. Income growth is being secured as a result of this corporate success but by the peasants-turned-workers in the developing world. While the working classes in the West might struggle, those at the top have been doing fine: owners and directors have enjoyed large pay increases and benefited from stock options and performance-related bonuses, while the financial community and investors gained from the buoyant mergers and acquisitions activity and share price rises.

The shrinking range of especially manufacturing jobs and stagnation of blue-collar wages in the West has arisen, as ever in the world of economics, due to a complex cocktail of events, but globalization has played a large part. In the good old days, western workers enjoyed a near monopoly access to western investment: American companies generally invested in America and British companies in Britain and they employed local labour because there was nowhere else to go. Most of the products were sold in the country of origin, but some were exported. Globalization, however, has changed that as work has been exported from developed countries. As a result, 'Distrust of globalization has probably never been higher in the past 60 years,' according to one Canadian columnist.[1]

It has been estimated that, as globalization has taken hold over the last two decades, the number of workers in what might be described as the market economy has doubled from roughly 1½ billion to nearly 3 billion, mainly as a result of the opening up of China and India, but also of the fall of the Iron Curtain in the early 1990s. The basic appliance of the rules of supply and demand would suggest that such a large increase in the supply of labour in a relatively short time, with output growing more slowly, will lead to job losses or wage cuts where wages are highest. It is natural that the bargaining power of labour declines in such circumstances, a position exacerbated by the fall in the strength of trade unions.

But as one American columnist noted,

Globalization isn't working out as promised . . . Americans were assured that new trade accords and China's membership of the World Trade Organization would mean better living standards for American workers. That's because China and other countries supposedly would buy American exports. In reality, American manufacturing jobs have been decimated, and the US is running an unsustainable and destabilizing trade deficit, especially with China.[2]

The phenomenon of job exporting started in manual, blue-collar jobs but is now spreading to many professions. In the 1980s and early 1990s the low earners fell further behind the middle class while the rich pulled ahead. Now the poor are keeping pace with the middle, but the rich are pulling away. The share of total income captured by the top hundredth in the US doubled from 8 per cent in 1980 to 16 per cent by the middle of this decade.

It is no wonder that most of the nervousness about globalization is directed at China. It accounts for one in five of the world's population and is more than four times the size of the US and three times the population of the European Union. Few in the West have been to China; even fewer can communicate in Mandarin. The mystery is enhanced because of the country's traditional policy of secrecy, which began to unwind only twenty-five years ago with a process of economic liberalization.

On all accounts – although the quality of official statistics is notoriously very low – China has made considerable progress during that time: the economy has increased twelvefold, and trade with the rest of the world by a factor of thirty. In the last decade China's GDP has overtaken that of Canada, Italy and the UK, and is on course to overtake that of Germany soon, making it the world's third-largest economy after the US and Japan. These figures, however, grossly understate the real size of the Chinese economy once adjustment is made for the country's relatively low cost of living. Such adjustments suggest the Chinese economy is perhaps four times larger than the crude figures – an estimate supported by China's capacity for electricity generation, estimated at around five times that of the UK.

China, and India too, are rapidly moving up the technological ladder. China is already graduating over 1 million scientists and engineers each year,[3] and it is estimated that, by the end of the decade, China will graduate more PhDs in science and engineering than the US. The plummeting cost of telephone calls means that all sorts of service-sector jobs, not just call centres, can also be exported. And although the negative consequences of the growth in China and India are currently focused on the very expensive labour markets of developed western countries, they have also been affecting workers in Latin America, South Africa and the more developed areas of Asia too.

The impact of globalization is far more pernicious than the shifts in trade or industrial structure we saw a generation ago. Then, one industry such as coal mining would be in decline, or one firm would close or relocate, but now the impact on the West is much wider than this. As a constant flow of manufacturing workers in Britain lose their jobs as Chinese imports rise, they will seek employment in other sectors, such as retailing or construction, depressing wages in those sectors too. Some blue-collar workers find this transition and the required retraining hard, but accountants, sales people and drivers, for example, will find a switch to other sectors more manageable.

The downward impact on the income of many households would have become more apparent in the last decade had it not been for rising house prices (making many people feel richer), rapid increases in consumer borrowing and the increase in the economically active proportion of the working-age population. It is also true that the industrialization of China and other countries has prompted dramatic deflation in the prices of many goods. For example, in the UK, the average annual price decline was 20 per cent for IT equipment, 6 per cent for clothing, and 5 per cent for toys, between 2000 and 2006. These offsetting trends could not continue for ever, and now they are diminishing, the disadvantages of globalization and technological advance will become more apparent to more people.

It will then become clearer that globalization is about massive waves of income redistribution: from workers to consumers, as they can shop around ever more widely for cheaper goods; from expensive labour to cheap labour, as employment expands rapidly in developing countries; and from energy users towards energy producers, as the demand for energy soars in developing countries.

The industrial structure of countries is constantly changing. The decline of traditional industries such as coal mining, iron and steel and textiles and clothing was, of course, firmly in place for decades in the UK and elsewhere before it became fashionable to talk about China. Now unfashionable state intervention often masked or delayed the decline, but the trends were clear. In Britain, manufacturing employment peaked at 9½ million fifty years ago and is now just 3 million, and a million of those jobs went in the last decade under the Labour government.

Not all industry has declined in the West. The share of finance and business services, for example, has grown substantially – and is now twice as large as manufacturing in the UK. Even though heavy industry has been decimated in the West, other sectors, such as publishing, pharmaceuticals and motor vehicles, are expanding. The statistics can also deceive – when a manufacturing company outsources its IT, catering or cleaning, the manufacturing sector appears to decline while business services increase, yet the same quantity of goods is being produced by the manufacturer.

Workers in developed countries do not panic about globalization on a week-to-week basis, but the medium-term consequences could be considerable. Alan Blinder, a former US Federal Reserve vice-chairman, said about off-shoring in a congressional testimony, 'We have seen only the tip of a very big iceberg,' adding, 'Tens of millions of additional American workers will start to experience an element of job insecurity and downward pressure on real wages that has hitherto been reserved for manufacturing workers.'[4] He predicts that the key labour market divide going forward will not be between high-skilled and low-skilled workers, but between services that can be delivered electronically from off-shore and those that cannot be. He estimated that between 22 and 29 per cent of all current American jobs might potentially be offshorable. Perhaps people in the West should become waiters or brain surgeons rather than typists or researchers.

The problem is that, beyond words, there is relatively little that governments can do. Social benefits can be increased at the margin for some of the victims, but sharply increased public expenditure is not a long-term solution for ageing societies with rising unemployment. Taxes could be increased for shareholders, company owners and the senior executives who are profiting from globalization, but globalization has simply made entrepreneurs and their capital more mobile. They can be expected to move to the areas of lower taxation if one area were to raise their taxes – indeed some companies have already moved their headquarters to Ireland.

We might expect the calls for trade tariffs and protectionism to intensify and become more widespread. And expect a range of social concerns to be raised – should we be trading with countries that allow child labour and have inadequate workplace safety regulations? While such social differences between the developed and developing world remain, labour costs in the West are always going to be higher than elsewhere.

Underpaid Women

'Scandal of women who earn 25% less than men' *Evening Standard*

The evidence appears to be compelling. A headline such as 'Scant progress on closing gap in women's pay' vividly sets the tone, and one American lobby group has claimed that 'The typical female college graduate in 1984, who is now in her mid-forties, has lost a total of $440,743 in the years between 1984 and 2004' due to the gender pay gap. But are working women *unfairly* paid less than men?[1]

Despite the strident nature of these headlines, the figures suggesting that women earn significantly less than men are not all they might seem at first glance. There are a range of statistical issues to consider. First, there is the difference between median earnings (half the people earn more than this and half earn less) and mean, or average, earnings, with the gap based on median earnings invariably being smaller than that based on mean earnings. In Britain, for example, the gap shrinks from 17 to 13 per cent when switching to median hourly earnings, as the figures remove the impact of the very high earners, who tend to be disproportionately male. The median figure is preferred by most analysts as it gives a better indication of the situation for a typical person – lobby groups use the average as it gives a larger figure.

Second, women's total weekly earnings, measured in pounds or dollars, will be below the level achieved by their male counterparts as full-time men tend to work longer hours than full-time women. Third, the impact of part-time workers on the pay gap can be significant as part-time women are disproportionately represented in jobs where the pay is around two-thirds that of part-time men for every hour worked.

The gender pay gap also widens as any given cohort of men and women grows older. For school leavers the gap is negligible but it rises steadily up to the age of about forty. This is partly because as women get older they are more likely to have spent time out of the labour market caring for children or elderly dependants. There is some evidence that the gap between male and female earnings declines again during people's forties and fifties due probably to the pay of very high-earning men slipping back.[2]

Despite the complexity of the measurement issues, the gender pay gap figures are often presented as if the gap is due purely to 'discrimination' against women. The equal pay web pages of a major British trade union start:

We are campaigning to end discrimination against our women members. Workers should be paid fairly regardless of age, gender, sexual orientation, ethnic or national origin, creed or disability. The 2006 annual earnings survey shows that the mean full-time hourly gender pay gap is 17% with no change over the last 12 months.[3]

On closer analysis, it becomes clear that only a small percentage of this gap arises out of what might reasonably be called discrimination.

Pay discrimination occurs when a man and a woman, who have similar qualifications and are doing similar jobs, are paid different rates. Because the pay gap as measured by statisticians is an aggregate concept, not matching person against person, there are lots of reasons other than what most people would see as discrimination that could explain, and justify, its existence. Most notable among these explanations are differences in the pattern of male and female employment (in other words, they do different sorts of jobs), previous employment histories, childcare responsibilities and levels of qualifications.

It remains the case that many women during their twenties and thirties will take some time out from work to have children, and recent legal cases have supported the common-sense argument that a forty-year-old man with a full employment record with the corresponding experience can expect, other things being equal, to be paid more than his female counterpart who has taken a long period out to have children.

Each generation of women has done better on pay relative to men than the previous generation, but it is true that the pace of improvement has slowed in the last decade or more. One possible explanation for the stabilization of the pay gap could be that discrimination, as defined in the wider world away from lobby groups, no longer exists. Fifty years ago, British employers sometimes operated a marriage bar preventing women from working once they were married. And before the 1970 Equal Pay Act, it was routine for collective agreements to have women's pay rates below those of men. Probably, the gap now between men's and women's pay largely, if not totally, reflects factors other than discrimination.

In the absence of any figures from governments that highlight pure discrimination, a number of academics and lobby groups have conducted research attempting to analyse the relative importance of the various factors contributing to the causes of the gender pay gap. Even so, it is difficult to come up with a definitive break-down. The Equal Opportunities Commission in Britain published research that identified four main causes of the pay gap: discrimi-nation, education, labour-market rigidities and working patterns. They believe that discrimination, which includes what they call 'systematic disadvantage', in other words, the work women choose to do being paid less than the work men choose to do, accounts for just over one-third of the pay gap. Another third was due to different lifetime working patterns, in other words, the tendency to work part-time and to look after children, and about one-tenth was due to women spending less time in education.[4]

Identifying and measuring these reasons is very difficult, and such studies are controversial. One American (female) researcher concluded that 'There is no proof that discrimination is the cause of the remaining pay gap. It is possible that the average man, brought up to view himself the main breadwinner, is more committed to his job than the average woman.'[5]

A survey of equal pay reviews in the UK commissioned by the Equal Opportunities Commission concluded that among employers that have conducted an equal pay review, just 5 per cent said that they had actually discovered any such pay gaps. Many of these gaps were modest – most were reported to be less than £1,000 annually.[6] Perhaps surprisingly, public-sector employers were more likely to have a gender pay gap than their private-sector counterparts.

Another piece of research suggested that a significant part of the difference might be accounted for by the fact that women 'are too scared to ask for a pay rise'.[7] The survey said that two-thirds of women had never put in a request for more money even though 80 per cent believe they are underpaid. Men, in contrast, were generally much pushier when asking for money. This speci-fic example would support the view that there are systematic differences in personality – essentially that many women are less competitive than many men, tend to be less self-confident, less motivated by money and less effective in negotiation – which contribute to the choices made in life that can lead to the existence of the pay gap. One survey suggested that four in ten women aimed to be financially dependent on their partner, relying on his income, savings and pensions to be secure in the future.[8]

Some of the differences between the sexes are visible long before the young people have entered the workplace. At A-level, the exam for eighteen-year-old school leavers in Britain, three times as many boys as girls sit physics while twice as many girls sit the exam in English literature. When it comes to apprenticeships, there are fifty boys for every girl in the construction sector and 250 for every girl in the electro-technical sector.

At university, men outnumber women by five to one in computer science and engineering courses, while women outnumber men by at least two to one in education, languages and subjects allied to medicine (excluding medicine itself and dentistry). There are very few occupations that have roughly equal numbers of men and women. Men dominate in computing, the police and sales and marketing, while women dominate in office support staff, primary-level teachers, care assistants and hairdressers. It is impossible to know whether the pay in the jobs dominated by women is lower on average because women dominate.

The pay gap in America has, however, been narrowing, but arguably not for the reasons anticipated or hoped for. The blue-collar and manufacturing jobs where men dominate have seen considerable downward wage pressure for more than a decade, while women, who are more prevalent in service-sector jobs such as healthcare, have seen wage rises, albeit from lower levels. One article, 'Rise of the women who earn more than their men',[9] told us that almost 40 per cent of women who work full-time are paid more than their husband or live-in boyfriend, hinting at progress being made by women in plugging the remaining gap.

But those who lobby to close the gender pay gap argue that new policies, such as compulsory pay audits for all organizations and legislation to tackle the culture of long working hours, which tends to discriminate against women, are required.[10] They argue that it is important 'to challenge the myth that gender equality has now been won and . . . [believe] – that continuing gaps are the result not of free choices made by women and men but of an unequal society'.[11]

If, though, the blatant forms of discrimination are no longer contributing much to the gender pay gap, sensible policy initiatives to close it are hard to find. Britain's Women and Work Commission published its 'Shaping a fairer future' report in 2006 and concluded that women are not making full use of their skills and that the primary cause is the culture of schools and workplaces.[12] Policies such as reducing gender stereotyping in schools and encouraging women to study male-dominated subjects, and making more senior jobs available to those who want to work part-time, are worthy initiatives but hard to implement. Their success is hard to measure.

Perhaps the biggest culture change required to close the gap is not in the attitudes and aspirations of women but in those of men. Perhaps a society with more male home-makers would be more appealing than one with more female lorry drivers. Meanwhile the stage looks set to remain clear for the chauvinist comedian who believes in equal pay. He must be a believer in fair pay, he says, because he lets his female staff work longer hours so that they can earn the same as his male employees!

It's All Too Much
'The age of rage' *Sunday Times*

'It is a profound privilege to die from stress-related diseases,' says a professor from Stanford University. The point he makes, of course, is that in developed countries we have never had it so good, and that worrying about stress is itself a sign of how charmed our lives are. As a society we have wealth, job choice and travel opportunities unimaginable only a generation ago, and in our free time we can gamble, drink, surf the internet and watch television on super-sized plasma screens to our heart's content. We have legal safeguards against many of society's ills, and the hard toil and infectious diseases that filled the Victorian graveyards with youthful corpses have all but gone. And yet it seems we are as miserable as sin and bogged down with stress.

Stress is, apparently, a serious problem, at an all-time high, killing us or costing us a fortune and putting companies out of business. There seems to be no corner of society, no group of people, that avoids being afflicted. One survey from BUPA, the private health company, suggested that around 7 million British people, equivalent to one in four of the working population, have been so anxious that they have been to the doctor for medication. One-third of the worriers said that they were losing sleep, a quarter said they were getting annoyed with others, becoming withdrawn or being driven to alcohol or overeating.[1] Another survey suggested that 9 million working Brits, one in three, have taken time off work because of stress. Nearly 4 million workers claim to be very stressed in an average week.[2]

There have been many other surveys on the topic of stress, giving the impression that almost every trade union or professional association has consulted its members on the topic. In addition, a good number of tables purporting to rank jobs according to their stress level have been produced and are a favourite for the media.

We learn that 38 per cent of men are unhappy at work and that 27 per cent of managers in the construction industry have sought medical help for stress, anxiety or depression.[3] A survey conducted by the National Union of Teachers found that work-related stress is the main health and safety concern for four out of five schools, with 40 per cent of teachers reporting high levels of stress.[4] The report said that high stress levels could be as damaging as ageing thirty years or becoming obese. Another survey of teachers in England said that stress was responsible for one-third, over 200,000 days, of teachers' sick leave in the latest year, up by 11 per cent in the past five years, costing schools £19 million.[5]

Business leaders in Sweden should spare a thought for their counterparts in Taiwan. Apparently only one-quarter of the former believe that stress levels are increasing, compared to 90 per cent of those in Taiwan. Stress levels were broadly related to the amount of holiday that they had – in Thailand, Taiwan and Malaysia it is typical to have fewer than ten days each year compared to over twenty in Europe – and also reflected the pace of economic change.

Call centres, where huge teams of people handle a seemingly never-ending flow of customer calls, have been described as the twenty-first-century sweatshops. With their workers referred to as battery hens and galley slaves, they are a frequent source of scare stories in the press. The call centres, which have mushroomed in the last decade with the shift towards the twenty-four-hour society demanding banking and other services at any hour of night or day, now employ approaching 1 million people in the UK, nearly one in thirty. Managers have threatened staff with wearing disposable nappies if they visit the toilets too often, and one worker was disciplined for taking two six-second breaks between calls. Despite such stories, studies suggest that stress is no higher for call-centre workers than others, and clearly some employers go to considerable lengths to look after their staff.[6]

But all these figures need to be taken with a large pinch of salt. Surveys can, of course, mislead, and statistics can lie, especially in an area as fluffy as stress, where the nature of the survey and the wording of the questions can heavily influence the results obtained. One particular problem is that virtually all the surveys are based on self-evaluation, making it very difficult to compare between groups of workers or between surveys. If teachers appear top of the stressed professions, for example, does that mean that their jobs are more stressful or just that they are more sensitive to stress? Or was the question in that survey different, prompting the higher positive response? It is also quite possible that certain personality types may be attracted to, or carefully avoid, the higher-stress/lower-stress occupations. Nonetheless, the responses to the surveys and the trends suggest that something is going on and to a sufficient extent to affect the broader economy.

One study by Sweden's Karolinska Institute, the university charged with giving out the medical Nobel prize, estimated that depression gave a reduced quality of life for 21 million people around Europe. As it costs the economy roughly 1 per cent of national income, over €100 billion a year, it is one of the largest health-related economic problems in Europe and has implications for the redirecting of healthcare resources.[7] A study by Britain's Health and Safety Executive, the government body responsible for health and safety regulation, suggested that about half a million workers suffered from work-related stress in the latest year, the largest category after backache.[8]

Stress clearly disrupts the lives of some people who seek medical or psychological help. There is also evidence that some types of stress can be related to the development of coronary heart disease and the occurrence of heart attacks. The National Heart Foundation of Australia has, for example, concluded that there is 'strong and consistent evidence of an independent causal association between depression, social isolation and lack of quality social support and the causes of coronary heart disease', adding that the increased risk contributed by such factors is of similar order to that contributed by smoking or hypertension. It found no consistent evidence, however, for a similar association between other types of stress – acute and chronic life events, work-related stress and so-called Type A behaviour or hostility.[9]

One extraordinary study showed that heart attacks rise on the days of important football matches. A British study found that there was a 25 per cent increase in heart-related hospital admissions on the day that England lost a World Cup match on penalties to Argentina in 1998. And to suggest that it is not the losing that matters, a French study revealed an increase in heart attacks in France in the days following their victory in the final of the same tournament.[10] Stress can also, it seems, lead to premature ageing and shrink the areas of the brain that control memory, attention and the ability to make decisions.

The manifestation of the stress can harm others too. According to one newspaper headline, a study showed that 'A bad day at work harms your children'. It advised leaving youngsters in childcare for a little longer while the parent recovers from the strains of the working day. Often the stressed person expresses his or her frustration in some form of rage. The incidents that are picked up by the newspapers normally get generous coverage, often with good justification. The case of a cyclist punching a 69-year-old, who subsequently died, for reprimanding him for riding the wrong way down a one-way street in London and the woman who killed a grandmother by pushing and kicking her when she was just trying to save a parking space at a car boot sale are examples of inexplicable rage – presumably brought on by some form of stress.

People suffering from stress and anxiety while flying can display symptoms of air rage, or sky rage, which can put passengers and crew at risk. One survey suggested that 15 per cent of flyers had experienced stress or air rage while in the air – this made it a more common complaint than dehydration, fatigue or nausea. The Civil Aviation Authority's figures showed a 59 per cent increase in the incidence of disruptive passenger behaviour on flights in the latest year.[11]

Road rage is inconsistently defined, and there is little scientific evidence available, but there is enough anecdotal information to suggest that it does occur, perhaps with increasing frequency, and does contribute to an important, if small, portion of road safety problems. One American survey of road rage (which incidentally concluded that Miami is the least courteous city for drivers, followed by Phoenix and New York) identified that stress, frustration and bad moods, in addition to running late and being impatient, gave rise to the phenomenon.[12]

There is no simple explanation of the increase in stress levels, but many theories abound. Technology is thought to play a part. If we keep our mobile telephones and computers turned on, we irritate others with our devotion to the devices and feel harassed by the desire for a quick response. Yet we feel vulnerable if we switch them off! Many academics put the increased stress down to the rapid pace of change in society. The term 'hurry sickness' has been coined to cover the physical and mental consequences of our increasingly pressured lives. Public-sector workers, such as teachers and nurses, are thought to suffer because they work in highly structured, hierarchical workplaces, where there is a lot of account-ability and face-to-face contact with the public.

International comparisons are few and far between but can shed light on the issue. One study of English and French teachers showed that they have much in common – both cited classroom behaviour, the low social status of teaching and the lack of parental support as causes of stress. But there were also differences – 22 per cent of English teachers' sick leave was attributed to stress com-pared to just 1 per cent in France, and more than half of the English teachers, as opposed to a fifth of the French sample, reported recently having considered leaving teaching.[13] In general, French teachers work shorter hours and are not required to be in school when not teaching, perhaps accounting for the differences. Surveys of teachers have also highlighted assessment inspections and the pressure to perform in exam league tables as exacerbating work-related stress.

But, even though many people feel 'stress', and for some it clearly gives rise to genuine problems, others might justifiably feel that the real problem we face is a booming stress industry that needs to make us feel worse by exaggerating how bad the problem is. There is a National Stress Awareness Day held in Britain – normally in early November if you're interested – and there is even an International Stress Management Association, a charity (with branches in the US, UK, Brazil and elsewhere) that exists 'to promote sound knowledge and best practice in the prevention and reduction of human stress'.[14] A web search will deliver a very long list of organizations and consultants that will offer individuals and businesses various solutions for their stress problems, including training in 'listening skills'. You can buy stress-relief sprays, aroma-therapy solutions, teas, pills and oils, which claim that 'in no time, you'll feel the weight of the world leave your shoulders'.[15]

Some commentators have even suggested that the word 'stress' should be banned on the grounds that it is too waffly, suggestive and unhelpful. Before using it, we should rethink and try to use a more accurate word. Do we mean overwork, acute boredom, or something more medical, such as depression or anxiety? Are we not in danger of making a mountain out of a molehill?

The good news is that, although the newspapers fill their pages with stories of stress and depression, they do occasionally give advice on how to cheer ourselves up. One bunch of researchers claimed a significant increase in happiness among people who followed ten simple steps. So, picking up on their recommendations, our advice is to: have a laugh every day; do a good turn; treat yourself; halve your television viewing; count your blessings; say hello to a stranger; look after something you've planted; do some exercise; phone or talk to a friend; and find some 'talk time' to spend with your partner. If you do, you will on average be 22 per cent happier in a month's time![16]

Games of Chance
'Pole "too dangerous" for firemen' *Daily Telegraph*

All workplaces have their hazards, television studios no less than many others, even if it is building sites, foundries, sawmills and kitchens that first spring to mind in this connection. Nevertheless it must have come as a shock to his fans when the *Daily Telegraph* broke the story that Noel Edmonds, a former radio disc jockey and television host tolerated by millions, was suffering from a repetitive strain injury (RSI). 'Raw deal! Noel Edmonds injures his elbow lifting the telephone,' the headline ran. Edmonds claimed he had contracted the injury from lifting an old-fashioned telephone used as a prop on his successful television show *Deal or No Deal*. The show draws out to inordinate length a string of blind guesses 'contestants' must make to come away with a sum of money that may be one penny or £250,000 depending on the breaks. No skill is involved and the whole charade could be accomplished in moments without altering the probabilities or the outcome. But that's hardly the point. Matters are complicated by telephone interventions at various times from a 'banker', who offers the contestants the chance to cut and run for some amount less than the remaining stake. This happens a dozen or so times during the course of the forty-five-minute show.

So Edmonds was suffering from RSI due to lifting a telephone handset weighing perhaps half a kilogram every few minutes for half an hour or so. What are we to make of this? Should we sympathize with the £3 million-a-year presenter? Was he a genuine victim of RSI? Or was he just making a name for himself as the world's best-paid malingerer? Perhaps it was simply a bad case of inverted snobbery. For, as Edmonds confided to the newspapers, 'After 40 years in entertainment, I can at last boast that I have suffered an industrial injury.'

The suffering star took advice from an orthopaedic consultant – a consultant with enough time between appointments, apparently, to be a 'huge fan' of the daily afternoon show. He was given steroids and told to modify his hand action, which is standard treatment for the real thing.

RSI is not a condition in itself, but a catch-all term describing carpal tunnel syndrome, tendonitis and other conditions where a repetitive action leads to cumulative physical damage to nerves, tendons, muscles or bones, usually in the upper limbs or back. Because pain is only felt gradually and there is often no visible injury, the condition can be relatively serious by the time it is recognized and require prolonged treatment. The same factors also make it easy to doubt the reality of the condition – a doubt understandably reinforced when a miraculous cure is sometimes effected by nothing more than an employer's financial settlement. Typical sufferers are not television presenters but workers at the

other end of the wage scale, such as hairdressers and people processing cheques. In the United States, RSI costs companies more
than $20 billion in compensation claims each year, according to
the Department of Labor, while in Britain the Trades Union
Congress estimates that 5.4 million work days are lost.

As Edward Tenner points out in his book on technology's
'revenge effect', *Why Things Bite Back*, 'The human being did not
evolve to perform small, rapid, repeated motions for hours on
end.'[1] But the contrast even between the few examples mentioned
so far raises the questions: how small and how rapid are these
motions, how great the strain and how oft-repeated must it be to
sustain the injury? Can you get it 'from opening too many bottles of
wine at a Christmas party', as RSI sceptic Paul Aichroth teasingly
insists?[2]

The truth is that different actions may give rise to different
injuries. A single over-enthusiastic cork-pulling may cause a painful
stretched muscle or a damaged tendon which will take days or
weeks to heal. But this is not RSI as suffered by thousands of
people in clerical jobs involving far smaller, more frequent actions.
Here, the problem may lie with traditional repetitive actions such as
scissoring and chopping. But with ever more widespread computer
usage, it is inevitable that RSI has become identified as a technological complaint. This is made clear in Germany, where RSI is
known as *Mausarm*, or mouse arm.

In the 1980s, Australia was swept by an epidemic of RSI so
severe that it dented the nation's economic prosperity. Prompted
by a trade union focus on occupational health in lieu of pursuing
the usual wage claim, numerous measures were taken to alleviate
the claimed suffering, but even now it is impossible to know
whether the phenomenon had a genuine physical basis or was no
more than a bad case of mass hysteria, egged on by the interest
shown by the medical community. The epidemic duly tailed off,
but whether due to workplace improvements or simply because
there were no more susceptible people left to experience it cannot
be told.

Despite spectacular outbreaks, RSI is not as prevalent as is sometimes claimed. There are several reasons for this. One is the greater recognition of this kind of workplace injury, which has led to improved design of items such as computer keyboards and the introduction of regular breaks (an option clearly not open to Noel Edmonds, with his gruelling schedule of recording three programmes a day a couple of times a week). Another is that a proportion of those claiming to suffer from RSI are undoubtedly malingerers seeking compensation or time off work. There are, in addition, people who seize on RSI as an outlet for other psychological problems such as stress. Whether they are real or imagined, RSI complaints have been almost invariably associated with employment rather than home or leisure activities.

This distinction is now becoming blurred. Many of the new technologies that are liable to give rise to RSI are personal. The new scare stories concern 'BlackBerry thumb', suffered by people sending prolix emails on their BlackBerry or other brands of personal digital assistant (PDA), and 'iPod finger', sustained from over-enthusiastic stroking of the rotary dial on Apple Computer's popular MP3 player. Mobile phones may cause similar injuries in users who send too many text messages, while the compulsive sending and checking of messages is a growing addiction problem.

'Growth of PDA-related injuries a concern', *USA Today* announced, reporting warnings from the American Physical Therapy Association about improper use of the devices. The article noted that one hotel was offering stressed guests 'a special Black-Berry Balm Hand Massage'. The *Independent on Sunday* talked of 'CrackBerry addicts' who crash their cars or ruin their marriages because they can't stop using the gadgets. Up to one-third of users show addictive behaviour, according to research done at the University of Northampton.

Because PDAs such as BlackBerrys are often supplied for work, some employees are beginning to sue their employers when these complaints arise. But with iPods and mobile phones, users generally have nobody but themselves to blame. 'iPod finger' made its debut as a medical condition following a warning by the British

Chiropractic Association in late 2005. Closer inspection of the story, however, revealed an admission by the association's Dr Carl Irwin that few actual injuries had yet been reported – but it was 'only a matter of time'.[3]

'Millions more' are at risk from texting, according to a *Daily Express* article addressed to the nation's 'text-maniacs'. The British Chiropractic Association had already warned in 2004 of the dangers of excessive text messaging. Apparently without irony, it suggested that you might avoid problems if you were to 'shrug your shoulders' before and after texting.

Ever since Pac-Man and Space Invaders, computer game consoles have been another focus of concern, because of both the repetitive actions they demand and the sometimes addictive nature of the games. As the leading manufacturer of such games, Nintendo became associated with an RSI condition inevitably known as 'nintendonitis'. Its games now carry copious instructions to rest the hands, take breaks and so on, but, it seems, sometimes to little avail. With only a few shopping days left to Christmas, the *Guardian* reported on the company's latest Wii game controllers, 'Nintendo steps in after slew of "wiinjuries"', describing how innocent bystanders had been left 'battered and bruised' by the game's motion-sensing remote control unit. Apparently, extravagant actions by players of the game combined with a loss of grip at the crucial moment have led to the units flying across rooms and striking priceless vases and grandparents in their path. Enthusiasts have posted images of their 'wiinjuries' on the internet. Nintendo responded by offering users more robust versions of the wrist straps supplied with the game.

The injuries occasioned by these personal hi-tech gadgets may be just as real as those sustained from poorly designed equipment in the workplace, but they are often borne with more fortitude because of the cachet the user gains from possessing the object. Thus, while the devices proliferate, Britain's principal charity for RSI sufferers, the RSI Association, has ceased to operate for lack of financial support.

But you don't even need to use these devices to be at risk,

according to the London *Metro*. 'Using iPod or phone in a storm "could kill"' was the front-page headline picking up on a report from three doctors in the *British Medical Journal* of a girl hit by lightning while making a call in a city park. According to *Metro*, the lightning provoked a heart attack, and the girl 'was found lying on her back. One arm was stuck rigidly upwards and her burnt-out phone was clutched in her hand.' Fortunately, she escaped complete technological martyrization, surviving with injuries including the loss of hearing 'in the ear she used to listen to her mobile'.

The *Metro* article went on to mention three phone users in China, Korea and Malaysia described in the *BMJ* piece who had been struck dead by lightning. The good doctors wrote that 'education is necessary to highlight the risk of using mobile phones outdoors during stormy weather', but they said nothing about the risk of wielding non-headline-grabbing metallic objects such as umbrellas. Nor was any attempt made to establish whether the risk of injury or death was materially increased by carrying a phone. Deaths due to lightning strike are surprisingly high. The National Weather Service puts the average US death toll due to lightning at seventy-three people a year; the global figure must be over a thousand. Given the high ownership of personal technology, it is remarkable that the *BMJ* authors could find only three cases worldwide where the victims were using mobile phones.

How confusing all this is. Is it a disgrace that people are allowed out in storms without realizing the danger? Or ought we to defend our right to roam in all weathers from the do-gooders? British newspapers have recently carried reports that schools have banned children from playing with conkers, that drivers have been prevented from parking their cars under fruit trees, that firemen may no longer slide down poles, that cats may no longer be rescued from trees, and that hanging flower baskets must no longer hang if they do so over people's heads, all these things supposedly decreed by zealous health and safety officials.

If a single person were seriously hurt or killed by any one of these curious hazards, the newspapers would naturally be eager to report the story. But in the meantime the media stance is one of pious disparagement of the people whom the *Daily Mail* terms the 'health and safety killjoys'. Perhaps things *have* gone too far in the name of risk reduction. A new chairman of Britain's Health and Safety Commission began his term with an unexpected attack on the pedants in his industry. His advice, passed on in a *Daily Telegraph* headline, was for us to 'Get a life and take sensible risks'. OK. Now what, exactly, is a *sensible* risk? The Institution of Occupational Safety and Health proposed one answer to that question when it sponsored the 2007 World Conker Championships.

6. Law and Order

Since 9/11, terror has become a big concern for ordinary people in ordinary places and everyone has a view on the merits of the 'war on terror'. But just how scared should we be of a terrorist attack? And can a government ever pitch its advice at the right level without scaremongering or appearing to ignore the risks? What are the consequences of real wars? Traditional crime, however, has more day-to-day impact on people and stories about murderers roaming our streets seem designed to scare. The early release of criminals from prisons adds to the worry.

Terror Alert
'MI5 head warns of 1600 plotters' *Financial Times*

Fancy seeing the Pyramids? If so, the opening line of the travel advice of the web pages of the UK's Foreign Office will probably put you off: 'There is a high threat from terrorism. Attacks can be indiscriminate and against civilian targets, including places frequented by foreigners.' It doesn't sound very promising, does it? But then again, there is similarly gloomy advice for other places, such as Morocco or Turkey, where Europeans seek some winter sun in their thousands. The situation is worse in other potential holiday destinations such as Thailand and Indonesia (including Bali), as in both cases the Foreign Office advice omits the reassuring phrase 'Most visits are trouble-free'.

Is the situation that bad? Is the Foreign Office erring on the side of caution? It does say that it does not warn against travel to every country where there is a risk of terrorists operating – for the obvious reason that it would cover virtually the whole world, 'serving only to cause panic and disrupt normal life'. And there are countries that it advises against all travel to, including the likes of Chad, Ivory Coast and Somalia. It also advises against all travel to parts of another twenty-five or so countries – including Albania, India, Indonesia, Israel, Pakistan, Russia and Sri Lanka. That said, although detailed figures are not given on the website, the reality is that in countries like Egypt and Turkey far more British nationals die from natural causes (like heart attacks among the elderly), drowning, road and rail accidents, and natural disasters, such as earthquakes, than from terrorism.

The Foreign Office advice reflects – or perhaps along with other government agencies operating in the domestic environment stirs up – the sense of fear in which a large proportion of the developed world lives. During the time of writing, Britain's Home Office assessed the security threat to Britain from terrorism as being 'severe'. This is the fourth point on a five-point scale, going from low, moderate, substantial, to severe and finally critical. 'Severe' means that an attack is 'highly likely', while 'critical' means that an attack is expected 'imminently'. You wouldn't guess from watching the people wander the streets that we were on as high a level of alert as possible for that length of time without the authorities having knowledge of an 'imminent' attack. The US Department of Homeland Security had the country on the 'elevated' national threat level, the third notch on a five-point scale. Apart from asking all Americans to be 'vigilant', it scarily said that 'everybody should establish an emergency preparedness kit as well as a communications plan for themselves and their family'.

Such a level of concern is reflected in the many alternative surveys that have been conducted assessing perceptions of the terrorist threat. One study showed terrorism to be ahead of all other worries in both Europe and the US, with 94 and 97 per cent respectively of those polled believing it to be an important threat.[1] Another survey showed that 90 per cent of Britons and 84 per cent of Americans felt that their country is likely to be the target of a terrorist attack in the near future.[2] A third put the likelihood of an attack a little lower – about two-thirds of respondents in the two countries thinking that an attack was somewhat or very likely in the next twelve months.[3] Of course, the response depends on the exact wording of the question that is asked, but it is clear that concerns are there and they seem to be affecting our daily behaviour – roughly six out of ten Americans and Britons now look twice at other passengers on public transport.

But the figures are not high in every country. While the levels of fear in France (84 per cent) and India (82 per cent) are close to those seen in the US and the UK, other countries are lower – for example, Germany (47 per cent) – and some are much lower – for example, Hong Kong (12 per cent) and Hungary (17 per cent). Worries about terrorism are highest in countries that have already suffered an attack. It is only those countries that have to date been spared attacks that have citizens with greater worries than terrorism – for example, the dominant concerns in Hong Kong are SARS and bird flu.

Furthermore, concern about terrorism is not evenly spread within countries. One American survey showed that nearly a third of those who lived in big cities said they were 'personally very concerned' about an attack, compared to only one in eight of those living in small towns or rural areas.[4] In New York, 69 per cent of people are 'very concerned' about another terrorist event, only fractionally down on the percentage recorded in October 2001 in the wake of the twin towers attack. The concerns of New Yorkers about terrorism remain high, but across much of the US concerns diminish as the vividness of the memory of the events of 9/11 fades. As if the fear of the terror act itself was not enough, surveys tend to find that a majority of residents in developed western countries feel that their country is not well prepared to respond to a terror attack.

Even economists are getting in on the act of worrying about terrorism: a prestigious survey of America's dismal scientists showed that they believed the threat of a terror attack was the biggest short-term problem facing the US economy.[5] Most people think that the failure to find a successful conclusion to the Iraq war has increased rather than decreased the perceived chances of terrorist attacks. One large survey spanning thirty-five countries found that 60 per cent of those polled shared this view, with only about one-quarter believing that the war had reduced the chances of an attack or had had no effect. In Britain, in contrast to the government view, 77 per cent of those questioned thought that the terrorist threat had risen since the 2003 invasion.[6]

The fear has had some odd consequences. One of Berlin's top opera houses came under fire for cancelling a controversial production of Mozart's *Idomeneo*, which was to show the severed heads of the Prophet Muhammad, Jesus and Buddha, due to concerns about Islamist attacks. German politicians condemned the cancellation as self-censorship, cowardice and damaging to the principle of free speech. The decision came in the wake of the riots following the publication of cartoons of Muhammad in a Danish newspaper. There have been reports of other, seemingly absurd, reactions in Germany designed to avoid offending the 3½ million Muslim residents. These allegedly include a request to darken a school gymnasium when Muslim girls are working out and a woman being told to change the name of her horse from 'Muhammad' to something less troubling, such as 'Momi'.

Much of the concern of westerners is focused on the concept of 'a Muslim problem'. One poll in Britain suggested that 53 per cent of people felt threatened by Islam, a rise from 32 per cent in the wake of the 11 September terrorist attacks on America. The appearance of a so-called clash of civilizations is supported by the fact that there has been a near doubling, to one in five, in the proportion of Britons who believe that 'a large proportion of British Muslims feel no sense of loyalty to this country and are prepared to condone or even carry out acts of terrorism'.[7]

But just how real is the threat? Some of the headline figures are, indeed, pretty scary. The roll call for global terrorism in 2007, compiled by the National Counterterrorism Center in the US, included over 14,000 terrorist incidents, 22,000 deaths of non-combatants, with many more thousands wounded and kidnapped.[8] The figures are high enough, but the trend is even worse: the figures for 2006 were well up on those in 2005, which in turn were a hefty increase on the previous year. Part of the increase in 2005 is explained by definitional changes to the figures. In the light of the American government's increased focus on the threat from terrorism, the authorities decided that the State Department's annual publication needed to be changed, effectively ending a twenty-year run of consistent data.

The definition of 'international terrorism' was shifted from one of 'involving citizens or territory of more than one country' to a new definition of 'terrorism' meaning 'premeditated, politically motivated violence perpetrated against non-combatant targets by sub-national groups or clandestine agents, usually intended to influence an audience'. This might sound trivial but it has made a large difference to the figures. As the new definition has been brought in, the figures have increased. Some government critics cried foul, suggesting that the changes were only made to make the numbers larger, making it easier for the government to justify its policies. The old figures were criticized, however, as they failed to count some clear cases of terrorism, including the Van Gogh assassination, the Philippine super ferry and the blowing-up of a Russian aircraft. While a simple aggregation of terrorism incidents is hardly a perfect metric for measuring the scale of the problem or the success in tackling it, such a list does provide a useful basis for analysis.

The figures show that the Near East and south Asia are particularly hard hit by terrorism, accounting for 75 per cent of the attacks and 85 per cent of the fatalities in 2007. Nearly two-thirds of the non-combatant fatalities worldwide in 2007 occurred in Iraq, with India, Afghanistan, Sudan and Sri Lanka collectively accounting for another large proportion. Several categories of civilians, including police, religious figures and journalists, bore a disproportionate brunt of terrorism. Over half the victims killed or seriously injured in 2006 were Muslims. Away from Iraq, Afghanistan and a handful of other mainly African terror hotspots, the number of reported terror incidents fell in 2007, continuing the recent trend.

The ex-Iraq numbers are not that large. This is reflected in the detailed information of attacks on the website of the UK's Foreign Office – it lists only a couple of dozen terrorist incidents from the previous three years, focusing mainly on incidents in generally terrorist-free areas. A little over 500,000 people die each year in England and Wales yet typically only a dozen or two Britons have died as a result of terrorism in recent years. Annual deaths from terrorism have been much lower than deaths from transport accidents (3,000), falls (3,000), drowning (200), poisoning (900) and suicide (over 3,000).[9] Twenty-eight non-combatant US citizens were killed by terrorists in 2006, of which twenty-two were in Iraq and three in Afghanistan. It is pretty clear that, so long as you stay away from the world's insurgent hotspots, the chances of being caught up in a terrorist event are minuscule.

But to what extent can we ignore the threat? One view is that the reaction of western governments to the terrorist threat is exaggerated. Terrorist attacks can never amount to more than a 'big, bloody nuisance', as one columnist put it – and we should carry on with our lives as normal. An alternative view is that the government should do more, introduce new security measures and make more arrests, in order to minimize the possibility of further attacks.

The low fatality figures quoted above would appear to support the former argument. It has been pointed out that in most years more people die in their baths than at the hands of international terrorists, and that more Americans have been killed by lightning or an allergic reaction to peanuts than by terrorists. The argument continues that the cost of hasty and ill-considered anti-terror measures and the impact of panic on liberal institutions are far greater than the cost of the terrorism itself. But even a convincing argument against panic does not mean that there is no need for a vigorous policy to combat terrorism. In terrorism, as in crime more generally, the number of incidents is contained by the policies in place to combat it. Terrorism might after all be like a disease that starts with only a few people and becomes an epidemic, at which point it gets out of hand. Perhaps we should consider ourselves fortunate that terrorists are, with some notable exceptions, generally so inept.

The statisticians are doing more than publishing figures, they are playing a role in maintaining safety levels in society by using their skills in risk analysis, profiling and screening, coupled with the rapid identification of disease clusters in the event of biological or chemical attack. Meanwhile we are left with the near-impossible task of judging the tiny risk of an apocalyptic event. With the British newspapers saying in the summer of 2006 that there are at least 1,200 home-grown Islamic fanatics under surveillance by the security services in Britain, it is no wonder that many people remain nervous. If that wasn't enough to worry about, by the end of 2006 MI5 was telling us that there were 1,600 'terror plotters' up to no good in the country[10] and by February 2007 the number had risen to 'more than 2000'.[11] That 'inflation rate' is certainly enough to get the pulse racing.

Bang Bang
'Debate rages over number of civilians killed' *Independent*

Television images and newspaper reports give the impression that violent conflicts and uprisings of one sort or another are sprouting up across the world. Yet the people who keep the tally of such things reckon that the last two or three years have seen the number of wars drop to the lowest level since the mid-1960s. It seems that only about half the number is taking place now compared to the peak in the early 1990s – some twenty-eight wars were counted in 2006 compared to fifty-five in 1992.[1]

Notwithstanding all the methodological difficulties in counting and classifying such activities, the downward trend in the last decade or so represents a stunning turnaround from the seemingly inexorable rise over the preceding twenty years. Data are also collected for 'armed conflicts' which are of lesser severity or which for other reasons do not qualify as full-scale wars. These have also been on a downward trend in recent years although the data have only been collected for a decade or so. A different source collects figures on the number of 'political conflicts' and assessed that there are around 270 live, of which 10 per cent involved a high level of armed violence and 30 per cent involved occasional violence.[2]

Although the number of conflicts might be declining, very little is known about how many people fall victim to this organized violence. Most data collection efforts are focused on battle deaths, ignoring civilian deaths, especially those which may result from the indirect consequences, such as failing economies and collapsing health systems. The second-round effects of conflicts are laid bare in the example of the Democratic Republic of the Congo. A study in the *Lancet* estimated that nearly 4 million people have died there since 1998, and that less than 2 per cent of the deaths were the direct result of violence, with most people succumbing to disease and hunger.

The difficulties of counting war dead came to a head in October 2006 when the *Lancet* (again) published a controversial study regarding the number of dead in Iraq since the US-led invasion in March 2003.[3] It suggested that more than 600,000 people had been killed since 2003, equivalent to 2½ per cent of the population, and much higher than other estimates derived from counting bodies in mortuaries or tabulating media reports of deaths. The widely quoted Iraq Body Count, one such compilation of media reports, gave a death toll of about 50,000 over the same period.[4] Experts in the field typically say that body-count methods underestimate the true count by a factor of at least five, but there has been no 'scientific' corroboration of this.

Although President Bush, who described the estimates as 'not credible', along with the US commander in Iraq and Iraqi officials questioned the methodology, the figures seemed to confirm the widely held impression that Iraq was descending into what the researchers called 'blood-thirsty chaos'. They surveyed nearly 2,000 households at forty-seven sites across Iraq, asking about births, deaths and migration in and out of the areas. The mortality rate had more than doubled since the invasion, and more deaths, which were mostly confirmed by death certificates, had been caused by gunshot wounds than anything else.

Arguing about the exact number, which will never be known, is to miss the point. In any case, the researchers did give an admittedly wide range of the estimate of the number of deaths from 390,000 to 940,000. Rather, it is the scale of the carnage hinted at by the survey that is important. Even a figure close to the bottom of the *Lancet* range would be roughly ten times as great as the 'official' estimate of civilian deaths – 30,000 to 50,000 was typical of the figure coming at the time from the administrations involved in the war. Yet even the low figures have the power to shock: one estimate, 50,100, of the number of Iraqi dead made in the summer of 2006 prior to the *Lancet* study was described in one newspaper as 'staggering'.

Needless to say, such figures of Iraqi dead are very politically sensitive. The US general Tommy Franks was famously quoted as saying, 'We don't do body counts,' and, at least until late 2005, the Pentagon claimed that it did not keep a running total of Iraqi deaths. It refuses to make public the figures that are collected, presumably for fear of inflaming concerns about the war. The sensitivities were emphasized by the news in October 2006 that a leaked memo from the office of the Iraqi prime minister to the country's Health Ministry had asked that it stop providing mortality figures to the United Nations.

Deaths among the Allied troops are, in contrast, logged in meticulous detail. By mid-2008, nearly 4,500 coalition troops had been killed in Iraq: over 90 per cent were Americans and the majority of the remainder British. The lists of servicemen deaths on the US Department of Defense and British Ministry of Defence websites are collated on other sites run by interested parties. The coalition has so far been far less enthusiastic when it comes to publishing either death rates (the number of dead relative to the number serving) for its military personnel or the number wounded. While any individual death is regrettable for those immediately involved, from the point of view of the media, public opinion, government policy and military planning, it is arguably more important to have the death rates that measure the risk of death for personnel located in any particular area.

Some independent analysts have tried to compile such figures from official sources, but this can be difficult without being sure how many forces of various types are stationed in each country at any one time. One such study suggested that the death rate (the number of deaths per thousand years of serving personnel) of British soldiers based in Afghanistan was six times higher than for their peers in Iraq in 2006, double that for those who were involved in the initial invasion of Iraq in 2003.[5] The author of the report said that 'The commentary we are getting from politicians about the conflicts does not do justice to the threat our forces face.' The authorities resisted demands for the publication of figures showing the extent of injuries to the forces on active duty.

The pattern of declared military expenditure by the world's governments has followed a slightly different path from that of conflicts. Expenditures (in inflation-adjusted terms) peaked in the early 1980s and, after a period of stability, fell in the early 1990s at the end of the Cold War. By the mid-1990s, expenditure was only two-thirds of the level in the late 1980s. More recently, however, and especially since the September 2001 attacks in the US, military spending has been rising more strongly. Countries in many regions of the world have been increasing their expenditure, but the rises have been more modest in Central and South America and in western Europe, notably in Brazil, Mexico and Germany, where expenditure has been cut back.

The US spends almost as much on military activities as the rest of the world combined. The country's spending is at its highest level since 1969 even though the number of armed forces (soldiers and civilians) stands at around 2 million, less than half the number forty years ago. Employment in the arms industry is close to 4 million, a million more than it was at the height of the Vietnam conflict. After the US, the big spenders are the UK, France, Japan and China – together they account for a further one-fifth of global expenditures. The top fifteen budgets together account for over

80 per cent of the global total, with NATO countries being the dominant spenders. The large budgets of Russia, China and India are difficult to assess accurately due to both a lack of transparency in public and corporate spending and the difficulty of choosing an appropriate exchange rate for the purposes of comparison.

Per capita annual expenditures vary enormously between countries, ranging from nearly $1,500 in North America, and $540 in western Europe, down to just $18 in Africa. It has been estimated that developed countries spend roughly ten times as much on the military as they do on development aid for the poorer countries[6] – a ratio that many people find hard to understand when large chunks of the world are suffering from poverty and ill-health.

More positively, the spending by the United Nations on peace-keeping operations is now at a record high, reaching just over $5 billion in the year to mid-2006, roughly double the amount at the turn of the millennium and surpassing the previous peak of 1994. Roughly 70,000 soldiers, police and military observers were serving in sixteen peacekeeping operations at the end of 2005. Over 40 per cent of the peacekeepers are located in Pakistan, Bangladesh, India, Nepal and Sri Lanka, with six sub-Saharan African countries accounting for another 20 per cent. A good part of the increase in budgets in the last year is accounted for by the missions to Congo and Sudan.

When servicemen return from active duty you would think that their problems were behind them, but many media reports suggest that is not the case. Some stories suggest that soldiers have difficulty getting appropriate medical treatment, and that the failure to give them priority means that thousands are unable to return to the front line. It is quite possible, however, that the psychological consequences of fighting in these wars will be greater than the physical consequences – one British charity dealing with services welfare, Combat Stress, again saw a record number of veterans in the latest year suffering from anxiety and depression. It said that 'soldiers face a mental health time-bomb', having bottled up the trauma.

One particular problem facing ex-servicemen is the so-called

'Gulf war syndrome', referred to by one newspaper as the 'mystery plague that wrecks 8,000 lives'. The existence and nature of the syndrome is a subject of considerable debate as, while there is incontrovertible evidence that rates of ill-health are greater for Gulf war veterans than across the armed forces in general, there is no evidence of an increase in mortality or the occurrence of any well-defined medical condition.[7] Symptoms attributed to the syndrome have been wide-ranging, including chronic fatigue, loss of muscle control, migraines, dizziness and the loss of balance, memory problems, muscle and joint pain, sexual problems, indigestion, skin problems, mood swings and shortness of breath. The British and American ex-troops have the highest rate of excess illness and are distinguished from the other nations by higher rates of pesticide use, use of anthrax vaccine and somewhat higher rates of exposure to oil-fire smoke and chemical alerts. Among the most likely potential causes not yet excluded are combustion products from depleted uranium munitions, side-effects from anthrax and other vaccines, parasitic infectious diseases, the spraying of insecticides over tents and exposure to chemical weapons such as nerve gas or mustard gas.

The combination of multiple possible causes, multiple symptoms and the background of higher reported cases of stress disorder means that we are unlikely ever to have clarity on the story. That was certainly the conclusion of fifteen years' research by scientists from the Royal Society, the British science academy, who concluded that there was 'little value in conducting further research'.[8] This will be of little reassurance to those veterans of the current Iraq war who are already revealing a range of serious health issues.

Lock 'Em Up
'How Britain has become a land fit for criminals' *Daily Express*

Is jail an expensive way of making bad people worse or the best place for persistent, violent and dangerous criminals? David Green, director of think tank Civitas, wrote of a deepening sense of crisis hanging over the British prison system, contrasting the mounting public concern over short sentences for serious offenders with parts of the political elite and judiciary expressing anxiety about the size of the inmate population and the supposedly excessive use of custody.[1]

Under the tabloid headline 'How Britain has become a land fit for criminals', we were told that the government has substituted the fight against crime with a war against prison, and that untruthful and misleading anti-prison propaganda has silenced all reasonable opposition. The article added, for good measure, that the criminal justice policy is maintained by lies and that misleading statistics and other obfuscations are used to engineer the public's consent to a sentencing policy that undermines their safety – a potent cocktail indeed. While the government's policy is so confused, the public is justified in feeling concerned about safety even if, notwithstanding the steady trickle of innocent people tragically murdered by ex-convicts, the personal risks are low.

The prison problem arises because most politicians, particularly on the left, would rather be remembered for building hospitals than prisons, even if it leads to overcrowding as more people are committed. Overcrowding means that there is increasing pressure, especially from the more liberal sections of society, for the early release of prisoners. But an increase in the early release of prisoners boosts the already high reoffending rates especially if the probation service is so stretched that they are inadequately assessed and not fully rehabilitated, in part as a consequence of the overcrowding. It adds up to a tricky policy area for government and a most fertile area for scare stories.

The release of dangerous criminals on to our streets – Scotland has one of the highest prisoner reoffending rates in Europe, with half of released prisoners back behind bars within two years – is a sign that the government is failing in its duty to protect the public. Add to that the apparently slack security that reportedly allowed 4,000 prisoners to walk out of prisons in the last five years, and it is a wonder that we can sleep at night.

The England and Wales prison population has risen sharply to 84,000, doubling in little over a decade. Meanwhile, the level of crime has generally been falling, suggesting that the higher imprisonment rate is a success. The combination of the increased chance of going to prison (acting as a deterrent) and more criminals being in prison (where they are unable to reoffend) makes the streets safer. The latter point would be consistent with the Home Office view that roughly half the crime in the country is committed by just 100,000 people. Instead, however, the view promoted by the anti-prison lobby, which has become widely believed across society, uses international league tables showing the number of people in jail per head of population to suggest that the country's penal system is in crisis. 'Britain tops European jail league' is the sort of headline that typically follows the release of new figures, on this occasion based on a press release issued by the Howard League for Penal Reform using numbers published by the Council of Europe.[2]

Other sets of figures, such as that published by the International Centre for Prison Studies, show broadly the same conclusions, namely that England and Wales have more people in jail per head of population than any other country in western Europe.[3] Within Europe, the rate is only surpassed by some of the central and eastern European countries, such as Poland, the Czech Republic and Hungary. The lobbyists would have us believe that judges and magistrates are deploying a rather barbaric instrument while their counterparts in Europe are opting for a more gentle approach.

The prison overcrowding seemingly adds weight to the argument that too many people are imprisoned. The cause is boosted when some of Britain's senior judges, for example Lord Chief Justice Lord Woolf in 2002[4] and his successor Lord Phillips in 2006,[5] say that judges should resist the temptation of sending

Europe's prisoners

	Prison population rate, per 100,000 of population★	Prison population rate, per thousand recorded crimes
England and Wales	142	12.1
Spain	140	**45.9**
Scotland	132	**14.6**
Portugal	128	**35.5**
Netherlands	123	**12.3**
Italy	98	**25.8**
Germany	96	11.0
France	91	11.6
Belgium	88	10.1
Ireland	85	**34.9**
Greece	82	**19.0**
Sweden	75	5.1
Finland	71	8.6
Denmark	70	6.6

Source: ★ ICPS, www.prisonstudies.org, 6th edition, selected countries, and www.civitas.org.uk, selected countries, 2001 figures (countries with higher rates than England and Wales are marked in bold)

criminals to jail, especially for short sentences. The *Daily Mail* responded by calling Lord Woolf 'The burglar's friend'.

A close look at the figures, however, suggests that the very foundations of this argument – that England and Wales have a disproportionate number of people in jail – could be fundamentally flawed. The number of prisoners in relation to the volume of crime, rather than in relation to the population, a ratio that the Home Office has decided not to publish, gives a different impression. Thankfully, Civitas has produced the numbers.[6] They show that the authorities in England and Wales send fewer people to prison in relation to the number of recorded crimes than the EU average. Spain, Portugal, Italy and Ireland all send at least twice as many criminals to jail in relation to the number of recorded crimes than England and Wales, which is in line with France, Germany and the Netherlands. Only the Scandinavian countries are incarcerating significantly fewer people. In other words, it is the relatively high level of crime in England and Wales that is responsible for the high prison population. It is not obviously the case, as the Prison Reform Trust press release entitled 'England and Wales – Western Europe's jail capital' says, that 'the statistics confirm that our courts are far more punitive than our closest European neighbours'.[7]

The British rate of incarceration, however, is only a fraction of that seen in the US, where the rate has more than trebled in the last twenty-five years. It is now just short of 500 prisoners per 100,000 population, meaning that one in every 200 people is in prison. Over 2.1 million Americans are in jail (pending trial or serving short sentences) or prison compared to under 1½ million a decade before.

There is no single reason why the number of British prisoners has risen so steeply in recent years. The appointment of Michael Howard as home secretary in the last Conservative government coincided with the start of the rise that continued under Labour, following their election in 1997. Labour's stance was much more ambiguous, however, as the government tried to reconcile the election pledge to be 'tough on crime, tough on the causes of crime', with the view, supposedly supported by the civil servants in the Home Office who had been brought up on dodgy ratios, that too many criminals were being sent to prison.

The number of people found guilty by the courts has remained comparatively static, and there has not been an increase in the number of serious crimes. But there has been a change in the pattern of offending, with an increasing number of people with long conviction strings and who have failed to comply with non-custodial sentences or have breached release conditions appearing before the courts.

Whatever the explanation for the trends, the building of prison spaces in England has failed to keep up with demand. This has led to overcrowding, with occupancy levels, based on official capacity, at over 100 per cent. The overcrowding puts pressure on prison management and disrupts the smooth running of prison regimes, raising the threat of rioting and higher rates of prisoner suicide. The increased churn of prisoners interrupts training programmes and undermines education, training and rehabilitation. But such help is vital due to the profile of the prison population – prisoners are much more likely than the general population to have run away from home as a child, have no qualifications, suffer from two or more mental disorders and be drug users.

Prison is not a cheap option. Figures released in 2005 for English prisons showed that the cost per prisoner ranged from £14,000 to £47,000 depending on the prison. Under the headline, 'Are our prisons just like hotels?', the nightly cost of housing a prisoner in Swansea prison, described as a grim Victorian jail, was reported to be £112, more than the average cost of a room at one of the city's top hotels.[8] While the cost of prison is known with some certainty, the cost of not putting criminals in prison is very uncertain, and estimates tend to be in very wide ranges.

Whatever the overcrowding problem now, it is set to get worse. Official forecasts of the prison population suggest that England will be short of 6,000 spaces by 2011, even after the government's commitment to increase prison capacity by 8,000 places. One prison reformer was quoted as saying that the forecast of the prison population hitting 100,000 was 'chilling' and meant we were living in 'gulag Britain'.[9] Yet it is hard for ministers to avoid the overcrowding problem by sending fewer people to prison. The then home secretary's announcement in 2006 that muggers, minor drug dealers and shoplifters would either be spared prison altogether or receive a hugely reduced sentence was met by the headline '60,000 will be spared prison' and naturally gave rise to some concern.

Prison overcrowding panics people because it means that an increasing number of offenders are released back into the community before the end of their term, possibly to reoffend. An article entitled 'Number of freed lifers trebles in five years' quoted a member of parliament saying, 'The public are being failed by a system which allows murderers and rapists back onto the streets to commit more offences. A life sentence should mean what it says, but at the moment it just means a few years watching television in a comfortable cell.'[10]

In recent years several high-profile murders have indeed been carried out by criminals on probation, showing that it is difficult for the stretched professionals to assess accurately the danger posed by offenders. Stories such as 'Blunders that let Monckton killer escape supervision' hardly ease our concerns. In America, three-fifths of convicts from state prisons fail successfully to complete their parole. Governments have never found it easy to get the appropriate level of policy coordination among the various groups involved – police, courts, prisons and probation services.

But should it just be hooded youths and seasoned criminals that give rise to concern? In rapidly ageing Japan, a wave of crime by the elderly is the problem. The percentage of over sixty-fives incarcerated in Japan has tripled in the last decade and now exceeds 10 per cent of the total – four times the UK proportion and the highest pensioner incarceration rate in the industrialized world. Prison in Japan is becoming a place for the old and disabled who have slipped through the cracks of the welfare system. A recent article told the story of a man in his eighties who broke into a Tokyo home with the intention of stealing. He was confronted by the woman owner who fended him off with a glass ashtray and said, 'I tried as best I could to strike back.' She was a mere seventy-nine.

Murder and Crime
'A town where thugs rule' *News of the World*

The safety of you and your family is paramount, and there are few things that are more scary than thinking you are under threat from dangerous souls wandering the streets. Every day, it seems, the media will have another tragic story about an innocent person who was in the wrong place at the wrong time and met an untimely end. The sight of bunches of flowers being tied to railings at the scene of a murder is a moving and seemingly frequent occurrence on our news broadcasts. Crime stories are also strongly political.

The hyping-up of crime figures, selecting those that make the situation look worse, is a tried and trusted way of making any government look bad.

'Britain in fear: a town where thugs rule' described an area of east London where a young man was killed as being 'a chilling example of forgotten Britain – an inner-city hellhole of lawlessness where gangs rule by gun and blade'. One tabloid article headlined 'Why are murder rates on the increase in this once civilised country?' started:

In 1955 anthropologist Geoffrey Gorer wrote that 'the English are certainly among the most peaceful, gentle, courteous and orderly populations that the civilised world has ever seen'. Half a century later, it would be absurd to use those words about modern Britain, where savagery, aggression and lawbreaking are endemic. We have been turned from a land of harmony into one of fear.[1]

Fear perhaps, but a land of 'endemic savagery'?

Murder, or homicide, which includes murder, manslaughter and infanticide, is viewed as the gold standard of the crime statistics, reflecting both its seriousness and the fact that the figures are hard to distort and are little affected by any changes in data-collection regimes. During this decade, the underlying number of homicides in England and Wales has fluctuated around 800 to 900, but the headline figure has been higher on occasions. The figures for 2000/01 included fifty-eight Chinese nationals who suffocated in a lorry en route to the UK, and in the following year around 200 of the victims of Harold Shipman, a rogue family doctor who drugged predominantly older patients to death, were added, taking the total number of homicides to over 1,000. Some fifty-two deaths in 2005 were accounted for by the London terror bombing in July of that year. Such exceptional events should be, but not always are, excluded from the figures when assessing the trend.

Careful slicing and dicing of the data can make the trends in the serious crime figures bad news or good. An article entitled 'Homicides soar by a quarter under Labour' explained that, since 1997, the number of victims in England and Wales had risen since

Crimes recorded by the police, 2001

	Homicides	Homicides per 100,000 population
Australia	340	1.9
Canada	554	1.8
England and Wales	891	1.6
France	1,047	1.7
Germany	868	1.1
Ireland	59	1.4
Italy	818	1.5
Japan	1,340	1.1
Russia	33,583	22.1
Scotland	107	2.2
South Africa	21,683	55.9
Spain	494	1.1
US	15,980	5.6

Source: International Comparisons of Criminal Justice Statistics 2001, Issue 12/03, 24 October 2003, www.homeoffice.gov.uk. Some data relate to 2000.

the first half of the 1990s, and 'Killings up 35% under Labour' compared the number of homicides in 2005 with the number in 1997, the first year of Labour government. In contrast, the story headlined 'Murder rate declines but Home Office battles against belief that things are getting worse', which claimed that the murder rate for England and Wales was showing 'its first sustained fall since the 1960s', was equally selective but presumably more welcome so far as the government was concerned.

As in many other areas of public policy, there are questions over the independence of government-produced statistics and research. The Statistics Commission, a watchdog set up by the government in 2000 but since disbanded, and an independent review team established by the then home secretary both published reports in 2006 recommending changes to the way the crime statistics are produced. When the basic bond of trust has been broken, it is easier for the media to get the wrong end of the stick and for the public to panic.

Panic-inducing crime news is not restricted to the UK. The Irish are told regularly that there is a murder a week and a rape every day. One article, with the subtitle 'Welcome to Ireland, land of sex fiends and killers', was about losing the war against crime as the latest figures showed a large increase in the number of murders. Another, 'Blame game goes on in a society dogged by murder and violence', told the sad tale of South Africa, where there are more murders than in the US and fifty times as many as in western Europe. South Africa tops most tables of murder and violent crime rates although precise figures are unknown. It is reported that the government does not like releasing figures for fear of them damaging tourism and leading to sanctions ahead of the 2010 football World Cup. There are serious concerns about their quality too – the police crime statistics showed nearly 22,000 murders in the latest year, while the Medical Research Council puts the figure at over 32,000 and the Department of Home Affairs has a figure close to 30,000. The figures from Interpol are even higher.

But the trend is not adverse everywhere in the world. The number of killings in Montreal is down on the previous year's record low, and New York saw the murder rate drop to its lowest since 1963 on the back of the 'zero tolerance' policies pursued from the mid-1990s. New York is now the safest big city in America, while others, such as Boston, Houston and Philadelphia, see rising crime rates. The Houston murder rate rose by one-fifth in the year when 150,000 evacuees arrived following Hurricane Katrina.

Understanding what is going on is not helped by the fact that terms can often get confused, with reports switching between murder and homicide, and violent, serious and headline crimes. Violent crime is a very diverse crime grouping in the UK as it contains the full spectrum of assaults, from murder to pushing and shoving, which result in no physical harm, as well as sexual offences and robbery. A casual reader of a newspaper can easily be misled.

In the UK, as in most countries, there are two sources of crime data – police figures of reported crime and surveys of people asking how they have been affected by crime. The British Crime Survey is considered the more reliable measure of violent crime as the police recorded crime figures have been inflated over the last few years by changes in recording practices (including harmonization across police forces), increased reporting by the public (many people have seen no point in reporting crime unless it is serious or required for insurance purposes) and increased police activity.[2] The problem with crime surveys, though, is that they do not cover all crimes. The British one does not cover crimes against business, crimes where there is no direct victim (such as drug dealing), crimes against victims younger than sixteen and crimes that have involved death (in good part because the victims cannot be interviewed). Surveys do not give crime figures for local areas.

The picture is complicated by the fact that some types of crime will be on a rising trend while others will be declining. One article referred to George Orwell's 'Decline of the English Murder', which 'lamented the disappearance of middle-class crimes of passion', with their place being taken by murders 'that had a background not of stifling domesticity, but of the anonymous life of the dance halls and the false values of the American film', or, to put it in today's terms, of the hoodie and the celebrity stalker.

Certainly, the chance of someone in Britain being involved in gun crime is very small as it is largely confined to small pockets of inner cities – two-thirds of the shootings are in just six of the capital's poorest thirty-plus boroughs. Mostly the disputes are about drugs, and three-quarters of shooting victims are young and black. The more recent 'fashion' for knife crime is also very largely limited to certain age groups and locations. It is a similar story in the US, where both the homicide victimization rates and the offending rates for blacks are six to seven times higher than for whites. Statistics setting out the likelihood of different types of people dying as a result of homicide are readily available in America. One website coldly sets out the factoids: the 21.2 per 100,000 black people who died from homicide in the stated year compared with a rate of 8.3 for hispanics, 4.9 for whites and 3.3 for all women.[3] As 85 per cent of murder victims know their killer,[4] it is pretty clear that, unless you are keeping some bad company, you're pretty safe.

For all the hyping of crime, however, there is some evidence that British people are more likely to be subjected to some crimes than their counterparts in most other European countries. One source, the International Crime Victims Survey, carried out four times since 1989 using standardized questions and data-collection methods with a view to obtaining comparable results for the participating countries, suggests that England and Wales have larger proportions of the population than other countries who have been victims of assault, burglary and car theft, but not sexual assault.[5]

Percentage of people or households victimized in the latest year

	Assault	Sexual assault	Burglary	Theft of a car
Austria	1.9	1.7	0.8	0.1
Belgium	2.4	0.7	2.2	0.9
Finland	4.3	1.8	0.5	0.5
France	4.5	0.8	1.6	1.4
Italy	0.8	0.9	2.4	2.6
Netherlands	3.8	1.1	2.2	0.4
Sweden	3.8	1.5	1.6	1.3
Switzerland	2.6	1.4	1.5	0.3
UK: England and Wales	5.0	0.8	3.0	2.8
UK: Scotland	4.9	0.4	1.5	1.2

Data shown for a selection of the twenty or so European countries that took part in the survey. Germany, Greece, Ireland and Spain are among the countries not participating.

If anything, we might expect crime to play an even greater role in the future in media-induced panic. More and more countries are coming under pressure to introduce national crime figures broken down by town or administrative area. Only then will residents have a better idea of the risks that they face and will police and others charged with keeping law and order be able to best direct their scarce resources. As more data become available, more stories will be written. In America, many of the newspapers keep a close eye on how the crime figures are moving. 'Keeping monthly homicide statistics can be like watching a horse race. They're ahead. They're behind. They're neck and neck. But there are no winners. Only losers.'[6]

7. The Natural World

Early civilizations believed in a world ruled by angry gods with the power to unleash forces of destruction beyond our control. Today, we understand that these forces are natural and not divine. But for all our science, we still have a hard time predicting or controlling them. To make matters worse, the scale of human activity on the planet is now such that we are able to whip up global disasters all by ourselves – though perhaps also to prevent them.

Looking Up

'Ozone layer healing, but more slowly than hoped'
Washington Post

We have grown up worrying about the hole in the ozone layer. From the 1970s, depletion of this fragile layer of the Earth's atmosphere by man-made chemicals called chlorofluorocarbons had been forecast to expose humanity to unprecedented levels of dangerous solar radiation. Strong ultraviolet sunlight would penetrate the atmosphere, reaching the ground, where it would cause skin cancers and eye damage in humans, livestock and wildlife and impair the photosynthesis of plants. 'What will it do to our children's outlook on life if we have to teach them to be afraid to look up?' Al Gore wondered in his first essay on environmental apocalypse, *Earth in the Balance*.[1] Greenpeace ran an advertisement headlined 'GOODBYE SUNSHINE', showing a photograph of a baby shielding its eyes against the 'harmful radiation reaching the Earth's surface'.

Children are still able to look up. So what went wrong, or rather right?

Ozone was once regarded as a health-giving substance. In

Victorian times, it was used in the way that chlorine is now for cleaning, bleaching, purifying water and preserving foods. People were sent to the seaside for their health, where the air was said to be rich in ozone, although you are more likely to catch a whiff of it near high-voltage electrical equipment, which can convert small amounts of the diatomic oxygen that we breathe into triatomic molecules of ozone.

The ozone layer had been known for more than fifty years when it first became a matter of environmental concern at the beginning of the 1970s. It lies in the stratosphere, the dry layer of the atmosphere between 10 and 50 kilometres altitude immediately above the troposphere. Whereas the troposphere is dominated by physical processes which we experience as weather, the action in the stratosphere is chemical. The fear at this time was that exhaust chemicals from supersonic aircraft flying at stratospheric altitudes would destroy the ozone, which blocks strong ultraviolet light from reaching the Earth.

Simultaneously, scientists had begun to realize that ultraviolet light might be a factor in causing cancer. The coincidence was too great to ignore, and both the danger of ultraviolet exposure and the potential dangers of fleets of supersonic aircraft criss-crossing the skies made the headlines. Any substantial threat was quickly nullified, however, when the United States Congress halted Boeing's supersonic passenger plane development project, although the reasons for this were ultimately economic.

Meanwhile, the environmental scientist James Lovelock, later to become well known for the Gaia theory, had used a sensitive device of his own invention to detect minute concentrations of chlorofluorocarbons (CFCs) in the atmosphere. There was no other source for these chemicals other than the refrigerants, aerosol gases and foaming agents that had begun to be manufactured during the Second World War. A little later, scientists at the US National Center for Atmospheric Research discovered that chlorine atoms catalyse the breakdown of ozone in the atmosphere. Lovelock's gadget had been built to monitor pesticide levels, while the NCAR team were concerned about chlorine spewed into the atmosphere by erupting volcanoes. Nobody suspected a link between ozone depletion and CFCs.

But in 1974 two chemists at the University of California, Sherwood Rowland and Mario Molina, established that CFCs were the dominant source of chlorine that was indeed breaking down ozone in the stratosphere. The discovery was startling. It showed that the chemicals we had started putting into refrigerators, spray cans and air conditioners twenty years before could escape (due to inefficient factory processes and poor disposal practices) and drift lazily up through the atmosphere, taking years or even decades to reach the ozone layer. Even at concentrations of less than one part per trillion, these chemicals are there broken down into chlorine atoms, each one of which can take out tens of thousands of ozone molecules in a vicious cycle of destruction. When it appeared in *Nature*, Rowland and Molina's paper, however, was not one of those highlighted by the magazine's press office, and it was ignored by the world's journalists.

The attitude of the media changed abruptly in 1985, when Joe Farman of the British Antarctic Survey reported a significant loss of ozone above the South Pole. Both the extent of the depletion and its latitude came as a surprise to scientists, whose models had led them to expect to see the first evidence of ozone depletion in the upper stratosphere above the tropics. When Farman's findings were confirmed by NASA, the *Washington Post* reported the discovery and coined the phrase the 'ozone hole'. No matter that it described the seasonal, partial depletion of a very minor atmospheric constituent and the consequently increased permeability of the atmosphere to merely part of the sunlight spectrum, the 'hole' had an undeniable graphic appeal. It was a rent in the firmament that would allow evil ultraviolet light to pour in, withering our crops and mutilating our bodies.

The advent of the ozone hole was an undoubted spur to those negotiating the Montreal Protocol to limit CFC production, although discussions had begun as early as 1981. When the protocol was signed on 16 September 1987, twenty-four countries agreed merely to level off and then gently reduce their output, not to an outright ban. Yet the Americans had legislated a decade before to ban the use of CFCs as aerosol propellants in response to the research into the likely effects of supersonic aircraft – and American consumers had actually done much of the work first by refusing to buy them in any case. This, and not Montreal, was 'the first, and last, unequivocal application of the precautionary principle in the ozone story' according to Joe Farman.[2]

The idea that Montreal would fix anything was slow to take off. In 1988, after the protocol was signed, the science writer John Gribbin published *The Hole in the Sky*, a popular account of 'man's threat to the ozone layer'. 'This book is required reading for everyone who is concerned about the gigantic threat poised over us all,' trumpeted the cover blurb. Gribbin was convinced that Montreal's half-hearted measures wouldn't be enough. 'Tomorrow is too late,' he wailed.[3] In fact, of course, as Gribbin knew better than most, tomorrow would do pretty well because of the twenty-year delay built into the migration of CFCs up into the stratosphere.

The ineffectual original agreement was gradually strengthened at a sequence of later international gatherings, as more countries signed up, including the major developing countries, and reduction targets were made more onerous. Developed countries finally stopped making CFCs in 1993, several years earlier than originally planned. China is due to phase out production by 2010. In 1995, Rowland and Molina shared the Nobel prize. The Swedish Academy's citation gushed that the researchers had 'contributed to our salvation from a global environmental problem that could have catastrophic consequences'.

Not so fast. Even in the 1990s, it was not yet clear that the CFC deals would produce the desired effect. In 2002, NASA predicted that repair of the Antarctic hole would only be *detectable* by 2020. Annual monitoring since then has revealed no clear trend and suggests that atmospheric systems are more complex than scientists had hoped. The formation of the hole after each Antarctic winter is subject to disruption. The hole shrank significantly from 2003 to 2004 but grew in 2005 and then again in 2006. Temperatures in September 2005 were the lowest since 1979, accelerating the seasonal formation of a hole which in that year peaked at 24 million square kilometres. But the hole also healed again during October, earlier than in previous years, which scientists attribute to changes in local meteorological conditions, not to changes in levels of ozone-depleting chemicals. Such blips, according to the World Meteorological Office,

cannot be explained by changes in the stratospheric halogen loading, but are due to interannual dynamical variability. This variability will make it difficult to detect the onset of ozone recovery in Antarctica, and in particular it will be difficult to attribute any positive change in ozone to declining amounts of ozone depleting substances.[4]

The latest measurements offer a little more hope. The US National Oceanic and Atmospheric Administration announced on 23 August 2006 that the Antarctic hole had stopped expanding and is expected to have healed by around 2060. 'Healing' is a relative term, of course, just as the word 'hole' marked an arbitrary threshold of ozone loss. Joe Farman is less optimistic. Although very little chlorine-containing gas is now being released, what's there already can only decay very slowly. 'One third of it will still be there in 2100: that's an awful lot of chlorine.'[5]

The ozone hole clearly retains considerable scare value. Even the generation that has grown to adulthood since the Montreal Protocol was signed frets about it. Their fears may be seriously off target – two-thirds of a sample of people in one survey apparently believed that the ozone hole is causing climate change.[6] But the fact that they persist indicates that the ozone hole has become an icon. It offers a ready image of man-made environmental degradation that increased emission of carbon dioxide does not.

So it would be a shame to let it go to waste. Fortunately for the environmental Cassandras, there is still the Arctic to worry about. Although NOAA's latest estimate is that the smaller and less frequently appearing hole here will be repaired as soon as 2030, some scientists fear that it will continue to grow. A large Arctic ozone hole would lie far closer to major centres of population than the Antarctic hole, and pose a correspondingly greater danger to human health, exposing more than 700 million people to dangerous levels of ultraviolet radiation.

How can this threat be real if we have largely halted the release of CFCs? The potential difficulty this time is with natural chemical processes triggered by abnormally low temperatures in the stratosphere – due, perversely, to global warming affecting the atmosphere lower down. According to the environment writer Fred Pearce, the Arctic ozone layer is now on 'a hair trigger', with 'many researchers' expecting a 'giant ozone hole to form' as it did a generation ago over the Antarctic.[7] But the hole is not there yet. Predictions of a large hole for 2005 were later said to have been 'overstated'. The next year did see some worsening in the situation. But then in 2007, the hole shrank by 30 per cent. The folly here is to expect to see in each year's tidings a clear sign of what will happen in the future, when the overall picture is one where any long-term trend must be picked out from amid a chaos of short-term variations. Succumbing to this temptation has led to some silly analysis not only by the media but also by partisan scientists and sociologists of science over-reacting to a given year's new data.

In case a new hole doesn't appear – and the mechanisms of these processes are poorly understood at present – Pearce has another message of doom. Suppose we do successfully avoid or repair both ozone holes. This would once more ensure that less ultraviolet light reaches the lower atmosphere. This in turn would mean reduced production of another atmospheric constituent, hydroxyl, which mops up carbon monoxide and other pollutants. All of a sudden, it's a problem to fix the problem!

The ozone episode may or may not be over. So what are, or were, the costs? At the time of Montreal, the US Environmental Protection Agency predicted a 5 per cent rise in non-malignant melanomas for each 1 per cent loss of ozone, amounting to perhaps 20,000 extra American victims a year. The prediction for the life-threatening malignant melanomas was not so clear. Al Gore passed on reports that Patagonian fishermen were catching blind salmon. Yet others found there had been no 'demonstrated harm to people or other living things' by 1990.[8]

Ozone depletion has continued since then until possibly stabilizing today, and melanoma rates have indeed risen widely. The effects of ultraviolet radiation on the body are better understood than they were, but the delayed emergence of melanomas means that it is hard to establish their cause. Australia has the highest rates of skin cancer in the world and is situated beneath the outer edges of the ozone hole when it is at its maximum in each Antarctic spring. But this apparent correlation may arise simply because the country's largely Caucasian population is ill-suited to the sunny climate and enjoys spending too much time on the beach. Meanwhile, the advice is simple: put on plenty of sunscreen – the apparently cynical original retort of CFC manufacturers to claims that their product was the problem – and avoid, if you can, the temptation to travel to Antarctica in the spring.

The Short, Hot Summer of 2006
'New tornado terror today' *Daily Express*

July 2006 was glorious throughout much of Europe. For England and Wales, it proved to be not only the hottest and sunniest July but the hottest month since records began in 1914. Towards the end of the month, however, the novelty of the delightful weather was wearing off. On the 27th, having chronicled the heat wave relentlessly over the previous weeks, the *Daily Express* chose this headline for its front page: 'August is going to be hotter than July'.

On a day when other newspapers reported the news – Tony Blair being called to account over the Iraq war, intensified conflict following Israel's invasion of Lebanon – the *Express* saw fit to predict the weather in 120-point type.

'Britain's record-breaking heat wave is set to sizzle on with forecasters predicting an August of "extreme heat",' the story began. Reading on, though, it seemed that the forecasters themselves weren't so sure. 'The hottest day ever recorded happened in early August and I wouldn't rule out it happening again,' said one cautiously.

The headline was remarkable for two reasons. First, it showed how the British obsession with the weather could lead a national daily to forget itself so completely as to give up on reporting actual events in favour of entirely speculative prognostication. Second, August wasn't hotter than July. Far from it. It was one of the most miserable Augusts in quite a while. (Weather statistics record the recordable – sunshine hours, rainfall, temperature – which does not always reveal subjective things like miserableness.)

But the *Express* was not to be deterred by mere facts. On 19 September, there was once again so little going on in the world that the weather got the front page: '82°F Britain's glorious Indian summer . . . but gales on way'. The gales never came. On 2 November, after the first autumn frost, the paper tried another tack. A large blue box on the front page had the legend '−14°C' inscribed within it. (It helps to put warm temperatures in Fahrenheit and cool ones in Celsius if you want to make them look extreme.) Underneath the number was the warning: 'Big freeze will hit Britain this month'.

Well, did it? Did it hell. Temperatures for November were 1–2°C above average, rounding off what turned out to be Britain's warmest autumn on record.

Towards the end of the month, the *Daily Mail* observed that the weather had gone 'Balmy and barmy'. The recorded data certainly attested to the first claim. And there was no shortage of bizarre observations to support the second, from flowering snowdrops to horses flying through the air, lifted aloft by a mini tornado. These weather phenomena are noteworthy, even news-worthy for some. But were they freakish?

The most freakish-seeming event of the odd summer of 2006 was that September was warmer than August. This appears odd to us because it is not simply an extreme, but an anomaly, an upset to the natural order of things. Surely it can never have happened before that a summer month was trumped for temperature by an autumn one. Central England temperature records go back to 1659. September 2006 was warmer than the previous record holder, 1729, but there have been Septembers warmer than the preceding Augusts eight times before. It has happened on average every forty years or so – not that rare, after all.

So what is freak weather? How often should we expect it? And is it becoming more frequent? Surprisingly, perhaps, weather agencies are reluctant to offer definitions. What determines a freak event depends entirely on what's chosen as the normal range. Freak events therefore occur at a constant average rate, which is governed by the defined level of freakishness. When planning protective measures against floods and hurricane, governments find it con-venient to talk in terms of ten-year events, or hundred-year events, for example.

However, this model makes a number of possibly unrealistic assumptions. One is that we are dealing with a system in which, although individual events depart from the average, the average itself remains constant. Another is that this average is accurately known in the first place because we have a long record of data. Difficulties and misunderstanding arise if the record period is too short to be representative or if the underlying norms are changing. Public and media attitudes to such events, and towards policy designed to prepare for them and deal with them, may be coloured if this is felt to be the case. A former sense of fatalism will be replaced by outrage and demands to know 'why weren't we told?' and 'why wasn't more done?'

Thus, if global warming is a systematic trend influencing our weather, then we would expect that certain events – heat waves, hot summers, hot autumns, hot years, also droughts and floods –

should begin to occur more often. Extremes may become greater, which is to say that the frequency of freak events may increase if our definition of what is a freak stays the same.

It was not only Europe that saw exceptional weather in 2006. China experienced its worst typhoon for fifty years, and there were unusually frequent and severe tornadoes in Kansas. New York City and Japan were blanketed under the deepest snows on record, but Canada had its warmest winter. Phoenix, Arizona, and much of the south-western United States experienced severe drought. The worst floods for fifty years brought an abrupt end to drought in the Horn of Africa. Sydney had its hottest-ever New Year's Day.

And this is just one year. Yet according to the climatologist John Houghton, writing a few years ago about global warming, the 1980s and 1990s were also remarkable for the frequency and intensity of their extremes of weather. In 1987, for example, northern Europe experienced its strongest storm since 1703. The following year Bangladesh suffered its worst-ever floods. But, he adds, 'a note of caution must be sounded. The range of normal natural climate variation is large. Climate extremes are nothing new. Climate records are continually being broken.'[1] Lucky for the newspapers!

Houghton is at pains to distinguish between individual weather events and the underlying climate trend. It is possible to show very simply that these may not be as closely coupled as we are led to think by a media increasingly prone to blame every meteorological oddity on global warming. ('Summer heat waves may get much worse', warned the *Independent*, citing climate change as the cause in September 2006. Six months earlier, towards the end of the winter rather than the summer, the same paper announced 'UK winter storms "to get stronger"', also due to climate change.)

Assuming for the moment that weather is a very simple system (which of course we know it is not), we can use statistical methods alone to predict temperature extremes against a background of steadily rising temperature. Say we expect a temperature rise of 3°C over a hundred years (the average estimated by the Intergovernmental Panel on Climate Change in 2001). How much more often should we then expect a heat wave such as the one that much of Britain enjoyed in July 2006, when the temperature was up by 3.6°C on the average for the month? The answer is that we can expect to see this temperature reached or surpassed about one summer in three – not every summer without fail.

The European heat wave of 2006 prompted headlines, but also health warnings, something largely new in the media treatment of summer weather. These came in response to high temperatures three summers earlier. In 2003, 20,000 people are estimated to have died from heat-related causes in Italy, another 15,000 in France. The death rate in Paris was eight times the normal, many of those who died being neglected elderly relatives of families who had abandoned the city for their summer vacation. It was said to have been Europe's hottest summer in 500 years. But this does not necessarily make it a freak. Average temperatures have risen since the mini ice age of the seventeenth century, so summers that seemed freakish then might not compete with very hot summers today.

The fact that many people died as a direct consequence of the heat is nevertheless a serious matter. Calling it a freak event does them disservice as it appears to excuse us from responsibility for taking precautionary measures against a predictable and predicted event.

The mismatch between the probability of an event and our preparedness for it can reach absurd levels. How can it be, for example, that Britain in 2006 can suffer 'one of its worst droughts for 100 years after two years of below-average rainfall'? Is this remarkable at all? Is it fair enough that we have been caught unawares? Is it cause for outrage? We should expect (at least) two consecutive years of below-average rainfall twenty-five times in a century (on average). So there was nothing odd about this event, and the headlines proclaiming a drought were more a reflection of the increased demand for water due to population migration to drier parts of the country than of any genuine freak of the weather.

This mismatch can also have tragic consequences. Katrina was 'only' a category three hurricane when it struck the city of New Orleans on 29 August 2005. Category three hurricanes make land-fall in the United States every year or two. This one commanded attention first in the Gulf of Mexico, intensifying from category four to five as it turned north before weakening again only a hundred miles off the American coast. (Only three category five hurricanes have hit the US since records began in 1851.) Katrina killed more than 1,800 people and caused damage estimated at over $80 billion – making it America's most expensive hurricane and worst natural disaster – because the scale and severity of the hurricane at sea produced an exceptional storm surge, up to 30 feet at some points along the coast, which breached the poorly maintained levees of New Orleans.

But was it just a strong hurricane that took an unfortunate route, or is it a harbinger of worse to come? Prior to the European summer heat wave of 2003 and Hurricane Katrina in 2005, the environment campaigner Jonathon Porritt could write that 'it would be extremely difficult to demonstrate that anyone had yet died from changes in the climate specifically brought about through pollution from our industrial economies'.[2] But these extreme events have led some to stop equivocating. For the science writer Fred Pearce, the heat wave was 'the first single weather event that climate scientists felt prepared to say was directly attributable to man-made climate change'.[3] The evidence for Katrina is more ambiguous because it is the surface temperature of the sea that generates the hurricane. There had been spells of strong hurricanes long before other climate change effects began to be noticed.

Given its profusion of wild weather, we might expect that 2006 overtook 2005 in Atlantic hurricanes as well, as it had been predicted to do. Yet by the official close of the hurricane season on 30 November not a single hurricane had made landfall in the US. This non-event is not rare either – the last year to draw a blank was 2001. Much of the media eagerly marked the day. 'What hurricane season?' Fox News demanded to know. 'Storm predictions prove all wet as '06 season ends', exulted the *Orlando Sentinel*.

But others simply couldn't believe the good luck. The *Miami Herald* was so disaster-addicted as to keep faith with the discredited merchants of doom, warning, 'Forecasters predict 7 hurricanes for 2007'. A more sophisticated version of this view came from Kerry Emanuel, a meteorologist at the Massachusetts Institute of Technology. 'We may see some quiet years – this year may be quiet,' he said, before the 2006 season had got underway. But he added, 'We probably won't see a quiet decade again in the Atlantic.'[4]

Some scientists, including Emanuel, cautiously attribute the low Atlantic hurricane incidence in 2006 to the El Niño event, a warming of the eastern Pacific Ocean that affects winds in the Atlantic. (Others counter that similar conditions were present in hurricane-rich 2004.) The El Niño hypothesis was seized upon by the media, perhaps because the superstitiously named phenomenon hinted at the age-old tendency to attribute extreme natural events, or our deliverance from them, to supernatural causes. 'Thank El Niño for mild Atlantic hurricane season', entreated the Reuters news service.

In short, hurricane frequency shows no change from the long-term average. Some studies suggest that the strongest storms, categories four and five, are increasing at the expense of weaker ones, which is consistent with the expectation that climate change will produce more severe weather events of many kinds. But the data are inadequate to be able to say for sure, and scientific opinion remains divided.

Scientists expect that a major effect of climate change will be an increase in freak weather events, from the locally talk-worthy to major disaster-makers. But this does not mean that all freak weather – or even most freak weather events – can be blamed on climate change. For many, though, it remains a strong temptation to make the link anyway, as a lobby group of scientists did in the 2004 United States presidential election campaign in Florida. Battered already that season by Charley, Frances, Ivan and Jeanne, voters were then greeted by billboards with the slogan 'Global warming = worse hurricanes. George Bush just doesn't get it'.[5]

Becoming Unsettled
'You have been warmed' *Daily Mirror*

Climate change is arguably the most serious issue we confront in this book. It may not have a sudden or immediate impact but it does threaten to affect us all, which has made it the media's most sustained, enduring and infectious panic story. Newspaper usage of the phrase 'global warming' has been increasing by a steady annual 60 per cent in recent years. It was mentioned 16,755 times in the British press alone during June–August 2006, but it's the same everywhere.[1]

'Be worried. Be very worried', cautioned the cover of *Time*, showing a polar bear peering over the edge of a very small ice floe. Even the doughty *Economist* decided that 'The heat is on'. Both magazines dedicated special surveys to the topic in 2006. The flow of alarmist headlines has become so copious that one think tank was prompted to lash out against 'climate porn'.[2]

How much should we worry? Is climate change a greater threat than terrorism, as the British government's chief scientist David King has insisted in his effort to ram home the danger? Almost certainly, it is – and not only because the risk of being killed in a terrorist attack is actually very small, as we saw in chapter 6. But threat of what? With terrorism the nature of the hazard is clear, but with climate change we don't yet know quite what we face.

There is, however, no shortage of respectable oracles to warn that the worst will happen. The wrist-slitting testament of James Lovelock, *The Revenge of Gaia*, even Friends of the Earth found 'gloomy'. For Lovelock, 'the fever of global heating is real and deadly and might already have moved outside our and the Earth's control'. It is too late for sustainable development – 'what we need is a sustainable retreat'.[3] Al Gore's film *An Inconvenient Truth* is hardly less bleak. 'I look around for meaningful signs we are about to change,' says the former American presidential candidate forlornly. 'I don't see it right now.'

According to ever more extreme forecasts, temperatures may rise by up to five, eight, eleven . . . degrees Celsius over the next hundred years, disrupting agriculture, plant and animal life and our vacation plans. In Britain, we don't know whether to laugh or cry: 'The Med may get too hot for holidays', but, there again, 'Norfolk to be the new Med'.[4] But in already arid regions of the world the effects would be dire. The rising temperatures will melt the polar icecaps, raising sea levels by half a metre, a metre, 7 metres, 70 metres . . . The heat will push climate systems into overdrive, producing longer, drier droughts, heavier downpours, more sudden floods, more vicious storms . . . No wonder there's now a 'coalition of environment, development, faith-based, women's and other organisations' piteously terming itself Stop Climate Chaos.

The cause of all this is believed to be the increasing concentration of greenhouse gases in the atmosphere, most notably carbon dioxide (CO_2) produced by humankind's burning of fossil fuels. Believed, that is, by virtually all scientists – and disbelieved by a small minority who hold either that there is no trend of rising temperatures, or that if there is it is due to terrestrial natural causes or else solar effects.[5] However, the balance of likelihoods now leans very strongly towards man-made carbon dioxide, as we shall see.

In a trenchant 1995 sceptics' handbook, *But Is It True?*, Aaron Wildavsky quoted a 1981 paper in the journal *Science* by James Hansen of NASA's Goddard Institute of Space Studies in New York predicting that 'potential effects on climate in the twenty-first century include the creation of drought-prone regions in North

America and central Asia as part of a shifting of climatic zones, erosion of the West Antarctic ice sheet with a consequent worldwide rise in sea level, and opening of the fabled Northwest Passage'. Hansen added that evidence of warming due specifically to man-made carbon dioxide 'should emerge from the noise level of natural climate variability by the end of the [twentieth] century'.[6] Wildavsky's purpose in 1995 was to mock the fanciful nature of these visions. Yet in 2007 they are all happening. As late as 2003, the *Sunday Telegraph* gloated that climatologists' disastrous predictions for the Arctic icecap were falling 'foul of reality': 'The latest research points to a deepening of the polar freeze,' the article assured us. Since then, melting has accelerated faster than even many scientists were predicting.

It's a good instinct to doubt, and a better one to test for yourself. Try checking the temperature records where you live. Check the national records. Or maybe you don't think that temperatures measured here and there are a reliable indicator of the heat received by the Earth. Then ask gardeners and birdwatchers whether they've noticed any changes. Ask alpine ski resort managers how business is. Ask English viticulturists.

Ask yourself about the 2,000 or more scientists who contribute to the United Nations Intergovernmental Panel on Climate Change, the body that makes the most influential predictions in the field. Is it just a 'quango–cum–travel-agency for those whose salaries depend on keeping the world worried about global warming', as some columnists think? The vast majority work for universities or national institutions dependent on government funding. Half of them owe their salaries to the American taxpayer. How can the IPCC be a conspiracy when its findings so clearly do not suit the governments that support it? Wouldn't governments arrange matters so as to hear better news?

From chemical analysis of rock samples and ice cores which contain historically trapped gas, scientists believe that the concentration of carbon dioxide in the Earth's atmosphere was rather stable at around 280 parts per million (ppm) for more than 20 million years. In 1958, Charles Keeling of the Scripps Institution of Oceanography began taking direct readings at the summit of Mauna Loa in Hawaii, far from any source of pollution. Allowing for the carbon dioxide taken up by oceans and vegetation, each year showed a small, steady rise by an amount corresponding closely with the quantity of carbon-based fuel burned around the globe. When Keeling died in 2005, his employer called his figures 'the single most important environmental data set taken in the 20th century'.[7]

Carbon dioxide in the atmosphere was constant until about 1800. The rise began modestly in the nineteenth and early twentieth centuries at a rate of 0.25 ppm a year. When Keeling began his work it stood at 315 ppm. Now the annual rise is at least 1.5 ppm. When the figure was announced for 2006 – 383 ppm – the London *Metro*, armed with a quote from David King, made a poorly judged attempt to heighten the alarm: 'CO_2 levels "hit 30m year high"'. But the drama is not in comparison with the state of affairs long before the evolution of the human species, it is in the inexorable increase since the beginnings of industrialization.

None but the most recalcitrant petrolhead would contest these data or the deduction that this carbon dioxide must be man-made. But what about temperatures? The long view was laid out in 1999 by Michael Mann, a statistical climatologist at the University of Virginia. He pooled data gathered by modern instruments with temperatures going back a thousand years 'reconstructed' from analyses of tree rings, corals and ice cores. The resulting graph has become known as the hockey stick because of its sharply upturned right-hand end, representing recent rising temperatures after a long period of stability. It drew fire from climate sceptics for its use of proxy data gathered from disparate sources. But in the absence of anything better, it would surely be remiss not to attempt such a study at all – and besides, economists and politicians routinely use this method. Despite criticism, Mann's graph has been substantially confirmed by more recent studies, and the 2007 report of the IPCC features an improved version of the same basic trend line. This latest report expects temperatures to rise by between 1.0 and 6.3°C by 2100, with around 4°C judged most likely.

The hockey stick graph of actual and predicted rising temperatures and that for the concentration of carbon dioxide in the atmosphere look remarkably similar, strongly suggesting (though not proving) a correlation between the two. However, because the upturns in the two graphs are so recent – seen in only the last few decades over a span of ten centuries – there remain uncertainties about the extent to which temperatures will follow the rising carbon dioxide trend and the time delay in their doing so. These have vital implications, not only for understanding the scale of global warming, but also for deciding how to deal with it.

Climate studies indicate that if carbon dioxide emissions ceased tomorrow it would still be ten to twenty years before the last molecules of the gas were effectively distributed through the atmosphere to exert the maximum greenhouse effect. It would be another thirty to fifty years before the infrared radiation they absorbed was passed on via other constituents of the air to produce heating at the Earth's surface – although ice core studies of earlier increases in carbon dioxide suggest that the full temperature effect might not be felt for a thousand years.

Add to this uncertain wait the greater uncertainties (but potentially greater risks) associated with what have become known as tipping points – phenomena of positive feedback where an effect produced by warming in turn promotes further, perhaps sudden, warming. The list seems ever-growing: as polar ice melts, reflective snow is replaced by dark sea which absorbs more heat; as peat in the soil warms it releases methane, another greenhouse gas; if plants die from overheating, they cease to absorb carbon dioxide or, worse still, release it if they are consumed in forest fires; and so on. If we pass these points, it is claimed, it will be impossible to reverse the damage no matter what we do.

Let us be more positive.

First of all, will things actually get worse? Newspapers always emphasize the negative, so front-page headlines warning, say, of 'The century of drought' are to be expected. Potentially increased crop yields or reduced winter deaths in other parts of the world go unremarked. Nevertheless, there are sound reasons to expect that the human situation will become overall more acute, if not as desperate as the media portrays – reasons such as net loss of stable, temperate climate zones, a more energetic climate system powering extreme weather events and, not least, the upheaval of change itself. Smaller environmental changes than those we may be confronting have been sufficient to destroy local civilizations during the past several thousand years of relative climate stability. This time, we face either 'quick and possibly costly adaptation' or migration, 'which has become difficult or, in some cases, impossible in the modern crowded world'.[8]

Despite this, the Earth as a whole remains highly habitable, much of its surface amply adapted to human life. The parts that are best adapted will doubtless shift a little, but climate change over the next century need not be a catastrophe and could prove no more than a moderate inconvenience for most people. Other parts will become less genial, but it's not as if this is a novelty. Enough societies struggle to survive today in areas already maladapted to human life, whether due to natural forces or human intervention.

How do we adapt? The odd bedfellows of the Stop Climate Chaos campaign group reflect the uncertainty: do we go back to nature, do we try progress, do we just pray? Climate change is an issue that affects us all, and there is an understandable feeling that we should all contribute towards resolving it. But the present focus of personal effort on using low-energy light bulbs and switching off appliances on 'standby' seems woefully at odds with the scale of the problem. It may even be unhelpful. James Hansen has warned that without a government hand on the tiller, 'conservation of energy by individuals merely reduces the demand for fuel, thus lowering prices and ultimately promoting the wasteful use of energy'.[9]

We need to think bigger. Faced with a large problem, it sometimes helps to break it into more manageable chunks. In 2004, Stephen Pacala and Robert Socolow, an ecologist and an engineer at Princeton University, looked at the upward graph of carbon dioxide emissions, projected to rise to 14 billion tonnes of carbon burned per year by 2054, and the horizontal line if levels could be

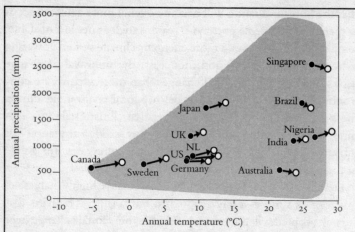

The tinted area of this graph represents a 'comfort zone' within which all the countries in the world are presently found, based on average annual temperature and precipitation data from the thirty years to 2000. Selected countries are highlighted. The arrows show how climate in these countries is expected to change using estimates for 2070–2100 from the IPCC Third Annual Review (2001).
Source: IPCC (TYN CY 1.1 and 2.0 data; A2 and B2 scenarios, DJF and JJA months data combined) and Mike Hulme, Tyndall Centre.

held where they are at present, at 7 billion tonnes a year. They divided the fat wedge between the two lines into seven equal thinner wedges, each representing a reduction of 1 billion tonnes a year by 2054. They then identified not seven but fifteen existing technologies that could each account for a wedge of carbon.[10] From staring disaster in the face, we were suddenly shown to have the luxury of choice in how to avoid it. The ideas are split between reducing energy demand (halving car miles, doubling car fuel efficiency, improving building insulation, for example), substituting carbon-free energy sources (nuclear, solar, wind), and capturing carbon dioxide (planting trees, sequestering power station emissions). What Pacala's proposal makes clear in its unideological way is that the solution to the problem is unlikely to be either entirely technological or entirely the self-denying ordinances of the dark green environmentalists. It's a mnemonic more than a prescription, but it shows that a start can be made.

How much it will cost to make such wholesale changes is anybody's guess. There will in any case still be an additional cost to adapt to climate change already on the way that mere stabilization of carbon dioxide emissions (as opposed to a cut) does nothing to forestall. And of course, doing nothing also carries an economic cost. However, there is in fact reasonable agreement among estimates of the cost of addressing climate change arrived at by sources ranging from Friends of the Earth to multinational accountancy firms. (There is, as you might expect, greater divergence in estimates of the cost of doing nothing, although this cost is reckoned to be at least as great as, and by some very much more than, the cost of mitigation.)

As climate change becomes a political and economic issue, and as it is increasingly realized that some climate change is inevitable, the phrase 'dangerous climate change' has entered the lexicon. But this is a largely meaningless concept. Norfolk's 'new Med' is presumably not 'dangerous climate change', but then Norfolk's new Med may be the Med's new Sahara. It is not sensible therefore to attempt to put a price on preventing dangerous climate change. However, economists do agree on the cost of limiting the global average temperature increase. Capping the rise at 2°C will come out at between 1 and 2 per cent of global GDP. This puts the price tag in the area of $500 billion to $1 trillion a year, or around a hundred dollars, euros or pounds per person per year – hardly unmanageable, especially if the load is distributed more equitably towards the rich countries responsible for the emissions.

Pigs Might Swim

'London-on-Sea: the future of a city in decay' *Daily Telegraph*

With its white beaches, scattered palm trees and lightly clad inhabitants, the tiny country of Tuvalu in the South Pacific Ocean looks in newspaper photographs like an island paradise. But there is trouble in paradise. The eight little atolls that make up Tuvalu rise only 5 metres above sea level and are in the front line of global climate change. While their politicians tour the world lobbying unsuccessfully for cuts in carbon emissions, Tuvaluans wait nervously for the next high tide that will wash salt water over their crops and round the trotters of their grazing pigs.

'Sinking islanders are facing mass evacuation', intoned one recent British newspaper headline, although of course neither the islanders nor their islands are actually sinking. It is the sea that is rising. According to Mark Lynas's colourful *tour d'horizon* of parts of the world already feeling the effects of climate change, *High Tide*, Tuvaluans now face the unenviable choice of whether to move and live 'cultureless and uprooted in a foreign country, or stay on the land of their forefathers and die'.[1]

Sea levels have risen by about 20 centimetres over the last century. They are rising on average (the effect is not evenly spread around the world's oceans) by 2 to 4 millimetres a year at the moment. The 2001 report of the UN's Intergovernmental Panel on Climate Change (IPCC) predicted that sea levels might rise by 49 centimetres by 2100.[2]

There are a number of sources of sea-level rise, although the relative contributions of each to the overall effect are still the subject of scientific debate. Probably the greatest contribution, though the one likely to be forgotten by most of us, comes from the thermal expansion of the oceans due to global warming. This is thought to account for about 60 per cent of the currently observed rise. Then there is the more theatrical effect of melting Arctic and Antarctic ice. Melting ice floes do not alter the sea level as they already displace water, but the ice sheets and glaciers on land that melt and run off into the sea make up the remaining

40 per cent. However, these ice sheets and glaciers are thawing faster than was once predicted, and over the next hundred years melting of the Greenland icecap alone could add at least as much again. As white ice melts into blue sea, the Earth's surface becomes that much darker, and so absorbs more sunlight, producing a greater global warming. In some scientists' view the reduced reflectivity of the Earth is now beginning to contribute more to global warming than our injection of carbon dioxide into the atmosphere.

A negligible additional factor in rising sea levels is due to melting mountain glaciers in temperate and tropical regions, such as the Himalayas, Andes and the fabled snows of Kilimanjaro, which some have predicted will disappear within as little as ten years. These add 100 cubic kilometres a year to the total, which may be 'more than the entire volume of Lake Geneva', but is still almost literally a drop in the ocean in terms of sea-level rise.[3] This melting is more significant for the fact that it jeopardizes the water supply upon which many mountainside communities depend. As much as 40 per cent of the world's population depends ultimately on Himalayan melt-water for its drinking supply, for example.

These figures seem modest: 49 centimetres is about up to the knees, and it'll take a hundred years, a slow rising tide by any measure. Certainly these figures are not scary enough for the media. *Time* magazine, in a special report on global warming in April 2006, explained these causes of sea-level rise, but the figure it chose to quote in its text for any actual rise was the 7 metres due to the melting of the entire Greenland ice sheet, 'swallowing up coastal Florida and most of Bangladesh'. (Elsewhere, a graph presented the accepted IPCC projections without interpretation.)

Fred Pearce, the veteran environment writer for *New Scientist*, chose the same lurid figure for an article in the magazine in 2000 based on the then forthcoming 2001 report of the IPCC. The piece ran under the preposterous headline 'Washed off the map: Better get that ark ready because sea levels are gonna rise.' Former United States presidential hopeful Al Gore's film, *An Inconvenient Truth*, spared us the ark but also could not resist the 7-metre deluge.

When the content of the story fails to provide drama, the art department is often happy to help. For instance, the *Daily Telegraph* in December 2006 reported the view of Stefan Rahmstorf of the Potsdam Institute for Climate Impact Research that sea levels might rise by a metre more than is generally expected over the next century. The article was generously illustrated with montages of sodden London landmarks. One showed water lapping gently against the masts of the Millennium Dome – at least 20 metres above ground level, never mind the usual high tide.

Even a 7-metre rise in sea level will not happen for quite some hundreds of years under the most pessimistic scenario. But this has not stopped even level-headed scientists from joining the more excitable media and showing us what the world would look like in this eventuality – a simple matter of plugging the relevant topographical data into a computer graphics package. The results – typically showing the coasts of Florida or East Anglia or the Netherlands – impose sea levels projected for hundreds of years hence on top of present-day cities and take no account of protective measures that would surely have been implemented during the passing centuries in these wealthy regions.

The morbidly curious might like to know at this point that if *all* the ice in the world were to melt it would raise the ocean level by 70 metres – a calamity that requires temperatures far in excess of even the most apocalyptic forecasts and even then would take thousands of years to transpire. Although there is not the remotest prospect of this happening, this too is a factoid routinely thrown in to juice up stories on rising sea levels and featured in the recent special reports of *Time* and *The Economist*.

Yet it's not as if the more modest rise is without consequence. A sea-level rise of no more than a metre would displace up to a hundred million people in Bangladesh, Nigeria, China and Egypt alone and inundate much productive agricultural land.[4] Interestingly, Florida and the Netherlands, with large populations living at or below sea level already, tend to be omitted from such round-ups, presumably because it is taken as read that they will be defended, for yes, prosperity protects even against the rising sea.

Sea-level rises are clearly felt most at the highest tides. It was a combination of high tides with unfavourable winds and atmospheric pressure that led to the disastrous coastal flooding in the Netherlands and East Anglia in 1953 and in Venice in 1966. This is a great help to the media, as news editors need equip themselves with nothing more than a tide table to work out when to run the story. The headlines can be used over and over. 'Highest tides in 20 years threaten coast towns this weekend' appeared in September 2006 in *The Times*, accompanied by a photograph of a man keeping 'an eye on sea levels' with the aid of a pair of binoculars.

Sea-level rise attributable to global warming is exacerbated in some populous parts of the world by the fact that the land is moving independently. Along the eastern seaboard of the United States and in south-east England, for example, the land is sinking at rates similar to those at which the sea is rising as land further north, once depressed by the weight of ice-age glaciers, seesaws upwards.

In such places bulldozers have been used to bank up protective shingle barriers. But these may be of little use. Astonishingly, each millimetre rise in sea level may push these barriers back by as much as a metre due to the complex workings of the processes of erosion.[5] On exposed coasts, this means that the shoreline can be expected to retreat by a pictorially gratifying 3 or 4 metres a year. Add to this the prospect of higher waves and stormier storms as the side-effects of global warming, and a few millimetres more of a calm sea has been transformed into a vindictive assault on our coasts.

It was King Canute's subjects who demanded that he command the sea to stop rising. The king politely turned up on the beach and, having already said there was nothing he could do, proceeded to demonstrate his powerlessness before the tide. Today, people in coastal communities appeal not to monarchs but to governments. Having for decades adopted the position that existing coastlines are to be defended, however, governments are increasingly shifting towards a policy of strategic retreat or, more euphemistically, 'managed realignment'. Major settlements will continue to be protected, but in some places, such as Wallasea Island in Essex, the sea is being admitted deliberately by breaching long-standing barriers. The aim is to sacrifice a coastal band of agricultural land to create a wide barrier of marsh which will offer a degree of natural flood protection. In some cases, the policy is defended not on economic grounds but because continuing to maintain the sea defence would cause wildlife habitat to be lost – cold comfort to the humans whose own habitat may be sacrificed in the process.

But for most of us, rising sea levels are the least of our worries among the effects of climate change. They affect relatively few people and are happening almost invisibly slowly, certainly far more slowly than the communities concerned are able to react. 'Sea level rise is such a slow process that once started it's almost impossible to reverse,' warns Mark Lynas in *High Tide*.[6] But his absurd nonsequitur gives the game away: there is nothing intrinsically unstoppable about something slow, indeed there is more time to stop it. Nevertheless, inexorability is an essential journalistic makeshift when things aren't happening with catastrophic speed. In March 2006, the *Baltimore Sun* – sea levels are rising comparatively fast at just over 3 millimetres a year in Baltimore as along the rest of the US eastern seaboard – attempted to alarm its readers by reporting the words of a local professor in environmental science: 'The seas are expected to rise slowly and steadily, but no one knows how soon or by how much.'

Indeed, scientific uncertainty is very high. The IPCC's 2001 report anticipated that sea levels would rise by 49 centimetres by 2100, but this is the midpoint of a range between 9 and 88 centimetres, an order-of-magnitude variation in estimates. This reflects the simple lack of knowledge of all that happens in complex natural systems. It's not clear yet, for example, whether the accelerating melting observed in the Arctic will be replicated in the Antarctic (which contains 90 per cent of the world's ice). At the moment it is generally thought that the Antarctic is in fact helping to mitigate rising sea levels by receiving larger net snowfalls each year than it loses due to melting. Nor is it clear how surface and groundwater around the world fit into the picture. These uncertainties are why the IPCC's 2001 predicted rise of 49 centimetres was in fact a reduction on the prediction of 54 centimetres in the IPCC's previous report of 1996. The estimate was cut again, to 43 centimetres, in the IPCC's most recent report in 2007, although some reputable studies published since the cut-off date for this report favour a significantly increased estimate of around 80 centimetres.[7]

We may not have taken the 20-centimetre rise during the twentieth century quite in our stride. It took the deaths of some 1,835 people in the Netherlands and 307 in Britain to prompt the launch of the Dutch Delta Works scheme of national flood defence and the construction of the Thames Barrier. But at least these so far adequate defensive measures were taken; the Venetians have yet to act to protect the Serenissima. This work will surely continue where it is feasible.

Meanwhile, populations that face more serious disruption are showing a good sense that evades the newspapers. The Tuvaluans have brokered a deal with New Zealand to resettle the country's entire population. Other, safer, South Pacific islands have also offered refuge. Are the islanders scrambling to escape? Hardly. New Zealand offered a quota of 300 immigrants a year, which would see the entire population of 11,000 resettled in little more than a generation. The Tuvaluans have suggested a lower rate of seventy-five people per year so that essential social services may be maintained on the islands. The Tuvaluans are in effect hedging their bets, which seems only wise given the high uncertainties in calculating future sea levels.

The Maldives are even lower than Tuvalu and home to more than 300,000 souls. Here the strategy is to concentrate areas of population into defensible enclaves. 'In Bangladesh the future has arrived,' according to the country's High Commissioner, Sabihuddin Ahmed.[8] 'Climate change will eventually threaten thirty to forty million lives [a quarter of the population] in Bangladesh. When these people's homes and crops are flooded forever, where will they go?' Where they go is indeed a serious issue, but there is time to plan. The timeframe over which sea levels are predicted to rise dangerously – in the Thames Gateway, the Netherlands polders, the Florida coast, and even in Bangladesh – is far greater than the duration of the typical housing policy or even the lifetime of some modern dwellings. The Netherlands needs no new technology to guard against sea-level rise. Scientists have estimated that spending $12 billion on raised earthworks and greater pumping over the century would be enough to deal with a 1-metre rise – that's about £10 a year for each Dutch citizen. If Bangladeshis grow wealthier at the predicted global rate, they too will be able to afford to safeguard many homes, greatly reducing the numbers of those who will need to migrate by the time that the forecasts become a reality.

Go with the Flow

'Risk of quakes adds spice to life' *San Francisco Chronicle*

Around the world, hundreds of millions of people live with the daily risk of extermination by the Earth's geophysical might – 500 million of them from volcanic eruption, 130 million as the result of earthquake, according to separate estimates (another – clearly incompatible – estimate puts 75 million Americans in thirty-nine states at significant risk from earthquake).[1] Many millions more are within realistic striking distance of the tsunami that would follow a massive geological upheaval under the sea. These numbers are growing faster than the rate of increase in global population. Every year, up to 80 million people are added to the numbers at risk from some kind of natural disaster, according to the United Nations' International Strategy for Disaster Reduction. It seems that we are choosing to live dangerously.

Even in these modern times, our violent planet has us in its thrall. Earthquake and especially volcano, with its visual sublimity, are two of the staple scenarios of the disaster movie. No hard sell is needed in order to inspire terror beyond the bare words – *Earthquake* came out in 1974, and *Volcano* in 1997. *Tsunami* followed in 2006.

For some, though, the cinema isn't close enough. Volcano tourism is a growing business. Mauna Kea on the Big Island of Hawaii competes with Vanuatu, with holiday brochures advertising the world's safest volcano. The volcanoes of Italy – Vesuvio, Etna, Stromboli – became essential stops for artists and writers on the Grand Tour. Today, thousands of tourists climb Etna's slopes each year. Injuries and deaths are a regular occurrence. Nine people were killed in 1979, and another two in 1987, when they wandered too close to active vents, adding markedly to the rather modest total of fifty-five recorded lives lost due to Etna's volcanic activity in all the preceding 3,500 years.

But these are mere teasers for the main event. Geological surveys indicate that there are about 500 known active volcanoes on land. Between them they are responsible for about sixty eruptions a year. Both the most violent and the most famous eruptions happened in the nineteenth century in Indonesia. The Tambora eruption of 1815 was the most powerful ever recorded, sending ash and gases into the atmosphere such that 1816 became known on the other side of the world as the year without a summer. Krakatoa famously destroyed an entire island in 1883. To these 500 may be added volcanoes under the sea about which much less is known, and the knowledge that volcanoes officially listed as dormant can explode back into life. The greatest likelihood of a human disaster today may come from a volcano that everybody considers to be harmless. Vesuvio was just such a volcano until its eruption in CE 79 took the lives of more than 3,000 inhabitants of Pompeii and Herculaneum.

The volcano has scarcely slept since. Worse still, according to *The Times*, 'Vesuvius has been saving biggest bang for the future'. The report was based on archaeologists' discoveries concerning not the eruption of CE 79 documented so colourfully by Pliny the Younger, but an even more powerful eruption known as the Avellino catastrophe which happened 2,000 years earlier. This eruption destroyed the Bronze Age settlement of Avellino but killed relatively few people. Paths found in the ash suggest that most managed to walk to safety.

Today, some 3 million people inhabit the area devastated by this eruption, which includes Naples, Pompeii, Ercolano and more than a dozen other towns. A fifth of them live in the 'red zone' on the lower slopes of the volcano, many in illegally built homes in the Vesuvio National Park. There might be enough warning of an eruption to allow for an orderly evacuation, but a sudden explosion would leave no time for all these people to escape, especially if, as was the case in 1983 at nearby Pozzuoli when residents feared that a small earthquake presaged a major eruption, they try to get away by car and get stuck in the traffic.

Mauna Loa on Hawaii, the world's largest volcano, erupts on average every ten years or so, but has not done so since 1984, leading to speculation that a big eruption is overdue, especially when seismic activity increased in 2002 and 2004. The major town of Hilo, the tourist coast and new housing on the volcano's slopes are all within four hours, and in some places just minutes, of being overwhelmed by lava. There is only one road out of the danger area, and, if that were cut off, there would be no means of evacuation other than by helicopter, which would be dangerous and slow. Nevertheless, land is cheap and building is legal, although discouraged by measures such as the withholding by the state government of utility services. The United States Geological Survey estimates that there has been more than $2 billion worth of construction since the eruption in 1984.

The mentality is the same in earthquake zones. 'Risk of quakes adds spice to life', headlined the *San Francisco Chronicle*, writing on the centenary of the earthquake and fire that claimed 3,000 lives in the city in 1906. Given a relatively gentle reminder of the ever-present danger in 1989 ($10 billion of damage, sixty-three killed), San Francisco has invested heavily in its infrastructure, but there remains a severe risk especially to housing from even a moderate quake. Less than one person in seven has earthquake insurance, according to the *Financial Times*. 'Most owners are simply trying to ignore the danger.' As at Mauna Loa, government interference – banning building or making insurance mandatory – would be seen as an infringement of liberty.

Reading this in New York or Paris or Berlin, you might puzzle at these people's fatalism while quietly congratulating yourself on living somewhere sensible. But you don't have to live along a major fault line for the press to give you the quivers. 'London could face quake of LA scale, say geologists', the *Sunday Times* reported in 1996. 'Britain "due a big earthquake"', the *Financial Times* echoed a few years later. But 'big' turns out to be relative – in the geological backwater of the British Isles it means a quake like the one in 1580 in which, it was said, 'two people were killed by falling masonry'.

Londoners do not much fear an earthquake as they go about their daily business, but then nor do San Franciscans or Angelenos. Why not? For many, the lifestyle benefits outweigh the risk. For others, economic necessity forces the gamble with nature. Plots of building land on the barren slopes of Mauna Loa have been advertised on the internet for as little as $400. Between major events, people believe that earthquakes and volcanoes are less of a danger than they are in fact, and a bargain is hard to resist.

What changes when the big one strikes? Does a rational reappraisal of the danger take the place of ignorance and denial? Is fatalism banished – or strengthened?

In 1995, the first known eruption of the Soufrière Hills volcano on the Caribbean island of Montserrat destroyed half the island, including its capital, Plymouth, and killed nineteen people. A decade later, more than £200 million has been spent redeveloping the island, but few of the 8,000 who left after the eruption – two-thirds of the population – have returned. A survey for the British Department for International Development found that, although most of the Montserratians who came to Britain 'might return home, hardly any are making active plans to do so'.[2] It is less the risk of another volcanic eruption that puts them off than the uncertainty of finding a home and a job.

The 1995 earthquake in Kobe claimed more than 6,000 lives and did $250 billion worth of damage, but it also awakened the Japanese generally to the truth that their buildings were not as earthquake-proof as they had been led to believe. How to prevent a recurrence was made obvious by studying the pattern of the damage. As is generally true in earthquakes, most of those who died were crushed by collapsing buildings. It was duly found that nearly all of these buildings had been put up before 1981, when building regulations were toughened. Rebuilt according to the new codes, Kobe at least should be far better equipped to withstand another earthquake of the same intensity.

But what of the capital, Tokyo, which, according to the *Financial Times*, 'is overdue a potentially enormous earthquake'? Since Kobe, the Japanese have greatly increased the number of seismic monitors to provide better warnings. But, according to Bill McGuire, the professor of geophysical hazards at University College London, 'nobody has ever accurately predicted an earthquake there'.[3] Although new buildings conform to the latest standards, older ones do not. McGuire estimates the cost of a quake may be more than $3 trillion to rebuild and 60,000 dead – grim, but less than half the toll of the last major Tokyo quake in 1923. Tokyo city authorities have also improved procedures for managing a disaster, but there is nevertheless a recognition, reinforced by experience at Kobe, where it was not rescue teams but simply people at the scene who saved most lives, that people 'ultimately have to be responsible for themselves'.[4]

Planning for catastrophic events that might happen at any time is not straightforward. A general warning may have no effect, while a specific warning can only be given on the strength of a firm prediction, which is often impossible to make. The massive eruption of Mount Pinatubo in the Philippines in 1991 was predicted and an evacuation successfully accomplished, saving thousands of lives. It is not insignificant that there was an American air force base in the affected zone.

When the Colombian Nevado del Ruiz erupted in 1985, by contrast, 25,000 died because the local agencies failed to act despite informed predictions in the month preceding the event. Those living near by had not associated the volcano with any danger partly because it is hidden from view behind other mountains. No evacuation was organized perhaps for fear of a backlash if no eruption came. The Ecuadorian volcano Tungurahua is one of the world's most active at the time of writing. An eruption in August 2006 destroyed villages and left one person dead and sixty missing. In this case, the area had been evacuated the previous month, but people had returned to their homes.

The Naples area authorities are trying to persuade red-zone residents to move out with inducements of €30,000 per household, rather than depend on an evacuation plan that would struggle to cope with a mass exodus. But if the experience at Pozzuoli is anything to go by, people might calculate that it is better to stay put and then demand the government build them a new town after the disaster. The regional president, Antonio Bassolino, wants the residents to go, but at the same time he would like tourists to come. It is even planned to convert some of the evacuated homes into hotels. 'Tourists obviously will leave at the volcano's first cough,' he says.[5] But volcanologists say he is reckoning without the likely influx of volcano rubberneckers. Neapolitan lives may be saved, but if the hotels fill up perhaps not many lives overall!

The Vesuvius eruption that destroyed Pompeii ranks a mere five on the volcanic explosivity index (VEI) analogous to the Richter scale. Like Richter's, this scale is logarithmic for intensity and also for the likelihood of an eruption. Thus, a six such as Mount Pinatubo or Krakatoa has ten times the power of a five, but whereas a five can be expected every decade or so, a six is a once-a-century event. We can expect a seven eruption every millennium, an eight every 10,000 years, and so on. These eruptions throw out so much ash and gas that, like Tambora in 1815, they can affect the entire planet. Even the Pinatubo eruption managed to depress the global temperature by 0.5°C for several years. The last eruption with a VEI of eight was more than 20,000 years ago. One need hardly

add that 'The volcano that could wipe out life on Earth', in the
Daily Mail's headline, is 'due to erupt any day now'.

Chilling News

'Will global warming trigger a new ice age?' *Guardian*

One of the most thrilling headlines of recent years was surely this
one tucked away on an inside page of the London commuters'
paper, *Metro*: 'British Winter Olympics in 2031?' Was the government about to fund a huge investment in refrigeration units and
snow-blowers so that our Olympians could at last realize their
potential on home soil? No need. It would all happen thanks to
natural forces. 'The "plus side" of climate change is that Britain
may be cold enough to host the Winter Olympics in 25 years'
time, a scientist has warned.' And you thought the weather getting
warmer was the plus.

The clue is in the word 'warned'. After all, we wouldn't need a
warning in order to enjoy a plus, would we? The real story concerned the decidedly less enticing possibility of a new ice age,
although space did not permit an explanation of how this might
come about.

With global temperatures on the rise by many measures, ice age
warnings have been out of fashion lately. But this was not always
the case. In 1973, the American magazine *Science Digest* wrote: 'the
world's climatologists are agreed ... that we do not have the
comfortable distance of tens of thousands of years to prepare for
the next ice age ... once the freeze starts, it will be too late.' A
couple of years later, a *New York Times* headline ran thus: 'Scientists
ponder why the world's climate is changing: major cooling widely

considered to be inevitable'.[1] Popular science books and television documentaries amplified the alarm. The most notorious of these, Lowell Ponte's *The Cooling*, claimed that 'cooling has already killed hundreds of thousands of people in poor nations . . . If it continues, and no strong measures are taken to deal with it, the cooling will cause world famine, world chaos, and probably world war, and this could all come by the year 2000.'[2]

What would bring on a new ice age? It depended on who you read, but there was no shortage of choices. Climatologist Stephen Schneider cited the possibility of an extreme snow deluge or disintegration of Antarctic ice sheets. Science writer John Gribbin's *Future Weather* discussed possible fluctuations in the output of the sun and dust in the atmosphere. The astronomer Fred Hoyle thought meteorites might do it.

All were writing during a cool spell in the world's climate. The 1910s to the 1940s had been unusually warm, creating dust-bowl conditions in the American Midwest. But thereafter, it was cooler than average long enough for climatologists to 'become used to the idea that the world was in a cooling phase', as Gribbin admits in a later, rather different book on climate change, *Hothouse Earth*.[3]

An ice age is perhaps the climatic change we can imagine most clearly, partly because we have evidence of what previous ice ages were like, and partly because it brings with it the visible transformation of water, the staff of life, from a usable liquid to an inaccessible solid – a dramatic and disastrous change of state that has no equivalent in global warming or other major climatic shifts. We have a folk memory of the Little Ice Age in the seventeenth and eighteenth centuries, reinforced in the paintings of Bruegel and Avercamp and in stories of the Pilgrim Fathers being helped through their first winter in the New World by the native Americans. And, at least in cultures that experience winter, we possess a darker mythology of the cold personified by ice queens and ice maidens, snowmen and Jack Frost, which has no warm-world counterpart.

Scientific evidence obtained from a range of sources indicates that ice ages occur every 100,000 years or so, punctuated by shorter interglacial periods lasting 10–20,000 years. Put another way, the Earth is a world of ice where, every now and again, circumstances conspire to produce a temporary thaw.

These circumstances relate to the Earth's changing position and orientation relative to the sun. It is only an approximation to say that the Earth orbits at a constant distance from the sun and therefore always receives the same quantity of solar radiation to heat it. In fact, the planet's orbit is slightly eccentric, and the axis about which it is spinning wobbles in various ways. These wobbles and eccentricities exhibit cyclical patterns called Milankovich cycles after the Serbian mathematician who spent his life investigating them. Calculating the periods of these cycles, and therefore how they overlap, is still no simple task, never mind explaining how much each of them affects the sun's ability to heat the Earth's surface, which is one reason why there is such uncertainty over what influences our climate.

In 1982, Gribbin was clear, however. Our interglacial holiday is almost over, and 'we are moving rapidly into an orbital configuration appropriate for a full Ice Age'. A string of bad winters might be all it takes: 'Northern Hemisphere summers are already cool enough for the ice-sheets to remain if once they become established.'[4]

There are shorter-term, but still severe, fluctuations in temperature that also challenge science. About 12,000 years ago, towards the end of the last ice age, there was a millennium-long cold spell known as the Dryas (after the tundra flower whose fossil pollen has been used to analyse the phenomenon). And then, 8,200 years ago, came a shorter cold snap. The prevailing theory is that both events were triggered when reservoirs of glacier meltwater gushed into the ocean, although the relevant dates don't correspond perfectly. This ice-cold water, the theory goes, interrupted the so-called ocean conveyor, the circulation of water (and heat) among all the seas, thereby preventing the Gulf Stream from warming the North Atlantic. Although scientists have known about the Dryas event for nearly a century, it is only since 1990 that it has been explained as a side-effect of a broader warming trend. Before that, it was simply viewed as the stuttering last gasp of the ice age.

Revived fears of a new ice age depend heavily on this still poorly understood mechanism thought to be responsible for the Dryas event. This time, fast-melting Arctic ice would flick the Atlantic switch. The popular term 'ice age' used in this context is misleading, as the change would not affect the entire northern hemisphere as a full ice age does, nor would it last as long as a full ice age. The world as a whole might get warmer, but northern Europe would cool – and quickly. Britain's climate might not become like that of the south of France after all, but more like that of Newfoundland. In 2004, around the time of the release of *The Day After Tomorrow*, the apocalyptic film loosely based on this scenario, the *Guardian* included a new ice age on a list of ten possible global catastrophes assembled on the premise that 'in this post-9/11 world of paranoia, no doomsday scenario is too outlandish to be taken seriously'.

Outlandish they may be, but predictions of a drastic cooling do deserve serious consideration. The conventional method of evaluating risk is to look at the probability of the risk combined with the impact of the threatened event if it does happen. The probability of an abrupt cooling, even in northern Europe, may be low compared to the likelihood of other climate change. But its impact – on agriculture, and on where and how people live – could well be more ruinous than a few degrees of global warming.

Unfortunately, we know little about how the oceans work. We have not had long to observe them, and there is only indirect evidence of their past behaviour, for example in ice core samples. Like the atmosphere, the oceans are a complex system in which huge forces are engaged. We know something of the ocean surface from satellite observations, but little about what goes on beneath, where the sheer mass of water, its movements and its stored heat are colossal. For example, just 3 metres of the oceans' depth has the same heat capacity as the entire Earth's atmosphere, yet the depth of ocean that effectively mixes with the atmosphere is ten to a hundred times greater than this. Even more than in atmospheric science, understanding relies on computer models, and some global-scale effects with vital implications for our future, such as the 'bipolar seesaw' under which one hemisphere is thought to warm if the other cools, are still poorly understood.

Wallace Broecker of the Lamont-Doherty Earth Observatory in New York State, who made the original link between the ocean conveyor shutdown and climate change, has pointed out that our circumstances now, near the end of an interglacial warm period, are hardly comparable with those at the end of the ice age when the Dryas event took place. He believes that it would take a substantial temperature increase of around 5°C to flick the ocean switch, a rise not expected to be seen even under the more pessimistic climate change scenarios until around 2100. And Craig Wallace, then at the Climatic Research Unit at the University of East Anglia, felt bound to disappoint the compilers of the *Guardian*'s catalogue of doom, announcing that, although his simulations suggested a weakening of the Gulf Stream by 10–50 per cent by this date, 'global warming will continue, which means the planet will still get hotter, only slightly less so'.

Recent findings suggest that the Gulf Stream may be slowing more rapidly than expected, yet the North Atlantic in general is actually warming – leaving our future climate as hard to predict as ever. Nevertheless, none of the UK climate scenarios to be published in 2008, based on the 2007 report of the Intergovernmental Panel on Climate Change, is expected to make a case for cooling.

What does the more distant future hold? What happened to that fateful 'orbital configuration appropriate for a full Ice Age'? Well, nothing actually. It's still coming. But exactly when is anybody's guess. The uncertainties in the Milankovich cycles leave plenty of scope for argument. Some believe that the Earth has already begun to cool, it's just that we haven't noticed because of all the warming! This view has prompted climate change sceptics to esteem our emissions of carbon dioxide as this 'wonderful and unexpected gift of the industrial revolution'.[5] According to Bill McGuire, professor of geophysical hazards at University College London, 'we should expect our planet to be plunged into bitter cold within the next few thousand years'[6] – but this was in a popular *Guide to the End of the World* published in 2002. In the same year, climatologists came to the more cheerful view that we are actually in the midst of a longer-than-usual interglacial period, and still have at least 50,000 years to go before the big freeze.

8. Our Declining Resources

A bare cupboard is a perpetual worry. In 1972, *The Limits to Growth* plotted downward graphs showing that oil and gas, gold, zinc, copper, lead and mercury could all run out within twenty years. They didn't. Now wheat, grazing land, fish and water are said to be in short supply. Will there be enough to go round? At the same time, there are less direct costs to human growth as we lose diversity, both cultural and biological, that holds for us a deeper, more spiritual value.

Wild Talk

'Earth faces extinction crisis' *Independent*

The newspapers have three basic stories about the diversity of nature. First, the good news: curious creature (or plant) discovered. Next, the bad news: pretty creature (or plant) on the verge of extinction. The third category comes across as more bad news: invading foreign species threatens our delicate flowers (or animals).

The good, the bad and the ugly, but often none is what it seems. A spectacular example of the good news came along in 2006. 'Discovered: Europe's first new mammal in 100 years', *The Times* announced. The Cypriot mouse was indeed an addition to the relatively short roster of European mammals, but it was strictly a rediscovery of a species previously thought to have gone extinct. Two harlequin frogs and six British butterflies were among other species coming 'back from the brink' in the same year.

The bad news may be misleading too, not because it is not bad, but because it is not news. Actual extinctions may be occasion for mourning but they are hard to date precisely and are rare for well-known species. There are no obituaries for plants and animals. Instead, we are reproached with picture spreads of exotic species, their mug-shots arrayed like war-dead, sometimes with dramatic red stamps across them declaring that they are 'endangered' or 'threatened'. 'Wave goodbye to hippos and polar bears', as the *Daily Mail* tearfully had it. More rarely, this story is generalized. 'Earth facing "catastrophic" loss of species' was a recent headline in the *Guardian*. 'Scientists call for action in biodiversity crisis: Warning that world faces next mass extinction.'

Outrunning both of these in frequency, though, in the British media at least, are stories of invasion and conquest, where one species comes into conflict with others. Favoured species tend to get written up on their way down ('Endangered birds being wiped out by grey squirrels'), those we dislike on their way up ('Moth that can kill humans is found breeding in Britain'). These articles express fears of human immigration by proxy, as a *Daily Telegraph* headline-writer could not help but reveal: 'Forget the plumbers, now Poland is sending us its rare butterflies'. But biology does not discriminate in this way. Whether we fancy a species or regard it as a pest, it is a species nevertheless. Invasion may seem to be good for local biodiversity, but often it is bad as the invading species can harm the survival chances of many indigenous species.

These vignettes suggest accurately enough that the balance of nature is always changing and that there will always be 'winners' and 'losers' among individual species of plants and animals. What they do not reliably show is the systematically increasing endangerment – and loss – of species from the Earth. In 1996 the International Union for the Conservation of Nature updated its 'Red Lists' of threatened species around the world. They counted 20 per cent of all mammals, for example, as 'vulnerable', 'endangered' or 'critically endangered'. When the lists were updated in 2006, seventy species of mammal had gone extinct, although those considered vulnerable or worse had held steady at 20 per cent. All other classes of species from birds to insects to plants were worse off to varying degrees, with amphibians especially badly hit, rising from 2 per cent threatened to 31 per cent.[1]

In press stories, the threatened species is often exotic, its existence threatened by practices such as tropical logging over which we tell ourselves we have no control. The creature's predicament is to be pitied, but there's nothing we can do. It was thus a surprise to have this normally rather abstract moral dilemma fetch up on English doorsteps when eleven local authorities used it as a reason to impose a moratorium on all new housing planning applications in parts of Surrey and the Thames valley, having been advised by the government's conservation agency, English Nature, that development would pose a threat to three heathland bird species living there. The entire front page of the *Independent* displayed heroic photographs of 'The birds that blocked 20,000 new homes'.

This brings home the big questions about biodiversity loss. How great is it? Which way is it heading? Is it our fault? What must we give up so that the Dartford warbler, the nightjar and the woodlark may prosper? And, shockingly perhaps, does biodiversity matter anyway?

There have always been species losses, most notably during five mass extinction events. Best known is the probable asteroid strike on the Earth that led to the extinction of 85 per cent of species including the dinosaurs 65 million years ago. The other extinctions all occurred more than 200 million years ago, including the super-volcano or asteroid that wiped out 95 per cent of species 251 million years ago. However, these catastrophic but infrequent events account for only 4 per cent of species extinctions over time. Extinctions occur continually due to natural selection. A species lifetime is typically a few million years, and most species that have ever lived are now extinct.

All these losses are more than compensated in the normal scheme of things by the rate at which new species evolve. Natural speciation is thought to give rise to three new species a year, although it is hard to be sure as scientists have not observed the process directly. This process has ensured that the present era of life on Earth is more diverse than at any time in its 600 million year history.

However, the current rate of species loss is very great, perhaps a hundred to a thousand times this rate of increase, as we humans compete against other species for food and water and destroy their

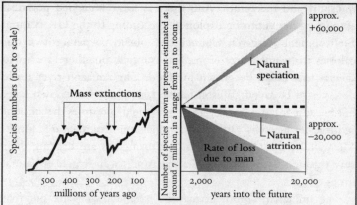

The left-hand side of chart shows the natural trend for biodiversity to increase, punctuated by the five major extinction events to the present. The data point in the centre shows the range in number of species thought to exist today. The right-hand side shows natural rates of both speciation and species loss as well as species loss due to man extrapolated from current estimates. The shaded areas represent uncertainty in estimates of rates of species gain and loss.
Source: Millennium Ecosystem Assessment/ Measuring Conservation for Biodiversity (Royal Society, 2003)/ E.O. Wilson, *The Diversity of Life.*

habitat. The 'globalization of nature', by which invasive species spread with either deliberate or inadvertent human assistance, is accelerating this loss.[2] Scientists estimate that the Earth loses on average a species a day, including roughly one bird and one mammal every year – 2007's mammal was the Yangtze river dolphin, the probable demise of which did occasion a rare obituary on the front pages of the *Independent* in August of that year. While recorded extinctions seem tolerably low, the loss of *populations* across what an economist might term a healthy 'basket of species' is much higher. WWF's Living Planet Index is such a basket, representing 1,300 land, freshwater and marine species, and it has declined by 30 per cent from 1970 to 2003.[3]

There are several good reasons to be concerned about this. Americans such as the biologist Edward O. Wilson have found that the argument that works best with Congress and organizations like the World Bank is a utilitarian one. We depend on plants and animals not only for food, but also for oxygen generation, water capture, protection against natural disasters, clothing, labour, transport and medicines. And there is huge untapped potential among species yet to be exploited. According to the UK Natural Environment Research Council, we obtain 90 per cent of our calories from just thirty crops, for example, but there are 1,650 species that could be grown for food. The Amazon river turtle deserves to be saved, Wilson has said, not only for its own sake, but because it tastes good – and could yield 400 times the amount of meat produced by cattle raised in the same area of cleared forest. Meanwhile, the pharmaceutical multinationals are hacking their way through the jungles of Central America in search of natural drugs.

The utilitarian argument may be extended to point out that benefits to humankind may be obtained not only from individual species but from biodiversity itself. The health of the planet may depend not so much on individual species but on the interaction between them, perhaps especially involving the vast numbers of microbial species in the soil. But quite how this may be so is not understood, and scientists' opinions have differed on whether a high level of biodiversity assists the working of the global ecosystem.

Quite different is the aesthetic argument more favoured in Europe that biodiversity should be preserved for our pleasure. We should look after species in the same way that we look after works of art – a loss may be afforded economically, but it is always to be regretted. If we grow to love our ecosystems, then that very familiarity will help to save them, even if it does mean that we try hard to preserve the glamorous species and ignore the dull ones.

Finally, there is a purely moral supposition that humankind has a duty of global stewardship. Upon this argument may depend the survival of those unfortunate species that we find neither useful nor pretty.

The problem with these arguments is that we don't really know what we are talking about. There are probably something less than 10 million species, although estimates range hugely between around 3 and 100 million, according to a 2003 report by the British Royal Society.[4] Only 1.7–1.8 million of these species have names, and even this figure is uncertain because there is no central catalogue and many species are certain to 'exist' only as synonyms. Most plants and vertebrates are named, but there are perhaps seven more insects for each of the million with a name already, while only 100,000 of the world's estimated 1.5 million fungi species are named. Still less is known about marine micro-organisms and microbes in the soil, the numbers of which cannot be estimated by the methods used for larger species. Then, within species, even many of the large and obvious ones, there are high uncertainties as to population numbers and trends. So when the 2002 World Summit on Sustainable Development set a target for the reduction of biodiversity loss, it did so despite the fact that '[n]o sound scientific basis currently exists for assessing global performance against this target'.[5]

Small wonder, then, that some species finds turn out to be previous losses (such as the Cypriot mouse). Others go straight from unknown on to the endangered lists. With so many species unknown, and the populations unknown of many of those we do know, it can only follow that estimates of rates of species loss and endangerment are little better than guesses. As the Royal Society confesses, 'The fate of organisms that have not yet been recognized by science cannot be measured.' Extravagant claims for annual losses of species in the tens of thousands attributed to Al Gore and Ed Wilson can most charitably be explained as fractions derived from the absolute maximum possible number of species on the globe.[6]

This ignorance makes it hard to direct conservation efforts appropriately. But there is another factor that may make them irrelevant altogether. Scientists have little idea of how many species we can afford to lose, not only because of the uncertainties in their estimates of species numbers and populations, but because of the fundamental nature of evolution.

The trend in biodiversity has been an upward one for millions of years as species achieve closer adaptation to their habitats. This raises a logical conundrum with practical consequences for our efforts to contain the damage we are doing to the Earth's biodiversity. If biodiversity always tends to the maximum, it becomes meaningless to talk about an optimum level of biodiversity. And if there is no optimum level, there's less point in fretting about loss of biodiversity when this is something that only temporarily sets back nature's 'aim'. We cannot logically say that we can afford no loss of biodiversity, except to the extent that the loss of one species might have a detrimental impact on connected species. Of course, it would be a shame if, amid the general carnage, we were to lose one species that held the balance of a whole ecosystem, or that might have offered us some miracle medicine.

Our modern successes in agriculture, industry and spreading our own species have so far killed off species equivalent to 100,000 years' worth of evolution. But does it matter? For utilitarian purposes, the answer is no. We need only a tiny fraction of species to support our lifestyle. Even on a higher plane, it is not clear that maximum biodiversity is necessarily a good thing – the strength of interaction between pairs of species may matter more, according to the population biologist Robert May. So our main reason to fear the loss of biodiversity may be sentimental. As the newspaper pictures remind us, we just like sharing our world with polar bears and Dartford warblers.

Setting aside dilemmas over which species to save and why, the problem of conservation is a practical one. The major environmental causes of biodiversity loss are over-harvesting, pollution, climate change, aggressive species invasions and human settlement. But they all come down to loss of suitable habitat. In the 1960s, Ed Wilson developed a 'theory of island biogeography', which shows how the number of species sustainable within a given area depends on that area. The theory predicts how many species we can expect to find on an island (or other area of habitat that is in effect isolated) of a given size. It also predicts how diversity will be lost if the habitat is reduced. Roughly, if an isolated habitat is cut to a tenth of its former size, it will be able to support only half the species it used to. The theory also shows how fragmented areas that look like a sustainable habitat on a map may not suffice if the species in question will not cross from one area to the next.

This is a major reason why, even in the admission of scientists, many conservation efforts have been unsuccessful to date. The areas devoted to wildlife have been too small and too broken up. Even the vast national parks of North America are proving too fragmented for some species, whose decline, though slowed, has followed the pattern predicted by Wilson's theory.

The answer is much bigger, better-located and better-regulated reserves. Ideally, we should focus on conserving habitat – then the species that live there will be saved automatically. But being the sentimental souls we are, we prefer to cherish glamorous species of rare orchid or the iconic panda. Fortunately, this is almost as good. If the Chinese succeed in saving the panda – despite the country's galloping industrialization, conservation efforts are doing well, and recent fieldwork has shown there are more pandas than were thought – it will be because they saved enough of its habitat, and with it hundreds of other species without really trying.

It is the same in the heathland of the Thames basin. Should we care more about the Dartford warbler than that 50,000 people are housed? Perhaps not. But should we then support these people's demand to be housed precisely where they fancy rather than somewhere else less critical to biodiversity? Again, perhaps not.

The Cod Delusion

'Cod and oysters: tastes our grandchildren may not savour'
Guardian

On 3 November 2006, it was widely reported that the world's entire commercial fishing stocks might be exhausted within our lifetimes. 'Study: Seafood could disappear by 2048', was how the *Chicago Tribune* led with the item. The paper neglected to say in which month of that year we'd have reached the bottom of the barrel. But it mourned: 'Clambakes, crabcakes, swordfish steaks and even humble fish sticks could be little more than a fond memory in a few decades.'

Most of the major American newspapers ran variations of the story on the same day, prompted by a paper in the journal *Science*. Often they used the word seafood rather than fish stocks, bringing home the human implications as forcefully as they could. Most cited the doomsday year 2048, and some printed a dramatic downward graph of fish supplies crashing to zero.

Something running out plays well in the newspapers, especially when there's nothing for people to see by which they might make a judgement on the matter for themselves. (It makes bad television for the same reason.) We can't see the fish in the oceans. But it was all too easy to picture the suddenly emptied supermarket counters replenished with turnips rather than turbot. Consumers can be forgiven for feeling a little confused. Hardly had we got used to the message that we should eat more fish because its protein and omega oils were good for us than we were being told to stop in the name of environmental sustainability.

The science behind the story is more subtle and leaves room for hope. In 2003, Boris Worm and his colleagues at Dalhousie University in Halifax, Nova Scotia, had reported that 90 per cent of large predator fish, such as sharks, had vanished from the oceans since 1950. This was about conservation, not the human food supply; indeed if predators were down, their prey – and our food – might prosper. But Worm's new paper in *Science* shows that this is certainly not the case. Worm and his team assessed a wide array of marine ecosystems and found them to be 'rapidly losing populations, species or entire functional groups' – that is to say, whole families of species.[1] Both absolute fish numbers and diversity in terms of numbers of species showed heavy declines. The authors' significant conclusion is that these two are bound up together such that over-fishing leads to loss not only of the species fished but of wider biodiversity, and conversely that reduced diversity in itself adds to the erosion of commercial fish stocks.

The results come from a statistical analysis of many previous studies, taking into account data gathered in different ways from different areas. In other words, it is not an analysis of directly collected scientific data, but an analysis of other people's analyses, what the scientists themselves call a 'meta-analysis'. This is not invalid at all, but it does leave the door open for sceptics to take issue, perhaps because a particular set of data is thought less reliable than others or because different data sets are not strictly cross-comparable. The papers had no difficulty finding scientists who did not support the study, one quoting a local professor who called it 'just stupid'.

The Dalhousie authors themselves concede that some of the data they have used may be unreliable. Figures from the United Nations Food and Agriculture Organization (FAO), for example, are supplied by member nations, some of which may distort the information they provide in what they see to be their own interests.

The assumption factored into the projection of the data into the future – that fishing and marine conservation practices will continue unchanged – is more problematic, as is the fact that the *apparent* correlation between biodiversity and fish stocks is not *proof* of a direct connection. These are standard difficulties with scientific statistics that use present-day data to try to tell us what will happen in the future. Against this, the authors can, and do, claim that if enough surveys are taken into the reckoning, and all are found to fit the overall pattern, then it would be foolish to dismiss the major conclusion.

The more glaring loopholes – chinks of light for optimists in the fishing industry – lie beyond the terms of reference the scientists set for themselves. For a start, Worm and his colleagues focus their attention on areas where there is the most detailed data, which is to say where we fish already, and on the species that are 'currently fished'. This seems at first like looking at a dug-out seam of coal and saying all the coal has run out. Fish are free to move within their ecological range, however, and so a loss in a monitored area can be taken to indicate a likely loss in other areas, although it is not a guaranteed loss.

Finally, the paper does not show the newspapers' simple graph of fish stocks hitting rock bottom in 2048 (the future portion of which is an extrapolation based on a business-as-usual fisheries model). Instead it shows a different set of downward curves only to 2004, representing groups of species 'currently fished', which portend potentially less dire consequences.

The Dalhousie research is both ambitious in scope and gloomy in tone, but predictions that we will run out of fish are nothing new. At the beginning of the last century, Britain reacted to depletion in the North Sea by sending its fishing fleets further north. Fifty years on, this led to a series of 'cod wars' with Iceland. Globally, though, the view was that there were plenty more fish in the sea. In the 1940s, even Rachel Carson, later to write *Silent Spring*, was emphasizing not man's depredations but the ocean's bounty in two books entitled *Food from the Sea*.

The global ocean catch grew from 19 to 85 million tonnes from 1950 to 1990, according to FAO figures, a growth factor rather greater than for the world population, accounted for by the fact that people are eating more fish than they used to. Since 1990, the catch has fallen slightly, and the 'dream anticipated by policy-makers in the 1970s' of a harvest of 100 million tonnes seems beyond achievement.[2] In 1997, the FAO warned that 60 per cent of commercial fish species were fully exploited, over-fished or depleted. By 2002, the figure was 75 per cent. National commissions warned of the worsening situation in American waters in 2003 and 2004. It now appears that the world reached a point of 'peak fish' around 1994, although the moment passed unnoticed, in marked contrast to 'peak oil', which we may be experiencing at the moment.

Assessment of the risk of losing a favourite food is not helped by a history of antagonism between conservation biologists and the fishing industry as well as the sheer complexity of the ecology. A US National Fisheries Institute spokesperson responded tartly to the Dalhousie findings: 'Fish stocks naturally fluctuate in population.'[3] Fishermen observe that warming oceans may be important, but this may simply be part of a denial mechanism by the fishing community to blame external factors rather than its own malpractice. There are frequent reports of exotic warm-water fish newly found in British waters, for example, while fleets have to go further north to find familiar species. But are the latter fish found in the north because they have migrated there due to climate change or because Iceland and Norway have better managed the resources off their coasts? It is impossible to say for sure.

For their part, policy makers often tread a middle line, which may be diplomatic but is perhaps not sustainable. In November 2006, for example, the International Commission for the Conservation of Atlantic Tunas cut quotas for Mediterranean bluefin tuna, but not by as much as the body's scientists were recommending, prompting environmentalists to repeat warnings that the fish would soon vanish entirely from these waters. According to the headline in the *Independent*, it was the 'Growth of sushi bars "driving tuna to extinction"'.

How bad is it really? It seems likely that individual consumption of fish cannot keep growing as it has been doing, but there is no reason to believe that we will be fresh out of all fish by 2048. There are grounds for optimism on many fronts. Much of the increased global demand has been met by fish farming, or aquaculture, which now yields 40 million tonnes a year, up from just 13 million tonnes as recently as 1990. There are severe problems with aquaculture as it is presently practised, merely the least of them being that the product frequently tastes like blotting paper. Using grain and fishmeal for feed is highly inefficient. It can take 3 tonnes of ocean fish to make meal to feed one tonne of farmed fish. Chemical and genetic contamination of the marine environment is also an issue. But aquaculture is a young industry that is experiencing many of the historical difficulties of intensive agriculture all at once. Imagine the chaos and protest that would follow on land if acres of forest, heath and wetland were suddenly turned over to wheat and cattle. In principle, farmed fish offer a more sustainable source of protein than livestock.

It is possible, though always politically unpopular, to scale back sea fishing. Norway did this with its cod fleets in 1989 and found that stocks bounced back amazingly quickly, so that by 1992 it was possible to relax the restrictions. The short-term economic and social cost was considerable, but not as great as the cost of ignoring the problem, which is what happened in Newfoundland, leading to the extinction of cod there and the permanent loss of the vast industry they once supported. However, regulations and quota systems must be enforced if they are to be effective.

A fifth of the global catch – some 20 million tonnes a year – is unwanted or disallowed under quota rules and is simply thrown back in the sea dead. Reducing this by-catch is a priority. Other efficiencies may be possible. At present, the harvesting of fish is allowed to proceed in an unconscionably crude way as Charles Clover illustrates in his book *End of the Line* with a dramatic comparison of how trawling might appear on land, indiscriminately killing and mangling as well as catching all kinds of animals. Fishing is an industry, not a romantic calling, and just as technology has helped us ruthlessly to track down ever more elusive stocks, so there may be technological means of selecting fish for harvest without damaging other species or the supporting ecosystem as much as we do now.

More and larger marine reserves would work not like safari parks but like game nurseries, providing refuge where depleted species could recover to sustainable levels so that we could then continue to harvest them from unprotected seas. Such reserves would also help to maintain the biodiversity upon which population levels of economically important species depend. As Worm notes: 'there is no dichotomy between biodiversity conservation and long-term economic development; they must be viewed as interdependent societal goals'. Encouragingly, while fish stocks decline when biodiversity is lost, they can also recover rapidly when diversity is high, making the fisherman's job easier once more.

Relatively little is known about the global diversity of species wherever they occur. The oceans, and especially the deep oceans, are far less explored than the land surface, so it seems probable that they harbour many unknown riches. Given this, it seems hardly likely that we have an accurate handle on the ocean's total potential for food.

There is much that consumers can do too. It is their conservative eating habits that drive up prices and bring favourite species to the brink, with cod in Stockholm at $175 a kilo and sushi tuna in Tokyo at $220. Change is not impossible. Herring, not cod, was once the over-fished staple in northern Europe. According to Mrs Beeton, the Romans would pay £15 for a one-kilo red mullet, a fish for which she was accustomed to paying a shilling. The market mechanism slows the growth in demand for such fish but does not put any block on their ultimate spiral to extinction. Here, the Marine Stewardship Council, set up by Unilever, owner of the Bird's Eye frozen food brand, and the WWF conservation charity, may help by prompting retailers, even counting the environmentalists' *bête noire* of supermarkets, Walmart, to sell more sustainable fish.

Meanwhile, we consumers should consider alternative species. During the cod wars, it was suggested that the British try pollack and whiting for their beloved fish and chips, but they never caught on. If we are to keep eating fish, we will have to become more eclectic in our tastes. Some fish, such as skipjack tuna and chub mackerel, are presently conspicuously under-fished. Variety on the fishmonger's slab (and more importantly in the vast quantities of fish taken for factory processing and fish-and-chip shops) would then more closely reflect diversity in the ocean. Marine ecosystems with more species are less liable to collapse than those with few species, so that the more we spread our harvest among different species, the better the chances that stocks will be maintained of them all. The overall gain is greater than the sum of the gains made by each species because of the beneficial effect of overall species richness. Furthermore, because of the observed potential for fish stocks to recover when they are given a chance, the switch away from present favourites need only be a temporary measure.

This potential has been dramatically demonstrated not once but twice in the last century as a side-effect of two world wars. By 1945, according to Mark Kurlansky's *Cod*, 'fish stocks in the European North Atlantic, after six years with little fishing, were at a level that has never been seen since'.[4] A big war would do the trick again. But binding international agreement on fisheries management seems preferable.

Not a Word

'Like ancient forests displaced by houses, language is ended too'
The Times

Any discussion about the death or loss of languages rapidly comes up against a fundamental problem of definitions making them hard to count and analyse. What is the difference between a dialect and a language? And do sign languages count? The consensus figure is that there are about 6,000 to 7,000 languages currently in use globally, but estimates in the academic literature range from 3,000 to 10,000. The practicalities also mean that it is impossible to keep an accurate tally on the number of moribund, endangered or safe languages.

Even so, the facts seem to be compelling and show a clear trend. We are told that the world is losing several languages every month and that 90 per cent of the world's languages will effectively vanish from day-to-day use by the middle of this century.[1] Most languages are losing speakers, despite the rapid global population growth. At least 500 of them are considered to be nearly extinct in that they are spoken by fewer than 100 people. It has been quipped that some Native American languages are only kept alive by a few old parrots on the Orinoco River!

It is a clear sign when only the elderly and a very small fraction of an ethnic group are speaking a language that it is effectively condemned to extinction. One American newspaper told the story of a German dialect spoken in Texas that is expected to vanish within thirty years.[2] The paper said of one elderly couple that 'the language will likely die with them', as their children had not been persuaded to learn it. The adverse dynamics can also affect languages with a larger number of speakers. It is estimated, for example, that there are 500,000 speakers of Breton over the age of fifty, but fewer than 2,000 under the age of twenty-five, so unless action is taken to save it, the language will effectively die out in the next half century. Even some languages used by very large numbers – such as some Indonesian languages with a million or more speakers – are at risk due to their speakers' age profile.

The loss of languages is a marked change from 10,000 years ago when – although no one knows for sure – there could have been one language for every 500 or so people on the planet. The expert community estimates that there could have been anything between 30,000 and half a million languages that have come and gone without trace. Isolation and the lack of trade and transport naturally bred linguistic diversity. Now, in contrast, it is estimated that there is one language for every million people. But, as ever, averages can lie and all languages are, of course, not in equal usage. Indeed, 95 per cent of them are spoken by just 5 per cent of people worldwide and perhaps as many as 350 languages, about 5 per cent of the total, have more than a million speakers.

It is the countries with the greatest number of languages that are losing languages the fastest. Brazil is home to around thirty nearly extinct languages, and the US has around seventy, but it is Australia in the lead with as many as 200 nearly extinct languages. Nearly 90 per cent of Australia's languages – those spoken by aboriginal peoples – are expected to perish with the current generation. A similar fate awaits many of Africa's tribal languages. Roughly one-third are said to be endangered, and it will be very difficult to save them since the vast majority have no written record.

The speed of loss is accelerating as languages become a victim of rapid globalization. New languages have traditionally appeared through pidgins and creoles, merging with other languages into families, sometimes taking on a written form. They grow and increase their influence, as did Greek and Latin, and then mutate. Accidents of history, such as colonization and trade, gave some, mainly European languages and in particular English, an importance well above their original geographical and cultural weight. But while some languages are vibrant and evolving, many more are being abandoned and few are being created, as the old dynamic has ground to a halt. When communities find that their ability to survive and advance economically is improved by the use of another language, native tongues naturally fade away, often rapidly as the young seek new opportunities. If languages are used just for religious ceremonies and bedtime stories, rather than trade and government, they are much more likely to die.

But how important is it to save languages? Some people feel this loss really matters – describing it as a disaster for humanity – believing it to be a more fundamental concern than a reduction in plant and animal diversity or the destruction of culture per se. One newspaper referred to the 'extraordinary interaction between language biodiversity', alluding to the fact that native tongues can also be rich in knowledge of the environment – flora and fauna – and of traditional, herbal medicines, knowledge that could be irretrievably lost.[3]

Languages can be full of cultural knowledge that facilitates different ways of understanding and discussing the world. For example, the Australian aboriginal language of Guugu Yimithirr does not have a concept of left and right, relying instead on the concepts of north, south, east and west. Your left hand, in other words, could be your north hand unless you are facing in the opposite direction, in which case it would be your south hand! The language requires a constant awareness of where one stands within the landscape geographically speaking – an alertness that is utterly lost in modern speech. One linguistics professor put it more starkly: 'If you lose your language, you lose a big chunk of your identity.'[4] UNESCO, the education, science and cultural wing of the United Nations, has responded to the concern by declaring the 21st of February as International Mother Language Day, in an attempt to promote linguistic diversity.

A few minority tongues have been saved and perhaps rejuven-ated. In 2005, the European Union added Irish Gaelic to its list of official languages – the hiring of translators and its use in speeches will help to preserve Ireland's native tongue, but at a cost to Europe's taxpayers of about €4 million. In Kahnawacke, a small community near Montreal in Canada, the use of Mohawk has been encouraged in schools, church services and even a local radio station. The University of Manchester is identifying and transcribing the many Romany dialects – spoken by small groups in many European countries – aiming to preserve the endangered language. Hebrew, essentially extinct for day-to-day communi-cation until the nineteenth century, is perhaps the most successful revived language as it is now spoken by over 7 million people – it is the official language of Israel and is studied in many Jewish communities around the world.

There would seem to be no such grounds for concern for the world's most popular languages – around ten of them have at least 100 million speakers. Yet even among those who use widely spoken languages, it would be wrong to underestimate the concerns about the future.

The Académie Française, for example, the pre-eminent learned body on matters relating to the French language, is not resting even though the language is spoken by over 70 million (and at least double that number according to French sources!). Notably, the Académie has tried to prevent the anglicization of the French language, suggesting that words such as walkman and software be avoided in favour of words derived from French. One of its past chairmen launched a campaign to try to make French the official language of European law and said that the defence of the language should be 'the major national cause of the 21st century'.[5] One suspects that, in downgrading world peace, the environment and global poverty, he might not be speaking for the French population as a whole. The campaign reflected the declining international clout of French – in less than twenty years, the proportion of EU documents originating in French has been more than halved. The French might see the use of their language fading but they pointedly say that the English must protect their language if it is not to be overrun by a bastardized Anglo-American.

There are conservatives in America who believe that English should be added to the endangered list. Their particular worry is that English will not survive the 'immigrant flood' of Spanish-speaking migrants. This seems an implausible scenario, but the American continent has a long history of immigrant languages killing off the indigenous ones. They argue that it would be unfortunate if future generations of Americans were unable to read Shakespeare in the original, but that rather presupposes that many people are reading it now!

None of these problems affects the most widely used language in the world, Mandarin Chinese, which is spoken by nearly 1 billion people. Nor should they really affect Spanish and English, which are a distant second and third, with about 350 million speakers each, followed by Bengali, Hindi, Portuguese and Russian, with between 150 and 200 million speakers.

English is not only the most commonly spoken second language but also the lingua franca in international business, media, scientific and academic worlds. That is just as well as there are concerns that the English themselves are becoming increasingly monolingual – in an ever-shrinking world, the ability to speak several languages should be prized. In 2004 the British government decided that learning a foreign language need no longer be compulsory beyond the age of fourteen, and modern language departments of universities are closing as demand for places tails off.

The English might be relieved that it is their language that is becoming the world's language, but it comes at a cost as the new global language looks less and less like English every year as it absorbs approximations and distortions. As distressing as this might be to many English people, such concerns are surely misplaced. While it is no doubt a bad thing to force people to stop using their language, it is hard to see why it is a bad thing if their language evolves – or even disappears – naturally. Our language is the one that we speak, that suits our needs, not the one that our ancestors spoke. Languages have always developed and expanded, withered and died, reflecting the ebb and flow of human politics, economics and migration. They fade away with little fanfare. The many language projects, such as those in Birmingham (collecting songs and phrases from African Caribbean patois) and in the north-east (saving old-fashioned words from the local dialect), are to be applauded but the realistic aim can never be higher than recording a little bit of social history for posterity.

9. Modern Science

Technology used to promise wonders. Now, it seems, it merely breeds distrust and fear. Arthur C. Clarke famously wrote that any sufficiently advanced technology is indistinguishable from magic. So why is the magic now black? Scientists insist that they are not moral agents, that their innovations can be exploited for good and ill. The public is dismayed at this abdication of responsibility and hankers for the days when scientists were heroes.

Frankenstein Foods
'Harvest of the damned' *Daily Mail*

On 16 February 1999, the *Daily Mirror*'s front page showed a picture of Tony Blair, whom it termed in the accompanying banner headline 'THE PRIME MONSTER'. What had the prime minister done that was monstrous? A subheading explained: 'Fury as Blair says "I eat Frankenstein food and it's safe"'.

'Frankenstein food', for those unfamiliar with British tabloid argot, describes foods derived from genetically modified crops, such as bread made from GM wheat, or soya milk in which some fraction of the soya is genetically modified. The term has become the inevitable media shorthand for this major development in agriculture, but in 1999 it was a new coinage.

By invoking Frankenstein's monster, the critics of this biotechnology, led by Greenpeace and Friends of the Earth, and backed by the organic-farming Prince Charles, played on age-old fears that, if we mess with nature, nature will mess with us: GM food is not merely modified, but mutated, and if you eat it, you will be mutated too. This is as absurd as suggesting that if you eat a hybridized tomato, you will become a human–tomato hybrid yourself. We eat conventionally hybridized produce all the time, and there have been no recorded instances of human–vegetable hybrids. Zeneca had launched a GM tomato paste without controversy. But vague unease was transformed to widespread public fear in 1998 when laboratory research by Arpad Pusztai at the Rowett Research Institute in Aberdeen appeared to show impairment of the immune system in rats fed with genetically modified potato. (The research was later discredited.)

Americans had by this time had some years to get used to GM foods, but there had never been anything like the controversy seen in Europe. Yet the risks – to human health, to the environment – are essentially similar on both continents. There is no intrinsic biological difference between Americans and Europeans, and little aside from its scale between American and European agriculture. So the fact that panic in the European media was matched by indifference in the United States needs to be explained.

One factor is a recent history of biological food scares, especially in Britain, related to farming on an industrial scale, ranging from salmonella in eggs to bovine spongiform encephalopathy (BSE) in beef cattle. In the United States food safety is looked after by the Food and Drug Administration whereas in Britain at the time it was overseen by the ministry also responsible for agriculture, producing a clear conflict of interest. But perhaps the major distinction is cultural, to do with the closer connection felt (rightly or not) to exist in Europe between the field and the table, an orthodoxy to which both picturesque countryside and culinary tradition are intimately bound.

This bucolic scene seems to be in stark contrast to the vision of agriculture opened up by biotechnology, a young and optimistic industry eager to show its potential. The mid-1990s saw the successive introduction in the US of the FlavrSavr tomato, an insect-resistant corn and a herbicide-resistant soybean. Monsanto's insect-resistant corn promised to save farmers insecticide, while the herbicide-resistant soya would help the manufacturer sell more of its Roundup weedkiller. In 1996, just 1.7 million hectares were planted to GM crops. The figure rose to 11 million hectares in 1997, 28 million in 1998, and 40 million by 1999, an area the size of California. This astonishing growth continues at 10–20 per cent a year, and has spread from North America to Argentina, China and a number of other non-European countries.

Britain's anti-GM campaign shifted into high gear when the *Daily Mail* launched a 'Genetic Food Watch' campaign in January 1999, and began using the scare label 'Frankenstein food' on its stories. Consumer attitudes to GM technology hardened, and the supermarkets judged that greater commercial opportunity lay in organic produce, which it could sell at a huge premium, than in food required to bear labelling revealing GM contents that nobody wanted. By 2003, farm-scale government trials of herbicide used on GM rape and sugar beet indicated that widespread planting would be likely to damage the environment, and the campaign seemed to be over. 'The death knell sounds for GM', crowed the *Daily Mail* as Monsanto shut down its operations in Britain.

In the United States, meanwhile, GM food ingredients have become widespread without labelling regulations. Any European who has visited the country during the last decade will almost certainly have eaten GM food – an irony apparently unnoticed by the *Daily Mail* as it promoted Florida holidays to its fearful readers. Very occasionally, the American press has sided with the environmentalists, but the more general reaction has been bafflement and hurt that other countries don't want their hi-tech chow. 'Food that starving people won't eat: poor countries foolish to turn down genetically modified produce', was how the *Chicago Tribune* responded when the Zambian government rejected US food aid offered in the form of GM corn.

There are many reasons why people might be ambivalent towards GM food, some of them more rational than others. This transformation of agriculture raises environmental, economic, social and ethical issues, but the most pressing concern is always human health.

Yet health may be the least of it. In many instances, no GM substance would even enter the body. Sugar might be made from GM beet, for example, but the process of refining the crop into the pure and simple chemical substance we know as sugar eliminates all biological material. In any case, our stomachs are no strangers to modified foods. Agricultural produce has been 'modified' by selective breeding for thousands of years and by the deliberate creation of hybrids for nearly 200 years. A poll quoted in the ever-vigilant *Daily Mail* suggested that nearly three-quarters of people in Europe remain 'extremely wary' of GM food and prefer 'natural crops'. In fact, if they were given 'natural crops' to eat, they would quickly become both unhappy and possibly unwell.

According to the *Mail*, people's main fear is 'the lack of data proving that the "Frankenstein foods" are safe to eat' – something that can't, of course, be proven in the way that the paper seems to demand. One death from eating GM food would suggest (but not prove) that it is unsafe, but even the continued survival of 300 million human guinea pigs routinely eating the stuff in North America does not prove conclusively that GM food is safe. Nevertheless, it is the clearest evidence available that GM foods are safe in terms of human health.

Where the GM revolution is opposed in America, it is opposed less on health grounds than on environmental grounds. In 1999, a laboratory experiment at Cornell University showed that caterpillars of the monarch butterfly were damaged by consuming the pollen of corn genetically modified for insect resistance. The monarch butterfly is brightly coloured and migrates in huge flocks, making it something of an American icon. The research therefore excited unusual public alarm much as Rachel Carson's singling out of the symbolic bald eagle as a species at risk of 'collateral damage' from DDT had done in *Silent Spring* thirty-six years earlier. However, subsequent field experiments showed that the caterpillars mostly did not eat the GM pollen anyway. The danger to such species is in any case surely dwarfed by that from the conventional pesticides that GM crops would help to banish.

The monarch butterfly notwithstanding, the American farming environment is different from that of Europe, occupying vast tracts of land with inevitably depleted biodiversity. Europeans have developed a fondness for their cosier mixed countryside, which may lead them to forget that agriculture always has a detrimental effect on the natural ecology – that, in a sense, is its purpose. There remain unresolved issues to do with the invasiveness and persistence of GM varieties and their effect on other species, but GM crops may turn out to be no worse than conventional ones and, if planted appropriately, could be of comparative benefit to the environment.

The ethics of GM technology are harder to resolve – like the ethics of any commercial transaction between unequal actors. America complains that Europe is restricting free trade not only by refusing to import its GM foods directly, but also by banning produce that may have become contaminated with altered stocks, including from developing countries. As a result, those countries feel driven to refuse to take American GM seed even to feed their own people, as happened in Zambia. Critics say this argument is self-serving, that food is anyway in surplus, and that hunger can be better alleviated by addressing distribution. Light is seldom shed when a technical matter is raised to a 'moral' issue, a process eagerly assisted by both the biotechnology industry and the anti-GM lobby with their opposing messages of 'feed the world' and 'keep nature pure'.

The company at the forefront of the GM revolution, Monsanto, furthermore acted with what in hindsight seems extraordinary carelessness, completely misjudging the European market and failing to advocate a precautionary approach to matters such as the mixing of GM and non-GM soybeans, which would later make it impossible to introduce food labelling and consequently difficult for American farmers to export their crops. While the anti-GM lobby undoubtedly crusades with 'overtones of moral fanaticism', the pro-GM industry is not exactly short of self-righteousness.[1] The perception of corporate arrogance in turn allows environmental campaigners to present themselves as 'people's champions tackling giant American Goliaths' despite their sometimes illegal and destructive actions.[2]

In the developed world, even the basic utilitarian argument for GM food is weak. A report to the British government in 2003 could find no discernible advantage for consumers and 'limited' economic benefit.[3] This lack of benefit – admitted on occasion even by pro-GM interests – suggests that GM food may simply be a solution in search of a problem. It is an innovation that has come about because the technology exists, not because the market demands it.

This impression was heightened by scientists accustomed to their role as heroes of the so-called 'green revolution' that had seen agricultural productivity raised enormously during the twentieth century through improvements in chemical fertilizers, plant and animal breeding, and sowing and harvesting technology. In genetic modification, they thought they were simply continuing in this tradition, using the latest science to make these processes more exact and efficient. The public, on the other hand, perceived a fundamental step change. Scientists thought they were aiding the supply of food worldwide; consumers suspected a corporate profit motive. Scientists saw no other way forward; consumers saw organic produce as a viable alternative.[4]

Scientists accordingly took the benefits of GM technology as self-evident and focused almost entirely on the objection to it which they were best prepared to deal with – namely the possible risk to health. Statements such as that by Peter Lachmann, who produced the Royal Society's 1998 report on GM food, that 'the public furore about health hazards of genetically modified foods rests on no reliable evidence base and falls little short of mass hysteria' thus miss the point (possibly deliberately) for a public whose view of the issue was always more complicated, involving attitudes towards America, corporate monopolies, the countryside and so on.[5]

For the crux of British consumers' fears so adroitly exploited by the *Daily Mail* was never health or the environment or ethics. It was instead to do with perceived coercion. In 2004, it became apparent that the newspaper's campaigning had not succeeded after all, as a European Union moratorium expired and plans for new GM trials were announced. 'So we're going to be force-fed GM', the paper announced. A month later, it was: 'Frankenstein food?

You'll be made to like it', a strange headline for a report that was actually about GM animal feed – perhaps the paper's readers were more bovine than anybody had thought.

Today, we are faced with a situation where GM technology exists, works for some and is unlikely to go away. In February 2006, the World Trade Organization found for the United States, Canada and Argentina and against the European Union on the conduct of review procedures for GM crops. It ruled that there could be no more unreasonable European moratoriums. The *Wall Street Journal* welcomed the outbreak of 'Frankensense'.

Undeterred, the *Daily Mail* now warned that 'U.S. biotech firms' were going to 'blitz' Ireland with 'GM grapes, apples, bananas, vegetables and cereals'. Surprisingly, the article did not describe the Americans' secret plan to drop this provender from over-flying B-52s. A group of Irish chefs had banded together to resist the invasion. Now, you wouldn't necessarily ask a scientist to cook you a gourmet dinner, and nor would you generally ask a chef to spell out the dangers of scientific innovation. But again this did not stop the *Mail*, which quoted one of the restaurateurs making the nonsensical claim that soon 'it will be impossible to cultivate indigenous crops as GM seed is used in farms across the country'.

'The U.S. government last night claimed victory in a battle to force genetically modified food on to the dinner tables of Britain and the world,' was how the *Mail*'s story began. In Ireland, as elsewhere in the EU, foods with GM ingredients must be labelled, but the *Mail* immediately raised a new fear that 'the U.S. administration is considering bringing a second legal case to the WTO to get this abolished'.

Where will it end? The companies have learned from Monsanto's mistakes and now threaten to use GM organisms cunningly disguised in products that people might actually want. One recent innovation is a low-fat ice-cream made using a protein derived from a species of fish. As a perverse way of dealing with the problem of obesity, this concoction might seem to exemplify GM's predicament as a solution looking for a problem, but the market appeal of such an idea cannot be ignored. Anti-GM campaigners sense that, as *The Times* put it, 'manufacturers may be trying to introduce GM processes by stealth in the hope of making GM foods acceptable to consumers'. Once they're acceptable to consumers, of course, the game's up. No wonder the environmentalists are worried.

It seems certain that the future on both sides of the Atlantic, and elsewhere, must be one where GM, conventional and organic foods all have a share of the market. Then nobody can complain, neither the North American companies, which currently claim to be 'losing' sales worth $500 million essentially because they have been unable to persuade Europeans to accept their wares, nor the crop-slashing Greenpeace and its allies, who will be seen as irrational zealots if the rest of the consumer population can calmly exercise its option to reject GM in the shops.

Little Wonder
'Fears grow that tiny particles may pose major health risks'
Seattle Times

Who would be afraid of a technology that promises so much? Cars that don't need washing, lighter, stronger tennis racquets and golf clubs, bouncier balls, fridges and washing machines that eliminate bacteria, stay-sharp razors, perpetual air fresheners, stain-resistant clothes and self-cleaning socks. And that's just in consumer goods. In cosmetics there will be more effective anti-ageing creams and invisible sun lotions, in medicine, tiny diagnostic sensors that circulate in the bloodstream on the lookout for trouble, and drugs against cancer that go straight to the source of the problem. Improved foods will include milk that tells you when it's about to go off, cholesterol-blocking cooking oil and animal-free meat.

These wonders – and many, many others according to its enthusiasts – are the bounty of nanotechnology, a catchall term for a set of emerging techniques that may allow us to arrange atoms and molecules on the tiniest scale to make substances and objects that can do jobs that it is presently difficult or impossible to do by conventional means.

But Prince Charles for one is worried. 'Charles: "Grey goo" threat to the world', reported the *Mail on Sunday* in 2003, as news emerged that the prince had convened a private meeting to debate the new technology. The stimulus for the royal fears seems to have been the publication a few months earlier of *Prey*, the latest thriller by Michael Crichton, in which genetically modified bacteria breed a horde of nano-sized robots which consume all in their path, turning it into the mysterious grey goo that headline-writers found so helpful.

Prince Charles had already made a reputation for himself campaigning against genetically modified crops. By 2002, it seemed that he and his environmentalist advisers had GM crops on the run, as European consumers rejected the very idea. The *Daily Mail* had led the media campaign. In nanotechnology, they had all found a new dragon to slay.

Certainly, this is how the whiggish element of the British press read the situation. 'Spare us all from royal nanoangst', wrote the science editor of the *Daily Telegraph*. 'The only grey goo that really worries me is the stuff between the Prince's ears.' Under the headline 'The real goo', *The Times* fretted: 'Once a shining banner signifying progress, science has become a tattered flag . . . Grey goo is the purest Luddism.' The article bemoaned how we now worry over the 'defects real and imagined' of any new technology rather than hailing its benefits and regard everything as 'potentially dangerous and worthy of social control'.

Nanotechnology first reached the public consciousness with the 1986 book *Engines of Creation* by Eric Drexler, although it was the physicist Richard Feynman who first considered the possibilities in a 1959 lecture entitled 'There's plenty of room at the bottom'.[1] Drexler rhapsodized in more detail on the boundless possibilities of the 'next revolution' in technology, as well as colourfully describing some of its pitfalls – coining the 'grey goo' label as he did so.

Nanotechnology is simply the technology of doing things at the bottom of the scale – typically less than 100 nanometres (a nanometre is a billionth of a metre), or the distance spanned by about a thousand atoms. Many materials start to behave in different ways at this scale because their surface area is greatly increased. For example, a millimetre crystal of salt could be broken into a trillion nanoparticles with sides of 100 nanometres. These particles would have a total surface 10,000 times that of the original crystal and, if placed on the tongue, would release flavour faster.

Sun lotions work because grains of white zinc oxide reflect the sunlight and prevent it from being absorbed by the skin. Ordinary lotions use relatively large grains of oxide, which is why they appear white. But lotions recently introduced on to the market use nanoparticles. These still reflect ultraviolet, but not the visible light, so appearing transparent. Elsewhere, too, arranging familiar materials in more precise ways will allow their potentially attractive properties to be maximized. A nanometre-smooth surface would not allow dirt or water to stick, for example. It is not hard to imagine the applications that could follow from such extensions of material properties.

Nanotechnology offers several instructive points of comparison with the GM controversy. The simple Luddite view is that we are once again meddling with nature in a fundamentally new way. 'If you think GM is scary', burbled one *Daily Mail* headline: 'Chicken that tastes of anything you want. Drinks that change colour at the flick of a switch. Everlasting chocolate. This is the new generation of Frankenfoods being created by scientists. The consequences could be terrifying.' But the argument is more subtle than this. The GM debate pitched a Europe where several countries had new left-of-centre governments and heightened consumer expectations for the environment against a technologically progressive America, but nanotechnology has mobilized sceptics on both sides of the Atlantic. 'Fears grow that tiny particles may pose major health risks', warned the *Seattle Times* in December 2005. The American media took the broad view that development of the technology ought to proceed, but only with regulatory safeguards. 'Stricter nanotechnology laws are urged; report warns of risk to public', headlined the *Washington Post* in January 2006. The article added: 'current U.S. laws and regulations cannot adequately protect the public against the risks'.

In April, the Food and Drug Administration weighed in after learning that dozens of people had suffered from breathing problems in Germany after using an aerosol cleaning product called Magic Nano. The product was quickly withdrawn from sale. The following month, the Wilson Center, a Washington think tank, released a list of 231 products whose manufacturers advertised using nanomaterials or nanotechnology, sparking further alarm.[2] The British *Daily Mail* picked up the story. ' "Hidden danger" in anti-ageing cream', it shrieked. Nanoparticles in products such as L'Oréal's Revitalift, Lancôme's Renergie and Boots' Soltan sun lotion could cause 'untold damage to human health', it warned, listing chest complaints, heart attacks and cancer among the problems that might arise.

By the end of the year, the US Environmental Protection Agency was in on the action too, with plans to regulate the silver nanoparticles used for their bactericidal properties in domestic appliances and food containers. The *Seattle Times* noted these would be the 'First federal restrictions on new, growing technology'.

Even the technologically gung-ho Bay Area grew fearful. The *San Francisco Chronicle* hailed Berkeley's aim to impose 'the world's first local regulation of nanomaterials'. This would be aimed at the city's famous university and the Lawrence Berkeley National Laboratory, and at start-up firms that might spin off to commercialize their innovations. Researchers responded by pointing out that their laboratory nanomaterials were made in quantities too tiny to test.

In another notable difference from the GM story, scientists have joined the call for greater regulation, desperate to avoid having what they see as another potentially exciting and lucrative technology disappear down the plughole of ill-informed public fears. 'The spectre of possible harm – whether real or imagined – is threatening to slow the development of nanotechnology unless sound, independent and authoritative information is developed on what the risks are, and how to avoid them,' fourteen scientists wrote in the journal *Nature*.[3] Countries with large hi-tech sectors such as the United States and Switzerland have sponsored preemptive programmes of public dialogue. 'The development of nanotechnologies has become an ideal testing ground for the application of public engagement processes to science and technology,' proclaimed Britain's Nanotechnology Engagement Group, steeling itself for the battle ahead.

Less clear was what should actually be regulated – the technological processes, which are not exposed to the public, or the materials, many of which are already regulated at the macroscopic scale. The obvious answer emerges if we look at nanotechnology not as Drexler's 'coming era' of miraculous novelty, but for what it is.

Now, what follows may allay your fears about nanotechnology, or it may simply confirm them: think of nanotechnology not as a fundamental novelty but as chemistry rebranded. Nanoparticles are simply chemicals, and, as such, to be feared or exploited according to their properties. When a government scientist warns that 'it's been shown that free nanoparticles inhaled can go straight to the brain', he's omitting to say that thousands of 'ordinary' chemicals do this too.[4] Prince Charles spoke of 'technologies which work at the level of the basic building blocks of life itself', as if these were entirely new – and sinister.[5] But nanomaterials are not new, nor are they inherently sinister, or for that matter especially wondrous. Ordinary chemicals work at this level already. The banality of the products on the Wilson Center's list attests to that. In short, the hazards of nanomaterials may be treated by and large like other chemical hazards.

The more distant dream, or nightmare, of tiny robots using atoms and molecules as building blocks sounds worrying until you realize what an unbelievably difficult way of doing things it is. Nature has taken millions of years to get to the point where tiny cells are able to grow and divide. Thousands or millions of cells must do this continuously to grow a living organism. Yet to build one simple virus, to take a Crichtonesque example, atom by atom with each assembly operation taking just a second would take a week. Man has long found it more convenient to make things by manufacturing the chemical ingredients in bulk and then shaping them into parts which can be assembled into a product. The nanotechnologist's dream is to turn this process on its head: your home might have a kind of programmable manufacturing appliance into which you would simply load some generic raw material and out would pop the latest model of mobile phone, or a Prada handbag, or a pristine copy of *Prey*.

The central fear about nanotechnology is that there are, as the *Observer* put it, 'no new rules'. But need there be? Old rules may suffice in many cases. Beneath the noise of all the breast-beating, this is in fact how the regulatory drive begins to sound. A 2004 report from the British Royal Society and Royal Academy of Engineering recommended that nanomaterials ought to be regulated as for new chemicals. Berkeley's nanotechnology ordinance, now approved, simply requires companies to disclose the toxicology – to the extent that it is known – of nanoparticles as they must already for bulk hazardous materials.

Some nanoparticles may indeed prove to be harmful – it would be a surprise if none did. Nanofibres may behave like asbestos fibres. Nanomaterials slathered on the skin may be absorbed and have harmful effects. Like diesel exhaust particulates, nanoparticles in the air may enter the lungs. A more immediate concern may be the escape into the environment of hard-to-recover silver nanoparticles from discarded appliances. *The Times*'s apologist was thus somewhat overenthusiastic in his denunciation of the nanotechnology critics who supposedly threaten to bring the whole edifice of scientific progress crashing to the ground: of course, 'real defects' do need to be addressed, and this technology, like all others, will have to be brought under 'social control'. It increasingly looks as if the way this might be done is when somebody brings the first lawsuit.

Perhaps then we will know where to direct our distrust. When the Magic Nano cleaning product was withdrawn from the market, American newspapers reported on German officials' caution in assessing the problem. The assumption was that the cause of the alleged breathing difficulties was the aerosol vapour produced when using the cleaner, although 'they could not rule out whether the nanoparticles it contained also contributed'.[6] After tests by the German Federal Institute for Risk Assessment, however, Magic Nano was found to contain no nanoparticles at all. Consumers should perhaps worry less about new technologies and more about trading standards.

Exposed
'Nuked' *Daily Mirror*

In so many ways, it was made for the media. A former Russian spy, Alexander Litvinenko, is admitted to hospital exhibiting symptoms of poisoning following a visit to a London sushi bar. At first, the speculation is that he has been given thallium. Then X-rays seem to show pieces of 'dense matter' inside his body, perhaps a canister that has broken open. Finally, his condition undergoes a sudden deterioration and he dies, but not before preparing a statement blaming the Russian president, Vladimir Putin, himself previously head of the nation's secret service, for his death. The autopsy confirms that Litvinenko was killed by a

large dose of radioactive polonium, a substance only likely to
have been obtained with state sanction from a nuclear reactor.
'NUKED', screamed the front page of the *Daily Mirror* the next
day, a Saturday.

At this point the story abruptly changes gear. Now it is no
longer just an intrigue. It is all of a sudden a 'public health scare'.[1]
Over the weekend, the UK Health Protection Agency urges
people who had been to the sushi bar on the day in question to
contact a telephone helpline, though doctors insist they aren't at
any serious risk. 'Hundreds of people face being tested for traces
of deadly polonium,' the Sunday *Observer* writes. By Monday,
nearly 1,100 people have come forward. Eight are referred for tests
– 'at a secret London clinic'.[2] The sushi bar is closed down for
decontamination as other locations Litvinenko visited test positive
for polonium 210. Traces of radiation are found in other places,
including British Airways planes on the Moscow route. By the
end of the week, the number of calls from the public is nudging
3,000; twenty-four are referred for tests.

What made it such a perfect story? The suspicion of foul play –
the conclusion drawn by British official reports. The exotic poisons
– thallium features in a novel by Agatha Christie, while polonium
cost its discoverer, Marie Curie, her life. The story unfolded in a
gripping way, with each new morsel eagerly snapped up by a
public with an appetite already sharpened for such incredible tales
by the opening the same week of the latest James Bond film, *Casino
Royale*.

Above all, there was the dread word 'radiation', accompanied
on the BBC news and in the tabloids by its spooky mandala. And,
significantly, there was also the probability that, while all were
excited by the drama, no reader was really at risk. This is because
polonium 210 emits alpha particles, which have high energy but
very short range. In Litvinenko's body, the particles damaged his
internal organs over a period of weeks, leading him to exhibit the
series of puzzling symptoms that kept doctors guessing as to his
illness, but could not penetrate beyond, explaining why radioactive
poisoning was not identified sooner. He was finally buried in

what the BBC *Newsnight* programme described reassuringly as a 'radiation-proof coffin', although an ordinary pine one would have done just fine.

Alpha radiation does not spread through the environment. Contamination is therefore very limited. In the end the only people dangerously exposed to polonium were involved in the world of espionage. Sixteen other people received radiation doses of 'some concern', including some of the bar staff, where it is thought that the poison was administered. These people face a 'very small' raised risk of cancer in the long term, roughly equivalent to that if they were to live in Cornwall for a decade or two and be exposed to the high natural level of radiation from radon gas released from the local geology. There never was a risk to general 'public health'.

The Litvinenko episode was unprecedented in many ways, but it was not the only recent radiation scare. At the beginning of 2004, it was reported that American cities were being scanned for terrorist 'dirty bombs' – bombs combining radioactive material with conventional explosives that would spread radiation. In an attempt at reassurance, the newspapers conjured the unintentionally hilarious vision of scientists, 'dressed casually to blend in with people enjoying the Christmas and New Year holidays', roaming major American cities with golf bags weighed down with Geiger counters.[3] Yet they would have detected nothing if the poisoned Litvinenko had walked right past them in the street. Extravagant precautions such as this, and the HPA's offer to 'worried' members of the British public to call the hotline, are signs of a desperate urge to reassure far more than they are realistic means of damage limitation.

Radiation generally invokes fear regardless of its nature, origin or potency. During the polonium scare, the *Observer* noted that 'The last radioactivity incident of this magnitude occurred when the radiation plume from Chernobyl swept over Britain in 1986.' Yet that event was quite different in all of these qualities. Why does radiation inspire such terror? In *The Perception of Risk*, Paul Slovic suggests that part of the fear stems from 'transmutation'.[4]

Polonium is transmuted to lead when it emits its alpha particle, for example. Like the mutation of viruses that also makes us uneasy, transmutation is change of a kind we cannot readily comprehend. But what we fear most is surely the knowledge – one of the few things we do know about it – that radiation causes cancer.

This is true both of nuclear radiation, which involves the emission of particles or rays from radioactive material, and of some forms of electromagnetic radiation. Ignorance of the precise facts, however, means that we are indiscriminate when it comes to assessing radiation risks. We are apt to judge the risk not according to its physical nature but according to the context in which we experience it. Thus, we judge X-rays safe (which experts warn is not the case) and the hazard from nuclear power plants high when experts insist it is low. We may be agitated when manufacturers irradiate our food in order to destroy bacteria, but we regard radon leaking from the ground into our homes with 'apathy' because it is a natural occurrence.[5]

Excessive reassurance may be the contemporary response to potential nuclear radiation hazards, but in the past it has often been excessive denial. This provides one further reason why our fears persist. Early nuclear accidents at Windscale (later renamed Sellafield) and near Detroit were downplayed in a time still marked by collective optimism about a clean, modern source of energy. The meltdown of a reactor and release of radioactive gas in 1979 at Three Mile Island in Pennsylvania was less serious than either of these events, but by this time the environmental movement had sprung up, highlighting the issue of radioactive waste disposal as well as plant safety, and the tide of public opinion turned.

This accident was overshadowed on 26 April 1986 when a reactor failed at the Chernobyl nuclear power plant in the Ukraine, leading to a chemical explosion in which much of the 190 tonnes of nuclear fuel escaped into the atmosphere. The radioactive rain that drifted westward over Europe and beyond contained perhaps 100 times the fallout from the Hiroshima bomb. The disaster put the brakes on nuclear power globally and is still the cause of massive controversy.

Did just fifty people die as the International Atomic Energy Agency (IAEA) and World Health Organization (WHO) insist? Or was the figure 10,000 times that, more like half a million, as is now claimed by authorities in the Ukraine, a figure many times greater than maximum estimates given elsewhere?

The World Nuclear Association, an industry lobby group, puts the Chernobyl death toll at '31+', limiting the count to those who died in the immediate blast or from acute radiation within a year and omitting all subsequent radiation deaths. It thoughtfully offers a comparison with deaths in coal mines since that date, which add up to more than 3,000, mostly in China, with another 2,000 or so deaths related to oil and gas extraction.[6] But the IAEA/WHO calculate that deaths from thyroid cancer due to radioactive iodine and other causes directly attributable to the Chernobyl explosion will ultimately be comparable with this total, at somewhere over 4,000.

Chernobyl is now a destination for day-tripping tourists and home, if one is to believe the *Sun*, to 'a generation of "mutant" super brainy children'. But, further west, it continues to leave its taint. The British government, in characteristic fashion, first denied there was a problem with radioactive fallout and then put in place restrictions on the sale and movement of sheep that were grazing contaminated grass. Eventually, the restriction zone was narrowed, oddly enough to a small area 'just downwind from the huge international Sellafield nuclear reprocessing complex', a site already notorious for radiation leaks.[7] According to Brian Wynne of the Centre for the Study of Environmental Change at nearby Lancaster University, scientists originally claimed that the radiation was entirely due to Chernobyl, but later admitted that half of it came from 'other sources', namely Sellafield itself and atmospheric weapons testing. Today, sheep graze the contaminated grass without restriction.

Public response to electromagnetic radiation is less understandable. Electromagnetic radiation includes radio waves, microwaves, infrared, visible light, ultraviolet and X-rays. Only the last two of these are sufficiently energetic to produce the chemical changes in biological molecules necessary to cause cancer. Yet many people are more worried about the low-energy electromagnetic radiation from electrical appliances.

This fear was fuelled by a series of *New Yorker* articles on microwaves by Paul Brodeur, expanded in a book called *The Zapping of America* (1977). Brodeur returned to the magazine in the 1980s to give power lines the same treatment. On both occasions, he built his case on anecdotal evidence of 'clusters' of cancers, miscarriages, birth defects and childhood leukaemia.

Misleadingly using the terminology of *nuclear* radiation, Brodeur claimed that levels of electromagnetic radiation in New York City were a hundred million times the 'natural' background. This is like pointing out that light levels in Times Square at night are this much higher than 'natural'. The abundance of something harmless is of little consequence. Nevertheless, the widespread scare that Brodeur's articles provoked nearly stifled the infant microwave oven industry, while public protests prevented the National Weather Service from installing a weather radar on Long Island. As Robert Park put it in *Voodoo Science*, 'people feared the known dangers of howling wind and crashing ocean waves less than they feared the unproven hazard of silent, invisible microwaves'.[8] The adjectives are significant here: it is the familiar, palpable danger that we downplay in favour of the novel and imperceptible.

Extensive reviews of the evidence by the US National Academy of Sciences in 1996 and the National Cancer Institute the following year found no correlation between the claimed cause and effect. Even a 'cluster' of five children with leukaemia at the heart of the controversy was too small to have significance – it was random bad luck, not a correlation with anything. The two reports should have put the matter to rest. However, the story persists.

The fundamental flaw in the argument of those who believe that fields of any sort are the cause of their complaint is something called the inverse square law. This says that if you double your distance from a radiation source your exposure is reduced by a factor of four. So if you worry about the 10,000 volts surging through the power lines 10 metres overhead, you should also consider the 240 volts in the cable running by your desk and the 12-volt electric toothbrush in your hand.

It seems that some people are doing just that. 'Electrosensitivity' is a growing complaint. Sufferers experience headaches, skin irritation and fatigue. The symptoms may be real enough. But have they correctly identified the cause? Or is it a case of mistaken attribution as with some claimed allergies? As with power lines, much expensive research has been commissioned to find out.

The current focus of the debate is mobile phone technology and the suspicion that the microwave signals that pass between the hand-held receiver and the nearest phone mast may cause brain damage. The argument is superficially plausible because people hold the devices against the side of their head. But again, as with power lines, no evidence solidly supports a connection. It is impossible to prove a negative, however, and so doubts persist, and, as the *Financial Times* warned, with around 2 billion users, 'even a tiny individual health risk could translate into thousands of deaths'.

The HPA, which reviewed the available studies in 2000 and again in 2005, confusingly concluded that while the 'balance of evidence' indicated no effect on health, there was some evidence for 'biological effects'.[9] Good news, then, both for the complacent and the worried. The latter evidence comes from small-scale studies involving volunteers, and the cause of the effects is unclear. In a sign of the times, the HPA nevertheless advised a precautionary approach, echoed by the WHO. Such advice shows how official agencies are increasingly taking into account not only scientific evidence but also the vagaries of public opinion, evidence-based or not.

A larger study by the Karolinska Institute in Sweden has since shown that long-term phone users appear to have a greater chance of developing a particular nerve tumour. What made these results compelling was that the tumours appeared on the side of the head where the user holds the phone. But again, cause and effect have not been unequivocally linked, and other large studies have not replicated the results. The effect may stem from older models of phone no longer in use, or from some other factor entirely.

When computers began to enter the workplace in the 1980s, fears arose concerning the radiation from their visual displays. Research then – much of it commissioned by trade unions and coming from socially liberal countries such as Canada and Sweden – led to sensible measures to improve workplace design and office lighting and to ensure that workers took regular breaks, although no radiation hazard was ever established.

Computers were often imposed on workers who feared the loss of their jobs, but people mostly love their mobile phones. So this time around we might expect radiation fears to subside sooner. Nevertheless, the WHO estimates that $200 million has already been spent worldwide on research into the supposed dangers of mobile phones. As their usage expands, so the fears become more far-fetched. 'Do mobile phones kill sperm?', demanded one recent headline, reporting news that the Reproductive Research Center at the Cleveland Clinic in Ohio found that men who used mobile phones had lower sperm counts.

This study nicely illustrates some of the problems that arise with this sort of research. The sample comprised 364 men undergoing infertility diagnosis, hardly a typical group. They were divided into groups with high, medium and low sperm counts, and it was found that those who used a mobile for more than four hours a day were disproportionately likely to be in the low group. Ignored was the possibility that people with such a curious lifestyle might exhibit other traits which could better explain the results – poor diet, posture or working environment, for example. Furthermore, the researchers appear to have forgotten the inverse square law. Unless you have ears in your crotch, the radiation your testicles receive while using a mobile phone is less than from listening to your stereo. One other thing would explain the findings – talking bollocks.

10. They're Coming to Get You

What you don't know can't hurt you is what they say. The corollary must be that increased knowledge raises the capacity for endangerment. As we learn more about asteroids, there is more to fear. Sadly, the reverse does not seem to apply. We know nothing about alien life, but we fear this too. Why are tales of encounter with extraterrestrials so often couched in terms of threat? Wherefore the human predisposition to fear? Aliens might be able to show us a good time. What use is higher intelligence otherwise?

Expecting Visitors

' "Aliens could attack at any time" warns former MoD chief'
Daily Mail

In one of the most dramatic UFO sightings of recent years, a group of United Airlines pilots and other employees on 7 November 2006 reported seeing a grey saucer-shaped object hovering over one of the terminals at Chicago O'Hare airport before it shot up through the clouds. One of the group notified the air traffic control tower, but the controllers saw nothing, and nothing appeared on their radar. The airline and the Federal Aviation Administration said there was no further action to be taken, leaving the workers 'upset that neither their bosses nor the government will take them seriously'.[1]

The episode illustrates several traits common to the more plausible UFO sightings. It has apparently credible witnesses, here in the form of trained personnel accustomed to aerial observation. It was a sighting by a small group, not a lone individual or a large number of people spread over a wide area. Typically, their feelings are hurt when they are not taken seriously by officialdom. Finally, of course, there is the overwhelming likelihood that the object, although 'unidentified', was not an alien spacecraft but some highly localized weather phenomenon or a piece of debris held aloft in the breeze – or a hoax.

After all, it doesn't take much to produce a phenomenon worthy of investigation. A few months before the O'Hare flying saucer, the British Ministry of Defence leapt into action to investigate the sighting by several independent witnesses one balmy summer's night of a mysterious pattern of lights hovering above Seaham, County Durham. The effect turned out to have been produced by party lanterns which had escaped into the sky like hot-air balloons. The party-givers later reported their doings: 'Our garden lanterns started a UFO scare'. The news item added that the lanterns are now sold with a warning that they have been mistaken for UFOs.

With sightings like this, it is hardly surprising that UFO stories tend to be regarded by the press as little more than an amusement. But the frivolity disguises a sense of unease at the possibility, however remote, that one day a flying saucer may indeed turn out to be a spacecraft containing an alien intelligence. This possibility excites curiosity in many, anticipation in some, foreboding in others, and in a few, real fear.

It was ostensibly in an effort to assuage such public fears that the United States Air Force set up a programme to log UFO sightings known as Project Blue Book. Between 1947 and 1969 the military authorities examined 12,618 UFO reports. Recent British Ministry of Defence figures record 714 sightings in the six years 2001 to 2006, about the same rate of sightings per head of population as in America.

There is nothing disreputable about seeing a UFO, or unidentified aerial phenomenon, as the official jargon now prefers to put it. They are after all 'unidentified'. What is peculiar is to insist that a UFO is an alien spaceship when many other explanations are far more likely.

Many daytime sightings can be put down to unfamiliar aircraft and birds, weather balloons, satellites, odd cloud formations or other effects. Nighttime sightings of luminous shapes and patterns may be aircraft lights, reflections of ground lights from clouds, fireflies, meteors or luminous discharges in the atmosphere (a range of phenomena largely unfamiliar to the public among which even the 'well-known' auroras borealis and australis have been seen by relatively few people). Perhaps 80 per cent of all UFO sightings may be quickly placed in one of these categories. When a sighting cannot be explained so readily, the question is whether the alien spaceship explanation is *definitely more likely than any of these or anything else*. In other words, which is more likely: that a bunch of airline employees see, let's say, a piece of grey polythene borne aloft from a Chicago building site, or that they truly see a flying saucer?

Where a physical phenomenon cannot be identified, a UFO sighting may be put down to a hoax, hallucination or delusion, depending on the number of people who saw it and their circumstances. Again, the balance of likelihoods argument applies. Is it more likely that a bunch of airline employees choose to perpetrate a hoax, or that they see a flying saucer?

Of the 12,618 Blue Book UFO sightings, only 701 remained officially unexplained, meaning that they could not be firmly attributed to a physical or psychological cause. Most turned out to be due to America's own spy planes – hence the military interest in the field at all. Of the 714 sightings that came to the attention of the British Ministry of Defence in 2001–6, twelve were 'deemed to be worthy of further consideration', according to a defence minister answering questions in the House of Commons. Questioned under the Freedom of Information Act, the ministry wouldn't say what made them special, or what further consideration they actually received.

This is not to say that there are no other rational explanations for such anomalies. In one year, 1952, there was a freak level of 1,501 sightings logged by Project Blue Book, three times the average; 303 of them were 'unexplained', ten times the usual number. The fact that *Life* magazine ran a major feature on UFOs in that year, and that a film came out of *War of the Worlds*, in which aliens come to earth aboard a glowing meteor, may not strictly count as explanations, but they certainly cannot be counted out as factors in the result. And the fact that a disproportionate number of the sightings for that year remained unexplained may in turn be simply down to the fact that they were not properly investigated, as the Air Force unit responsible for the work was stretched far beyond its usual volume of work. More significantly, even in a period of acute state paranoia, not one of the UFOs was deemed a risk to national security.

There were other spikes in UFO sightings in 1957 when the Soviet Union launched its *Sputnik* satellite, and in 1978, when the film *Close Encounters of the Third Kind* was released. When *The X-Files* finally disappeared off our television screens in 2002, the whole idea seemed suddenly unfashionable. 'The Martians aren't coming: British UFO-spotting clubs may have to close because of a lack of sightings', read one headline.

Credence of UFOs is fuelled by the abundance of apparently credible witnesses, such as United Airlines pilots but also routinely including police and military officers. One such was Peter Horsley, a one-time equerry to Prince Philip who ended his career as deputy commander-in-chief of British Strike Command. He became interested in UFOs while working at Buckingham Palace in the early 1950s precisely because so many reports came from airmen. On the prince's nod, he was permitted to look into the 'more credible' reports, provided there would be no publicity.[2]

He did keep his counsel at the time, but his 1997 memoir is an unintentional casebook of military psychosis. At one point, he meets a general who believes that UFOs are alien spaceships come to warn us of nuclear war. 'This was heady stuff but I knew that there are always a number of senior retired officers who are attracted to all sorts of fringe cults, most likely out of boredom.'[3]

It seems it takes one to know one. Horsley is soon taken to meet a mysterious figure who wants an introduction to Prince Philip, for whom he has a message about humankind's depredations against wildlife and who he believes can help him in his mission to promote 'galactic harmony'. Horsley recounts eleven pages of 'verbatim' dialogue with this figure, full of curiously accurate details about developments in science and technology that took place from the 1950s to the 1990s.

Aside from his thoughtful personal appeal to Prince Philip, the (future) president of the (not yet founded) World Wildlife Fund, the figure's comments on our destructiveness in war were entirely characteristic of aliens' sermonizing, noted in other witness reports. It does seem a shame that aliens would come all that way to warn us of a danger of which we were already acutely aware at the time, rather than tell us something usefully prescient about HIV, CFCs or CO_2 emissions.

From time to time, these distinguished witnesses gain sufficient momentum to challenge the establishment (people very like themselves, of course) about the cover-up they suspect to be taking place. The *Daily Express* reported one gathering in Washington DC with the headline 'Don't tell the CIA but generals have proof ET exists and wants to make contact'. Appearing at the conference were men from the FAA, a cardinal from the Vatican and Britain's former Chief of Defence Staff, Admiral Lord Hill Norton, who believed that 'there is a serious possibility that we are being visited – and have been visited for many years – by people from outer space, from other civilisations; that it behoves us to find out who they are, where they come from, and what they want'.

During Congressional hearings on UFOs in 1966, the future American president Gerald Ford asked, 'Are we to assume that everyone who says he has seen a UFO's an unreliable witness?' Well, it might be a good start. For, again, which is more likely: that a military officer suffers from some delusional condition, or that he has been visited by aliens? 'Credible' does not mean should-be-believed-under-all-circumstances, and even men in uniform may have funny turns. Even if we accept that a person with military training is in general a more reliable witness than an ordinary member of the public, there are large numbers of military personnel and so there is still a good chance that a few of them are experiencing psychological difficulties. Add in the special conditions that might obtain, such as forms of stress or oxygen starvation in flight, and we might be tempted to say that military UFO sightings should be given no special credence at all.

Although aliens might seem inseparable from their vehicles, the creatures themselves present their own distinctive dangers. Ufology is essentially a harmless pastime – perhaps even useful, if it diverts bored air marshals from ordinary war-making. But aliens do claim human lives and minds. In the most spectacular case of 'alien abduction', thirty-nine members of the Heaven's Gate cult were found dead in April 1997, their souls having supposedly left their bodies in order to rendezvous with a spacecraft come to take them away.

More frequently, individuals report seeing and hearing things, or discover that they cannot account for periods of time, and attribute this to alien contact or abduction. One in ten Americans claims to have seen one or more UFOs, a far higher incidence than the few hundred sightings a year investigated by the Air Force. Polls routinely find that a majority of people believe there is intelligent life on other planets, and around half 'believe in' UFOs – although of course they'd be fools not to, at least while the U part still applies. But 65 per cent of Americans also believe that a UFO crashed at Roswell, New Mexico, according to a CNN poll in 1997, on the fiftieth anniversary of the most celebrated claim of an alien encounter. Nearly 4 million Americans claim to have been *abducted* by (not just to have seen) aliens according to another poll in 1992. Merely as tourism this is quite a figure – it's more Americans than visit France each year.

Aliens seem to be created in our own image. They are bipedal, they possess similar although superior technologies and have similarly dismaying ambitions of domination and control. Curiously, Americans' reports over the years have gradually come to concur on the key details of what aliens look like. Equally curiously, reports of aliens made by people in other cultures diverge from this norm.

This is to be expected when one considers the sources of inspiration available to these groups, while the disappointing general likeness of aliens to humans is not so much a failure of imagination, but a clue that aliens are not aliens at all but proxies for humans. Accounts of alien abduction closely resemble accounts of abuse, as Carl Sagan points out in *Demon-Haunted World*. Elaine Showalter adds that women's 'abduction scenarios closely resemble women's pornography'.[4] They may also reflect anxieties over conception and childbirth. The obsession with sex squares neatly with the idea of higher intelligence: of course these aliens want us for our bodies – they'd have no use for our inferior minds.

But wait. Why not genuine aliens? Consider alien visitations not as a problem in psychology, but as one in probability. How many aliens are out there, and would they find us? In 1961, Frank Drake, an astronomer at Cornell University, devised a formula to find out. The Drake equation is simply the multiplication of a set of chances. Start with the number of stars in our galaxy, the Milky Way. Take the fraction of those that have planets; take the fraction of those planets that are chemically suitable for life; take the fraction of *those* planets on which life actually does arise; now consider the fraction where that life evolves to intelligence; and then the fraction that develops appropriate communication (or interstellar travel) technology. Most of these fractions are small, some very small, so that multiplied together they amount to a very small chance indeed. Still, the number of stars in the Milky Way is several hundred billion, so that helps raise the odds. Present estimates of the number of civilizations out there potentially able to communicate with us range from effectively none to maybe 5,000.

This looks good, but now contact must be made. This brings in another series of long odds. The alien civilization must point their detection equipment our way – one planet orbiting one of several hundred billion stars. They must recognize the signal of our presence and they must then choose to act. Plus, there's one final, vital term from the Drake equation to consider – one that makes the equation a child of its time during the Bay of Pigs fiasco. This is the fraction of the lifetime of the planet during which its communicating intelligent life flourishes. Both the alien civilization and our civilization must overlap in time if we are to make contact. We have only had the ability to send communications into space for around fifty years, one ten billionth of the lifetime of the Earth. Based on the Earth experience, civilizations tend to last no more than 500 years, and perhaps it's the same on other planets. The chances of our connecting become incredibly tiny. Small wonder, then, that as John Allen Paulos cruelly puts it, 'innumerates are considerably more likely than others to believe in visitors from outer space'.[5]

That's When It Hits You
'Asteroid nearly rocks Earth' *Cape Argus*

You might want to put this date in your diary: 13 April 2029. It's a Friday. Friday the 13th. This is the day, NASA announced in 2004, on which the Earth is most likely to be struck by a civilization-destroying asteroid. On Christmas Eve 2004, the space agency quoted odds of one in 300 – an unprecedented level of risk – that we would be hit by the recently discovered 2004 MN4, a 400-metre diameter chunk of rock orbiting around the sun. Later that day it dramatically shortened the odds to one in sixty-three. By the end of Christmas Day, the chance of the planet being largely wiped out stood at one in forty-five. On the Torino scale, asteroid watchers' newly invented equivalent of the Richter scale, 2004 MN4 rose from a zero to a two and then to a four. These may be long odds for betting on a horse, but they are uncomfortably short when you consider what's at stake.

But at least there was twenty-five years to work out what to do about it.

Most asteroids are thought to be remnants of a failed planet. They generally occupy an orbit between Mars and Jupiter, but numbers of them are regularly dislodged from this orbit by the gravitational influence of the planets. Small asteroids reach us all the time but burn up in the Earth's atmosphere, where we see them as meteors or 'shooting stars'. A meteor that survives this process is termed a meteorite when it reaches the Earth's surface. There are presently around 3,000 designated 'near-Earth' asteroids the size of 2004 MN4 or larger. 'Earth will be hit by an asteroid large enough to wipe out most of the human race. That is a certain fact. We just don't know when,' according to Lembit Opik, a worried British member of parliament.[1] And while we are waiting for the big one, there are also a billion objects out there the size of a bus, quite large enough to do considerable damage to our planet. These are frightening numbers.

But consider what it must take for one of these asteroids to pose a real threat to us. First of all, the asteroid must be of sufficient size. Fortunately, the abundance of asteroids decreases sharply at larger sizes, so while there are indeed many out there, the billion or so bus-sized objects in fact represent a tiny minority of the total number of asteroids. Next, the asteroid must have enough energy to penetrate the atmosphere and do damage. This means that it must be both massive and fast-moving. Then, its composition must be right – a dense stony or metallic object will do more damage than a carbon-rich or icy one, which is more likely to break up high in the atmosphere.

Most obviously, the orbit of the asteroid must coincide with that of the earth. This is no small requirement. Space, as Douglas Adams pointed out in *The Hitchhiker's Guide to the Galaxy*, is 'big, really big'. So the chance of the path of one fairly small orbiting rock (the Earth) overlapping with that of a far smaller one (the asteroid) is always going to be extremely low. This overlap must occur not only in space but also in time. And again, the chance that our asteroid crosses the Earth's path at the precise moment that the Earth itself is at that point in its orbit is very small. In 1989, an asteroid missed the Earth by just six hours, which sounds close until you express it in terms of distance – 600,000 kilometres, well over the distance from the Earth to the moon.

Finally, even if an asteroid does strike, it may not have a catastrophic impact on us. Only a very rare large asteroid would have major consequences for humankind regardless of where it hit the planet's surface. Clearly, a rather smaller object could destroy a city like Los Angeles or Tokyo in a direct hit, but it is far more likely to fall in an almost entirely unpopulated region. If a meteorite falls into the sea, however, then the mortality due to the resulting tsunami is likely to far exceed that for an equivalent impact on land. A modest 100-metre asteroid might kill 10,000 people in a land impact, but the tsunami it would cause if it landed in the sea might kill 100 million. 'The United States is, by this measure, one of the most vulnerable nations on Earth, since it has numerous major cities close to sea level on two separate oceans,' observes the asteroid expert John Lewis.[2]

The good news is that these probabilities, each tiny on its own, must be multiplied together to calculate the overall risk. Since all the fractional chances stacked up here are extremely small, the multiplied total giving the overall probability of a lethal impact is minuscule. The practical risk could be reduced still further if we have forewarning of an impact.

Asteroid 2004 MN4 – whose notoriety duly earned it a proper name, Apophis – is bigger than the meteorite responsible for the geological feature known as Meteor Crater in Arizona and far bigger than the one that exploded in 1908 with the force of a thousand Hiroshima bombs in the air above Tunguska, razing thousands of square kilometres of Siberian forest.

So why were there not desperate headlines at the time warning of our impending destruction? Because the danger passed almost immediately. With the odds at one in 300, the NASA scientists seemed strangely keen not to alert the world to the danger but to offer reassurance. 'These odds are likely to change on a day-to-day basis as new data are received,' they announced. 'In all likelihood, the possibility of impact will eventually be eliminated as the asteroid continues to be tracked by astronomers around the world.'[3]

Now, 'in all likelihood' is hardly a phrase of scientific precision.

What did they mean? The newspapers were certainly puzzled. 'Asteroid impact alert for 2029? Perceived danger may go down as studies continue', the *Seattle Times* repeated dubiously. In fact, as we know, the odds rapidly shortened. But even then, the scientists remained apparently blasé: 'the odds against impact are still high, about 60-to-1, meaning that there is a better than 98 percent chance that new data in the coming days, weeks, and months will rule out any possibility of impact in 2029.'[4] This was a little bit different. But why should new data lean this way? Mightn't they equally be found to suggest that a collision is more likely?

After all, this does not happen for other statistics, although we might wish that it would. If, in a certain city, you have a one-in-a-hundred chance of being shot, that risk does not disappear as a gunman approaches you. A better analogy is one that omits human malevolence, such as emerging from a junction on to a main road in your car and having to cross traffic going the other way. You can risk the turn when you see another car approaching if that car is going to turn off the main road on to your road. As the car gets closer, you gather more data about it – you see it slow down, indicate, the wheels turn slightly, until at a certain point you are sufficiently sure it won't hit you to make your manoeuvre. A risk that once seemed great is in this way shown to be less.

Scientists estimate an asteroid's future trajectory based on observations of its orbit around the sun. Because of observational inaccuracies and limitations in the computer models they use, this path is not a fine line but a three-dimensional swathe of space. Where that swathe overlaps the Earth's orbit, there is a finite possibility that the asteroid will hit us. But as more data are obtained, the swathe can only become narrowed, and as this happens the likelihood that it now includes the Earth is reduced.

In the case of Apophis, somebody found some archived photographic plates of the asteroid dating from before its 'discovery'. Measurements from these promptly reduced the risk to zero, although closer examination later revealed a bias in the measurements which meant that the 'all clear' should not have been sounded at all. Two months later, the danger was finally eliminated with new data from the Arecibo radiotelescope.

Apophis is not beaten yet, however. Its orbit crosses ours again in 2036 and it is currently given a 5,000-to-one chance of hitting us. This led the popular television astronomer Patrick Moore to predict, in an article on space exploration milestones for the twenty-first century, that in 2028 as the asteroid approaches the Earth for the first time we might send up a nuclear device to deflect it from its course so that it does not score a hit second time around.

Asteroids are a new fear. Until recently, we simply did not know enough about them to worry. Two recent discoveries have changed our perceptions. The first was the scientific confirmation obtained in 1990 that an asteroid strike at Chicxulub in Mexico was the most likely cause of the extinction of the dinosaurs 65 million years ago. The second was the dramatic footage of the comet Shoemaker–Levy 9 breaking up and pummelling the planet Jupiter in 1994. At the same time, improved astronomical observation is enabling us to spot many more, especially smaller asteroids – and realize that they pass very close to Earth. Compare the 3,000 'near-Earth asteroids' known now to only eighteen known in 1981. Methods developed in order to evaluate the impact on human populations of nuclear weapons meanwhile allow us to estimate the damage that would be done if an asteroid did hit.

Now that we are learning more, the impact risk is apparently both rising (as we find more asteroids) and falling (as we discover, one by one, that they are not after all on a collision course with Earth). There has been a large drop in the estimated interval between globally catastrophic strikes. In the nineteenth century, this was put at 281 million years. In 1958, the pioneer asteroid researcher Ernst Öpik (Lembit Opik's grandfather) concluded that an object 500 metres in diameter – enough to trigger the end of civilization – could be expected every 590,000 years. This has altered to 5–10,000 years today.

These are still low probabilities of destruction, but there remains a disproportionate public fascination in them which may be explained by a number of other factors. Here is a natural hazard with no limit to the scale of its destruction – unlike more familiar terrestrial dangers of earthquake, volcanoes or tsunamis. 'They are the only credible natural threat to human civilization,' according to John Lewis.[5]

Where public alarm is far out of proportion to actual risk, it is hard to judge the effort that should be made to address the risk. Media coverage seldom helps. In 1999, BBC News warned that the Earth is 'due' to be struck by a 'giant asteroid' and that we must: 'Invest to avert armageddon'. The piece quoted Lembit Opik, whose humble aim was for the UK to contribute £500,000 towards a global initiative to obtain better astronomical data. 'If we saw an asteroid hurtling towards us,' he said, 'we would get 20 seconds and that's not even long enough for the Lord's Prayer. If we make this investment then we would get anything from two years' notice of an impending impact and that's long enough to divert the object.' On the first working day of the new millennium, the British government announced that it would fund a task force to look into the threat, while the then science minister Lord Sainsbury soothed: 'This is not something that people should lie awake at night worrying about.'[6] The major outcome was to set up the so-called Near Earth Objects Information Centre.

Meanwhile, astronomers' top priority is to log the thousand-plus objects a kilometre or more in size that their calculations tell them must be orbiting within the solar system, even though one-third of them are strictly 'undiscovered'. Smaller objects are more numerous, and so it is more likely that one will hit the Earth, but the damage they do is less, and of course it is harder to spot them. The chance of any meteorite, even a small one, hitting you personally can be estimated by considering the fraction of the area of the planet's surface you occupy. The Earth's surface area is 500 million square kilometres. Seen from above, you take up, let us say, an area about 0.5 metres square. This gives a chance of one in 2 million billion that any meteorite hits you (or the roof above your head), and a chance of one in 300,000 or so that it hits someone somewhere. Perhaps 50,000 meteorites a year reach the Earth weighing 10 grams or more. We would therefore expect one human life to be lost to meteorite strikes every six years on average. Why don't we hear more about these astonishing injuries and deaths? According to Lewis, the reason is that the death is often erroneously put down to more plausible natural mishaps or explained by superstitious beliefs.

Suppose the worst, and a big asteroid is found that really does have our name on it. Even then, the risk 'can be mitigated in much more concrete ways than is true of most hazards,' according to Clark Chapman of the Southwest Research Institute in Boulder, Colorado. 'An impact can be predicted in advance in ways that remain imperfect but are much more reliable than predictions of earthquakes or even storms.'[7] With ample warning, people could be moved away from the area of impact.

Launching a nuclear bomb into space to deflect an asteroid from its course is an option under serious consideration. But this carries its own risks. Some regard the supporters of this technological fix as fanatics. In 1994 Carl Sagan warned against the diversion 'through error or madness' of a premature nuclear bomb space mission 'for other, nefarious, purposes'.[8] The question we should ask ourselves is this: is the risk of our destruction through such misuse greater than that due to the undeflected asteroid?

An even greater danger, according to Chapman, comes not from a real asteroid but from panic spread by misleading reports of observations or predictions. News of a near-miss by a small asteroid given at short notice would be sure to stoke public apprehension of a real impact, for example. Reports of a scientific prediction (which later proves wrong or to have been misreported) that an impact will occur at a particular time and place would cause intense panic until (and perhaps after) the report was denied.

In the past, such false alarms have been avoided because scientists have kept apparently bad news to themselves until they had information to say that it was not news at all. In future, it is increasingly likely that these alerts will leak out, and we will have to learn to make our own judgements. It is perhaps worth noting, therefore, that at the time of writing, all asteroids known to NASA rank as zero on the Torino scale.[9]

A Sceptic's Toolkit

For those not inclined to credulousness, it is easy to be cynical about the media in its presentation of stories involving statistical or scientific information. We would rather encourage scepticism. With this in mind, we offer this toolkit for the interpretation of data or information that come our way:

- **Vested interest:** ask yourself who has made a particular statement. Why might they have done this? Are we being told the whole story?
- **Weasel words:** should ring alarm bells – especially emotive ones such as 'plague', or ones that put us on a one-way trip to disaster such as 'inevitable' and 'overdue'. It is inevitable that night follows day, but it is not inevitable that there will be a terrorist attack. You can be overdue for a meeting that started an hour ago, but a volcanic eruption, an earthquake or an outbreak of disease is only ever overdue based on arguments of probability. Other words may not have the obvious meaning. Government surveys of the 'work force' count anyone who has worked one hour or more in a week, so a boost in the numbers working could be down to children babysitting or students spending an evening behind a bar. Is this what you consider work?
- **Surveys:** who conducted it? Are they credible? Do they have an obvious motive? Who paid them? Whole fields of study can become unhealthily dependent on funds from one source, whether that source is commercial, governmental or charitable. Were the questions neutrally worded? How big is the sample? Too small, and the result may be skewed. Too big, and the authors may be trying to use sheer weight of numbers to persuade you. Is the sample size and margin of error shown? When a pet food manufacturer says that four out of five cats prefer their product, did they only feed five cats? How were the data collected?
- **Figures:** try to compare figures. Look at as many of the effects of a

change as possible, not just one. Compare the present with the past. Compare one country with another. If the data aren't there to make the obvious comparison, ask yourself what is being obscured.

- **Percentages and actual numbers:** people with a story to tell will choose the more impressive way of putting things.
- **Anecdote and statistics:** fears are spread by word of mouth, press and television reports based on harrowing individual stories; authorities frequently counter these with broad statistics. Meaningful comparison between the two is hard. Both may be 'true'.
- **Graphs and charts:** like words and figures, these may be subject to error or deliberate distortion. Don't automatically believe them because they look technical.
- **Timeframe**: this is an important factor that words like 'inevitable' gloss over. Sea levels are rising, but over a longer period than housing planning cycles, so there is time to adapt. Many data series have a long-run trend, a shorter cyclical variation and then (often erratic) individual data points. Be aware of each so as not to be tricked.
- **Why now:** ask yourself why the story is appearing now, and whether it would be equally newsworthy at another time. Global warming stories appear more in the summer. Travel fears play well as people set off on their holidays. Sex surveys are often released in time for St Valentine's Day.
- **Defeatism:** be wary when told there is nothing we can do about something. Why then are we being told about it? Is it merely to alarm us, or to put us in a state of fear?
- **Scare snobs:** distrust scares where an elite is trying to deny others advantages they already enjoy, for example environmental and health crises exacerbated by cheap flights, exotic food, private modes of transport, choice in medicine and education.
- **Scenarios:** many economic and scientific studies model a range of future scenarios. Make sure that the outcome described is not just the worst-case scenario.
- **Accentuate the positive:** don't discount the possibility that even if some things are getting worse, others may get better – which negative newspaper stories make it their business to do. It will get warmer in 100 years, but what might human ingenuity have devised by then? New

energy sources? Genetically modified human metabolism? Improved photosynthesis? Science fiction, you might say, and so it is – for now. But think what has been achieved over the last 100 years.

- **The big picture:** it's bad if 100 people die of bird flu, but in a country of 50 million, this is very few. How many died of everything else?
- **A sense of proportion:** try to keep one, even if the top brass won't. Ian Blair, the Commissioner of the Metropolitan Police, insists not only that Islamic terrorism poses a greater danger to Londoners than the IRA ever did, but also that it represents a 'far greater threat' than that faced during the Second World War. Does this seem remotely credible, or is somebody just bigging himself up?

During the real war, it's perhaps worth adding, a government poster advised: 'KEEP CALM AND CARRY ON'.

Notes

Introduction

1. Andrew Marr, *My Trade: A Short History of British Journalism* (London: Macmillan, 2004).
2. Charles Mackay, *Extraordinary Popular Delusions and the Madness of Crowds* (Ware, Herts.: Wordsworth Editions, 1995), p. 214.
3. www.psandman.com.
4. John Allen Paulos, *Innumeracy: Mathematical Illiteracy and Its Consequences* (London: Viking, 1989), pp. 51–2.
5. According to the quotations expert Nigel Rees, www1c.btwebworld.com/quote-unquote/p0000149.htm.
6. *The Times*, quoted in *RSS News*, June 2006.
7. http://en.wikipedia.org/wiki/GeorgeCarlin.
8. 'Living dangerously: a survey of risk', *The Economist*, 24 January 2004, p. 8.
9. 'Age of terror scaring Australian children', *The Age*, 26 September 2006.
10. Mary Douglas and Aaron Wildavsky, *Risk and Culture: An Essay on the Selection of Technical and Environmental Dangers* (Berkeley and London: University of California Press, 1982), p. 9.
11. Mackay, op. cit., p. xv.

Chapter 1. Sex, Marriage and Children

THE BIRTH DEARTH

1. 'Italian women shun mamma role', www.bbc.co.uk, 27 March 2006.
2. Donella H. Meadows, Dennis Meadows, Jorgen Randers and William Behrens, *The Limits to Growth: A Report for the Club of Rome's Project on the Predicament of Mankind* (New York: Potomac Associates, 1972).
3. Paul Ralph Ehrlich, *The Population Bomb* (London: Ballantine, 1968).
4. 'World population prospects', www.un.org.

FAMILY BREAKDOWN

1. 'Parents live apart to cash in on benefits system', *Daily Telegraph*, 16 December 2005.
2. '19 Minutes', *Daily Mail*, 19 July 2006.
3. 'A nation of unhappy families', *The Times*, 26 February 2007.
4. UNICEF, *Child Poverty in Perspective: An Overview of Child Well-being in Rich Countries*, UNICEF Report Card 7, 14 February 2007 (UNICEF Innocenti

Research Centre, 2007), available at www.unicef-icdc.org/presscentre/presskit/reportcard7/rc7eng.pdf.

5. 'Marriage rates fall to lowest on record', www.statistics.gov.uk, 21 February 2007.

6. 'Mamma's boys', *Observer*, 12 November 2006.

7. 'Do divorcing couples become happier by breaking up?', *Journal A*, Royal Statistical Society, March 2006.

8. 'How do you keep your teenagers out of trouble?', *Daily Telegraph*, 3 November 2006.

9. 'Marriage maketh man', *The Times*, 1 March 2007.

10. See for example www.caci.co.uk and www.experian.co.uk.

THE MARRIAGE SQUEEZE

1. 'A good man is harder to find', *Newsweek*, 2 June 1986.

2. 'Marriage by the numbers', *Newsweek*, 5 June 2006.

3. 'An iconic report 20 years later', *Wall Street Journal*, 25 May 2006.

4. *Home Alone?*, Unilever Family Report 2005, www.ippr.org.uk, 27 October 2005.

5. 'It's worth the wait', *Sunday Times*, 4 June 2006.

6. 'Forget Bridget Jones – meet Brad', www.bbc.co.uk, 9 November 2004.

SOMETHING FOR THE WEEKEND?

1. BRG Consult at www.consultgb.com.

2. www.durex.com/cm/gss2005results.asp.

3. 'Much more sex please . . . we're British', *Guardian*, 18 August 2004. Other variants on the title of the theatrical farce *No Sex Please, We're British* include the mutually contradictory 'No quick sex please, we're British' and 'No sex please, we're busy'.

4. *Guardian*, 15 August 2006.

5. Anne M. Johnson et al., 'Sexual behaviour in Britain: partnerships, practices, and HIV risk behaviours', *Lancet* 358 (1 December 2001), pp. 1835–42; Kaye Wellings et al., 'Sexual behaviour in Britain: early heterosexual experience', *Lancet* 358 (1 December 2001), pp. 1843–54.

6. Kaye Wellings et al., 'Sexual behaviour in context: a global perspective', *Lancet* 368 (11 November 2006), pp. 1706–28.

Chapter 2. Health

THE FAT THING

1. 'Overweight and obesity: defining overweight and obesity', www.cdc.gov, October 2006.

2. 'Overweight and obesity: home', www.cdc.gov, October 2006.

3. 'Quality and outcomes framework guidance: obesity', www.bma.org.uk, February 2006.

4. *Independent*, 22 April 2006.

CURRYING FLAVOUR

1. 'Is your curry killing you?', *Sun*, 2 February 2006. 'Chinese food can kill you' is a similar example from the *Daily Star*, 21 June 2001.
2. Hervé This, *Molecular Gastronomy: Exploring the Science of Flavor* (New York and Chichester: Columbia University Press, 2006), p. 94.
3. www.salt.gov.uk/salt_myths.html.
4. Harold McGee, *On Food and Cooking: The Science and Lore of the Kitchen* (London: HarperCollins, 1991), p. 545.
5. www.smartmobs.co/archive/2006/07/07/qr_code_hyper.html.
6. Joanna Blythman, *Bad Food Britain* (London: Fourth Estate, 2006), p. 172.
7. 'Salt debate leaves bitter taste', www.foodproductiondaily.com/redirect.asp?idc= 13228, 23 March 2006.
8. Joanna Blythman, *The Food We Eat* (London: Michael Joseph, 1996), p. 258.
9. www.italkali.com/english/home.htm.
10. www.salt.gov.uk/salt_myths.html.

A DEAD DUCK

1. Mike Davis, *The Monster at Our Door* (New York: New Press, 2005), p. 5.
2. www.who.int/csr/disease/avian_influenza/country/cases_table_2007_10_08/en/index.html.
3. Davis, op. cit., pp. 76, 8.
4. Quoted in ibid., p. 125.
5. Quoted in David Boyle, *The Tyranny of Numbers: Why Counting Can't Make us Happy* (London: HarperCollins, 2000), p. 80.

IT'S AMAZING WHAT THEY CAN DO

1. Laurie Garrett, *Betrayal of Trust: The Collapse of Global Public Health* (Oxford: Oxford University Press, 2001), p. 256.
2. www.bbc.co.uk, 26 February 2004.
3. www.statistics.gov.uk/CCI/nugget.asp?ID=1067&Pos=1&ColRank=208.
4. Geoffrey Cannon, *Superbug* (London: Virgin, 1995), p. xxii.
5. Garrett, op. cit., p. 248.
6. Garrett, op. cit., p. 258.
7. www.hpa.org.uk/infections/topics_az/staphylo/staphylo_FAQ.htm.
8. Paul Slovic, *The Perception of Risk* (London: Earthscan, 2000) p. 92.

COMPLETING THE COURSE

1. www.hpa.org.uk/infections/topics_az/Vaccination/cover.htm.
2. A. J. Wakefield et al., 'Ileal-lymphoid-nodular hyperphasia, non-specific colitis, and pervasive developmental disorder in children', *Lancet* 351 (28 February 1998), pp. 637–41.
3. www.cochrane.org/reviews/en/ab004407.html.

4. For measles cases see www.hpa.org.uk/infections/topics_az/measles/data_mmr_confirmed.htm and MMR uptake see www.hpa.org.uk/infections/topics_az/cover/vaccine_uptake_data.htm.

5. Committee on Safety of Medicines, Report of the Working Party on MMR Vaccine, 1999.

6. Stanley Feldman and Vincent Marks, *Panic Nation* (London: John Blake Publishing, 2005), p. 109.

Chapter 3. Passing the Time

ART IS DANGEROUS

1. *L.A. Life*, 8 October 1992.

CHEERS!

1. 'The unbearable lightness of being English', *New Zealand Listener*, 15 January 2005.

2. www.icap.org.

3. 'London women are shameless drunks', *Daily Mail*, 30 April 2003.

4. 'Quarter of children so drunk they have passed out', *Daily Express*, 17 November 2005.

5. 'Alcohol in Europe: a public health perspective', www.ias.org.uk, 1 June 2007.

6. Ibid.

7. 'The not-quite-so-grim neurology of teenage drinking', www.stats.org, 7 July 2006.

8. 'Who is minding the internet liquor store?', NBC News, 9 August 2006.

9. 'Selling alcohol online survey snares NBC', www.stats.org, 16 August 2006.

10. 'Drink data to show disorder fall', *Financial Times*, 6 February 2006.

11. 'Fewer men exceeding benchmarks', www.statistics.gov.uk, 28 November 2006.

THE DEATH OF CINEMA

1. Paulo Cherchi Usai, *The Death of Cinema: History, Cultural Memory and the Digital Dark Age* (London: British Film Institute, 2001).

2. 'The decline in average weekly cinema attendance: 1930 to 2000', *Issues in Political Economy*, 2002, vol. 11.

COLLECTORS' AGONY

1. Kevin Hayes and Ailish Hannigan, 'Trading coupons', *Significance*, magazine of the Royal Statistical Society (Blackwell Publishing, September 2006), pp. 142–4.

Chapter 4. Social Policy

GOLDEN OLDIES' TIME BOMB

1. 'Pensions crisis is much worse than firms say', *Scotland on Sunday*, 19 November 2006.
2. Europe Pensions Barometer 2006, AON Consulting, www.aon.co.uk, January 2007.
3. 'Brown's raid on pensions', *Daily Telegraph*, 16 October 2006.
4. 'The Whitehall pensions', *Daily Telegraph*, 6 November 2006.
5. 'The new pension crisis', *Wall Street Journal*, 18 August 2006.

CREDIT CRUNCH

1. FSA Financial Risk Outlook, www.fsa.gov.uk, 25 January 2006.
2. 'The iPod generation', *Daily Telegraph*, 18 September 2006.
3. OECD Economic Outlook no. 80, www.oecd.org, 28 November 2006.
4. 'Graduates fear debt more than terrorism', *USA Today*, 18 May 2005.
5. 'Money sickness syndrome', www.axa.co.uk, 20 January 2006.
6. OECD Economic Outlook, op. cit.

THE HOUSING BUBBLE

1. 'Global house prices are still rising', *Financial Times*, 30 December 2006.
2. 'No let-up in £45-a-day property price boom', *Daily Express*, 21 December 2006.
3. 'International Housing Affordability Survey', Demographia, 2006.
4. '£1.1 billion worth of mortgages', *Daily Mail*, 5 January 2007.
5. 'The UK house-price-bubble illusion', www.housingoutlook.
6. 'Pay no attention', *Financial Times*, 7 November 2006.

MIGRANT INVASION

1. 'Environmental migration', Optimum Population Trust, 2 November 2006.
2. 'International migration outlook', 2007, OECD.
3. Ibid.
4. 'Foreign labour in the UK', *Labour Market Trends* (ONS, October 2006).
5. Simon Briscoe, *Britain in Numbers* (London: Politico's, 2005).

LOSING CONTROL OF YOUR VEHICLE

1. www.statistics.gov.uk/StatBase/Product.asp?vlnk=618&Pos=1&ColRank=1&Rank=272.
2. Paul Slovic, *The Perception of Risk* (London: Earthscan, 2000), p. 140.
3. www.dft.gov.uk/pgr/statistics/datatablespublications/accidents/casualtiesgbar/roadcasualtiesgreatbritain2005.
4. www.rotor.com.
5. Slovic, op. cit., p. 26.
6. Cited in Simon Briscoe, *Britain in Numbers* (London: Politico's, 2005), p. 193.

7. Previous data may be found on www.numberwatch.co.uk/risks_of_travel.htm.
8. www.swov.nl (1998 figure).

DEATH BY PHONE

1. *The Register*, 1 December 2003, www.theregister.co.uk.
2. 'Association between cellular telephone calls and motor-vehicle collisions', *New England Journal of Medicine*, 13 February 1997.
3. www.bbc.co.uk, 22 March 2002.
4. *Daily Mail*, 4 November 2005.
5. 'Mobile phones and driving', www.dft.gov.uk.
6. 'Cost effectiveness of regulations against using a cellular telephone while driving', *Medical Decision Making* 19(1) (1999).

Chapter 5. The Workplace

NO WORK OR LOW PAY

1. 'Don't discount the positive side of globalization', *Toronto Star*, 31 December 2006.
2. 'And now for a word about globalization', *Arizona Republic*, 9 November 2006.
3. 'Profits of doom', *Financial Times*, 14 October 2006.
4. 'Economic challenges facing the middle class', Congressional testimony, 31 January 2007.

UNDERPAID WOMEN

1. 'Memo to John Roberts', Institute for Women's Policy Research, September 2005.
2. 'The gender pay gap', *Centrepiece*, summer 2006.
3. www.amicustheunion.org/default.aspx?page=2299, 22 January 2007.
4. 'Just pay', 2001, and 'Britain's competitive edge', 2004, www.eoc.org.uk.
5. 'Scant progress on closing gap in women's pay', *New York Times*, 24 December 2006.
6. 'Equal pay reviews survey 2004', EOC working paper no. 32 (spring 2005).
7. 'Women suffer pay gap', *Daily Mail*, 17 January 2006.
8. 'A third of women banking on men', *Metro*, 11 July 2006.
9. 'Rise of the women who earn more than their men', *Daily Mail*, 15 November 2006.
10. 'Progress on gender pay gap stalled', Fawcett Society, 21 October 2006.
11. '30 years on', Fawcett Society, 7 November 2005.
12. 'Shaping a fairer future', Prosser Report, Women and Work Commission, February 2006.

IT'S ALL TOO MUCH

1. 'Seven million Brits are making themselves ill with worry', www.bupa.co.uk/about/html/pr/150206worriedbritons.html, 15 February 2006.

2. 'High-stress lifestyle leaves millions lost', www.hbosplc.com, 22 November 2004.
3. 'The age of rage', *Sunday Times*, 16 July 2006.
4. 'Stress is more damaging than obesity', www.sec-ed.co.uk, 25 November 2004.
5. 'Teacher sick-days stress linked', www.bbc.co.uk, 13 December 2004.
6. 'Call centres under pressure', www.channel4.com, April 2005.
7. http://ki.se, 9 October 2006.
8. 'Work related ill-health affects 2 million', *Financial Times*, 4 August 2006.
9. 'Stress and coronary heart disease', National Heart Foundation of Australia, www.mja.com, 17 March 2003.
10. 'A health warning for older armchair fans', *Financial Times*, 30 June 2006.
11. Civil Aviation Authority survey, www.cnn.com, 8 August 2006.
12. 'In the driver's seat', *Auto Vantage*, 16 May 2006.
13. 'Is teaching the most stressful job?', www.bbc.co.uk, 27 March 2004.
14. www.isma.org.uk, www.ismabrasil.com.br and www.isma-usa.org.
15. www.hypnosisdownloads.com.
16. 'Ten steps to happiness', *Daily Mail*, 28 June 2006.

GAMES OF CHANCE

1. Edward Tenner, *Why Things Bite Back: New Technology and the Revenge Effect* (London: Fourth Estate, 1996), p. 173.
2. Stanley Feldman and Vincent Marks, *Panic Nation* (London: John Blake Publishing, 2005), p. 239.
3. *Guardian*, 8 December 2005; www.chiropractic-uk.co.uk.

Chapter 6. Law and Order

TERROR ALERT

1. 'Transatlantic trends', *Key Findings 2006*, 6 September 2006.
2. www.synovate.com/knowledge/infact/issues/200510/, October 2005.
3. 'Similar levels of fear of terrorism in USA and Great Britain', www.harrisinteractive.com, 6 February 2004.
4. *New York Times*/CBS News Poll, www.nytimes.com, 7 September 2006.
5. NABE Economic Policy Survey, www.nabe.com, 28 August 2006.
6. 'Worldwide poll shows 60% fear terror threat is worse after war', *Guardian*, 28 February 2006.
7. YouGov poll, quoted in *Daily Telegraph*, 25 August 2006.
8. NCTC Report on incidents, 2006, www.nctc.gov.
9. 'Deaths by age, sex and underlying cause 2004', HSQ 26, www.statistics.gov.uk, February 2007.
10. 'MI5 head warns of 1600 terror plotters', *Financial Times*, 10 November 2006.
11. 'Secret report: terror threat worst since 9/11', *Sunday Telegraph*, 25 February 2007.

BANG BANG

1. AKUF and the University of Hamburg, quoted in *Vital Signs 2006–2007*, Worldwatch Institute.
2. Heidelberg Institute for International Conflict Research, quoted in *Vital Signs*, op. cit.
3. 'Mortality after the 2003 invasion of Iraq', www.lancet.com, 11 October 2006.
4. www.iraqbodycount.org.
5. 'Afghanistan risk exposed', *New Scientist*, 9 September 2006.
6. www.oecd.org/dac.
7. 'Reflections on Gulf War Illness', *Phil. Trans. of the Royal Society*, 24 March 2006.
8. 'Veterans told: there is no Gulf syndrome', *The Times*, 25 March 2006.

LOCK 'EM UP

1. 'Prison really does work', *Daily Mail*, 20 June 2006.
2. 'England and Wales lead pack on European imprisonment rates', www.howardleague.org, 18 January 2006.
3. *World Prison Population*, 6th edn, International Centre for Prison Studies, King's College, London.
4. 'Lord Woolf: wild about Harry', www.bbc.co.uk, 17 January 2003; and 'Woolf warns of prison-riot risk', *Guardian*, 20 June 2002.
5. 'Too many in jail, says top judge', www.bbc.co.uk, 30 May 2006.
6. 'Prison population in EU countries', www.civitas.org.uk/data/prisonEU2001.htm.
7. www.prisonreformtrust.org, January 2004.
8. *South Wales Evening Post*, 4 March 2005.
9. 'Even more prisons needed, Reid told', *Guardian*, 27 July 2006.
10. *Sunday Telegraph*, 17 September 2006.

MURDER AND CRIME

1. *News of the World*, 3 September 2006.
2. 'Crime in England and Wales, 2005–6', www.homeoffice.gov.uk, July 2006.
3. www.wrongdiagnosis.com.
4. 'Easier to panic than do the math', *Toronto National Post*, 13 April 2006.
5. *European Sourcebook of Crime and Criminal Justice Statistics, 2003*, www.wodc.nl/eng.
6. 'Going off track', *Philadelphia Daily News*, 10 July 2006.

Chapter 7. The Natural World

LOOKING UP

1. Al Gore, *Earth in the Balance* (Boston: Houghton Mifflin, 1992), p. 88.
2. 'Late lessons from early warnings: the precautionary principle 1896–2000' (European Environment Agency, 2001), p. 80.
3. John Gribbin, *The Hole in the Sky* (London: Corgi, 1988), p. 143.

4. G. Braathen, *Geophysical Research Abstracts* 8, 09861, 2006.

5. *Chem@Cam*, summer 2006, p. 16.

6. www.esrcsocietytoday.ac.uk/ESRCInfoCentre/PO/releases/2002/September/public.aspx.

7. Fred Pearce, *The Last Generation: How Nature Will Take Her Revenge for Climate Change* (London: Eden Project Books, 2006), p. 51.

8. J. Firor, *The Changing Atmosphere: A Global Challenge* (New Haven and London: Yale University Press, 1990), p. 43.

THE SHORT, HOT SUMMER OF 2006

1. John Houghton, *Global Warming: The Complete Briefing*, 3rd edn (Cambridge: Cambridge University Press, 2004), p. 8.

2. Jonathon Porritt, *Playing Safe: Science and the Environment* (London: Thames & Hudson, 2000), p. 63.

3. Fred Pearce, *The Last Generation: How Nature Will Take Her Revenge for Climate Change* (London: Eden Project Books, 2006), p. 254.

4. 'Katrina and the waves', *Independent*, 23 August 2006.

5. Quoted in Roger A. Pielke, 'Disasters, death and destruction: making sense of recent calamities', *Oceanography* 19(2) (June 2006), pp. 138–47.

BECOMING UNSETTLED

1. Searched using the Factiva database, the phrase 'global warming' was used 16,755 times in June–August 2006, 10,547 times during the same months of 2005, and 6,196 times in 2004. Curiously, global warming is mentioned consistently less in the winter months. The comparable figures for December–February are 10,632, 8,411 and 5,055 respectively.

2. *Warm Words*, Institute of Public Policy Research, August 2006.

3. James Lovelock, *The Revenge of Gaia* (London: Allen Lane, 2006), pp. 3–4, 7.

4. *Daily Telegraph*, 28 August 2006; *Eastern Daily Press*, 28 July 2006.

5. Climate change protagonists sometimes argue that this renegade rump has dwindled to nothing, but see, for example, a letter from forty-one scientists in the *Sunday Telegraph*, 23 April 2006.

6. Quoted in Aaron Wildavsky, *But Is It True? A Citizen's Guide to Environmental Health and Safety Issues* (Cambridge, Mass.: Harvard University Press, 1995).

7. Quoted in Fred Pearce, *The Last Generation: How Nature Will Take Her Revenge for Climate Change* (London: Eden Project Books, 2006), pp. 24–5.

8. John Houghton, *Global Warming: The Complete Briefing*, 3rd edn (Cambridge: Cambridge University Press, 2004), pp. 143–4.

9. 'The threat to the planet', *New York Review of Books*, 13 July 2006.

10. S. Pacala and R. Socolow, 'Stabilization wedges: solving the climate problem for the next 50 years with current technologies', *Science* 305 (2004), pp. 968–72.

PIGS MIGHT SWIM

1. Mark Lynas, *High Tide: News from a Warming World* (London: Flamingo, 2004), p. 83.
2. Intergovernmental Panel on Climate Change, *Climate Change 2001: The Scientific Basis* (Cambridge: Cambridge University Press, 2001), p. 642.
3. Lynas, op. cit., p. 232.
4. Ibid., p. 114.
5. J. D. Orford and R. W. G. Carter, 'Examination of mesoscale forcing of a swash-aligned gravel-barrier', *Marine Geology* 126 (1995), pp. 201–11.
6. Lynas, op. cit., p. 114.
7. See, for example, E. Rignot and P. Kanagaratnam, 'Changes in the velocity structure of the Greenland ice sheet', *Science* 311 (17 February 2006), pp. 986–90.
8. 'For my people, climate change is a matter of life and death', *Independent*, 15 September 2006.

GO WITH THE FLOW

1. R. I. Tilling and P. W. Lipman, 'Lessons in reducing volcano risk', *Nature* 364 (22 July 1993), pp. 270–80; www.undp.org/bcpr/disred/documents/publications/rdr/english/c2/b.pdf; www.usgs.gov/newsroom/article.asp?ID=202.
2. 'After the volcano', *Guardian*, 18 July 2005.
3. 'Prophet of doom', *Independent*, 9 November 2005.
4. 'Tokyo prepares for "the big one"', *Financial Times*, 17 January 2005.
5. 'AD79 and all that', *Independent* (foreign edn), 2 October 2003.

CHILLING NEWS

1. Quoted in Aaron Wildavsky, *But Is It True? A Citizen's Guide to Environmental Health and Safety Issues* (Cambridge, Mass.: Harvard University Press, 1995), p. 370.
2. Lowell Ponte, *The Cooling* (New York: Prentice-Hall, 1976).
3. John Gribbin, *Hothouse Earth: The Greenhouse Effect and Gaia* (New York: Bantam, 1990), p. 13.
4. John Gribbin, *Future Weather and the Greenhouse Effect* (New York: Delacorte, 1982), p. 107.
5. Quoted in Robert L. Park, *Voodoo Science* (Oxford: Oxford University Press, 2000), p. 33.
6. Bill McGuire, *A Guide to the End of the World* (Oxford: Oxford University Press), p. 68.

Chapter 8. Our Declining Resources

WILD TALK

1. www.iucnredlist.org/info/tables/table1.
2. *Millennium Ecosystem Assessment* (World Resources Institute, 2005).

3. www.panda.org/newsfacts/publications/livingplanetreport/living planetindex/ind ex.cfm.
4. *Measuring Biodiversity for Conservation* (Royal Society, 2003).
5. Ibid.
6. Cited in, for example, Bjørn Lomborg, *The Skeptical Environmentalist* (Cambridge: Cambridge University Press, 2001), p. 249.

THE COD DELUSION

1. Boris Worm et al., 'Impacts of biodiversity loss on ocean ecosystem services', *Science* 314 (3 November 2006), pp. 787–90.
2. Tim Lang and Michael Heasman, *Food Wars: The Global Battle for Mouths, Minds and Markets* (London: Earthscan, 2004), p. 244.
3. 'Seafood could disappear by 2048', *Chicago Tribune*, 3 November 2006.
4. Mark Kurlansky, *Cod: A Biography of the Fish that Changed the World* (London: Jonathan Cape, 1998), p. 158.

NOT A WORD

1. 'Language cull could leave people speechless', *Guardian*, 25 May 2002.
2. 'Dying dialect gets a voice', *Houston Chronicle*, 27 November 2006.
3. 'Like ancient forests displaced by houses', *The Times*, 24 February 2007.
4. *Houston Chronicle*, op. cit.
5. 'France looks to the law', www.telegraph.co.uk, 25 October 2000.

Chapter 9. Modern Science

FRANKENSTEIN FOODS

1. Stanley Feldman and Vincent Marks (eds.), *Panic Nation* (London: John Blake Publishing, 2005), p. 160.
2. Frank Furedi, *Culture of Fear*, rev. edn (New York: Continuum, 2002), p. 174.
3. www.cabinetoffice.gov.uk/strategy/work_areas/gm_crops/index.asp.
4. Emma Hughes and Jenny Kitzinger, *Framing Genetic Research*, BA Festival of Science, Norwich, 2006.
5. Feldman and Marks, op. cit., p. 153.

LITTLE WONDER

1. www.its.caltech.edu/-feynman/plenty.html.
2. As of August 2007, the list includes 502 products: www.nanotechproject.org/index.php?id=44.
3. 'Safe handling of nanotechnology', *Nature* 444 (16 November 2006), pp. 267–9.
4. 'Welcome to the world of nano foods', *Observer*, 16 December 2006.
5. 'Small is hazardous', *Independent on Sunday*, 11 July 2004.
6. 'After illness, a closer look at nano science', *Philadelphia Inquirer*, 14 April 2006.

EXPOSED

1. 'The radioactive spy', *Guardian*, 25 November 2006.
2. 'Three people exposed to spy radiation are sent for urgent tests', *Evening Standard*, 27 November 2006.
3. 'Cities are swept for "dirty" bombs', *Daily Telegraph*, 8 January 2004.
4. Paul Slovic, *The Perception of Risk* (London: Earthscan, 2000), p. 266.
5. Ibid., p. 267.
6. www.world-nuclear.org/info/info6app.htm.
7. Scott Lash, Bronislaw Szerszynski and Brian Wynne (eds.), *Risk, Environment and Modernity* (London: Sage, 1996), p. 64.
8. Robert L. Park, *Voodoo Science* (Oxford: Oxford University Press, 2000), p. 148.
9. William Stewart (ed.), *Mobile Phones and Health: A Report from the Independent Expert Group on Mobile Phones* (IEGMP, 2000), p. 3.

Chapter 10. They're Coming to Get You

EXPECTING VISITORS

1. 'In the sky! A bird? A plane? A . . . UFO?', *Chicago Tribune*, 1 January 2007.
2. Peter Horsley, *Sounds from Another Room* (Barnsley: Pen and Sword Books, 1997), p. 172.
3. Ibid., p. 181.
4. Elaine Showalter, *Hystories: Hysterical Epidemics and Modern Culture* (New York: Columbia University Press, 1997), p. 196.
5. John Allen Paulos, *Innumeracy: Mathematical Illiteracy and Its Consequences* (London: Viking, 1989), p. 59.

THAT'S WHEN IT HITS YOU

1. 'Space evaders', *Guardian Unlimited*, 29 September 2004.
2. John S. Lewis, *Comet and Asteroid Impact Hazards on a Populated Earth* (San Diego and London: Academic Press, 1999), p. 132.
3. www.space.com/scienceastronomy/solarsystem/asteroid_fears_020326-1.html.
4. www.space.com/scienceastronomy/asteroid_risk_041224.html.
5. Lewis, op. cit., p. 146.
6. www.space.com/news/uk_asteroid_000104_org.html.
7. Clark Chapman, 'The hazard of near-Earth asteroid impacts on Earth', *Earth and Planetary Science Letters* 222 (2004), pp. 1–15.
8. C. Sagan and S. J. Ostro, 'Dangers of asteroid deflection', *Nature* 368 (1994), p. 501.
9. http://neo.jpl.nasa.gov/risk/.

How the English and Welsh Die

Over three-quarters of deaths are caused by the three main killers – heart disease, cancer and lung disease. The more newsworthy 'external' causes, prompting much panic, account for few in comparison.

	Total deaths in 2005 512,692	Deaths per 10,000
Circulatory system (inc. heart attack, stroke)	**183,997**	**3,589**
Neoplasm, tumours, cancers	**138,454**	**2,701**
Respiratory system (inc. pneumonia, asthma)	**72,517**	**1,414**
Digestive system	**25,213**	**492**
External causes	**16,411**	**320**
of which Transport accidents of which:	2,740	53
Pedestrian	*543*	*11*
Pedal cyclist	*126*	*2*
Motorcyclist	*486*	*9*
Three-wheel motor vehicle	*9*	*0*
Car occupant	*1,311*	*26*
Animal rider	*13*	*0*
Rail vehicle	*1*	*0*
Water transport accident	*24*	*0*
Air accident	*159*	*3*
Falls	3,006	59
Inanimate mechanical force	98	2
Bitten by rat	1	0
Bitten by dog	2	0
Bitten by other animal	11	0
Drowning	177	3
Accidental threat to breathing	469	9
Electric current	28	1
Smoke, fire and flames	252	5
Hornets, wasps and bees	3	0
Excessive natural cold	74	1
Lightning	2	0
Flood	2	0

	Total deaths in 2005	Deaths per 10,000
Accidental poisoning – alcohol	151	3
Accidental poisoning – non-alcohol	759	15
Intentional self-harm	3,172	62
Assault	323	6
Undetermined intent	1,484	29
War	1	0
Medical/surgical complication	373	7
Nervous system (inc. Alzheimer's, Parkinson's disease)	**15,209**	297
Mental and behavioural (inc. dementia)	**14,563**	284
Other deaths (inc. senility and SIDS)	**11,457**	223
Genitourinary system	**10,231**	200
Endocrine, nutritional, metabolic	**7,433**	145
Infectious diseases	**6,141**	120
Musculoskeletal system	**4,378**	85
Perinatal deaths	**2,432**	47
Skin	**1,788**	35
Congenital malformations and abnormalities	**1,292**	25
Blood disease	**1,096**	21
Eye and ear diseases	**44**	1
Pregnancy and childbirth	**36**	1

Source: ONS, Mortality Statistics, DH2, no 32.